Wasters

Wasters

SHANE ROSS
AND
NICK WEBB

PENGUIN IRELAND

PENGUIN IRELAND

Published by the Penguin Group
Penguin Ireland, 25 St Stephen's Green, Dublin 2, Ireland
(a division of Penguin Books Ltd)
Penguin Books Ltd, 80 Strand, London WC2R ORL, England
Penguin Group (USA) Inc., 375 Hudson Street, New York, New York 10014, USA
Penguin Group (Australia), 250 Camberwell Road, Camberwell, Victoria 3124, Australia
(a division of Pearson Australia Group Pty Ltd)
Penguin Group (Canada), 90 Eglinton Avenue East, Suite 700, Toronto, Ontario, Canada M4P 2Y3
(a division of Pearson Penguin Canada Inc.)
Penguin Books India Pvt Ltd, 11 Community Centre, Panchsheel Park, New Delhi – 110 017, India
Penguin Group (NZ), 67 Apollo Drive, Rosedale, North Shore 0632, New Zealand
(a division of Pearson New Zealand Ltd)
Penguin Books (South Africa) (Pty) Ltd, 24 Sturdee Avenue, Rosebank, Johannesburg 2196, South Africa

Penguin Books Ltd, Registered Offices: 80 Strand, London WC2R ORL, England

www.penguin.com

First published 2010
I

Set in 12/14.75pt Bembo Book MT Std
Typeset by TexTech International
Printed in Great Britain by Clays Ltd, St Ives plc

A CIP catalogue record for this book is available from the British Library

ISBN: 978-1-844-88251-9

www.greenpenguin.co.uk

Penguin Books is committed to a sustainable future
for our business, our readers and our planet.
The book in your hands is made from paper
certified by the Forest Stewardship Council.

To our mothers

Contents

Prologue

On a drizzly grey November afternoon in 2008, sipping coffee out of paper cups in the Insomnia Café across the road from FÁS headquarters on Upper Baggot Street in Dublin, we watched the comings and goings of the staff at Ireland's semi-state training and employment agency. The employees, shuffling in and out of the grim concrete building, looked like beaten dockets. Morale at the agency was low, and no wonder: it had been receiving some unwelcome media attention, following a series of probes by the Comptroller & Auditor General and the Public Accounts Committee into advertising and promotion spending overruns. There was a whiff of scandal in the air – a whiff that was soon to grow into the stench of rotting waste.

We eyed the building opposite and plotted our response in case any last-minute obstacles were placed in our way. It had taken months to prise open the doors of the FÁS fortress. No late stunts would have surprised us.

When the time came, we walked across Baggot Street, spoke to the receptionist and were met by the head of the Freedom of Information Unit, Michael Bowden. He escorted us into the creaky lift and up to the fifth floor.

Inside, FÁS headquarters was a depressingly poky place. An organization with an annual budget of nearly €1 billion, which we had reason to believe had been spending lavishly on the pleasures of its top brass, it was evidently doing little to provide comfort for the staff who endured the daily slog. We passed a series of small rooms: employees poked out their heads from behind dark corners to gawk at us.

At the end of a narrow, wood-panelled corridor, Michael ushered us into a room that overlooked the office car park. He introduced us to a young woman who was there to ensure we did not steal any of the documents we had come to inspect.

Our Freedom of Information Act request, which we had put together after receiving a tip-off from a trusted anonymous source, had sought 'all the details of the cost of travel, accommodation, etc., incurred by FÁS personnel and directors', as well as their spouses, on a visit to Florida in connection with the FÁS Science Challenge, a project that was intended to open doors to careers in science, technology and engineering. The Florida branch of the Science Challenge brought a small number of Irish students every year to the National Aeronautics and Space Administration (NASA) and the Florida Space Institute.

We never dreamed of the scale of the paperwork that our inquiry would throw up. A large table was piled high with row upon row of documents covering the transatlantic trips – and much more. The credit-card statements and receipts relating to our FOI query also contained fascinating details about spending in other areas by FÁS chief Rody Molloy, Corporate Affairs boss Greg Craig and other executives.

Michael showed us the files, asked politely if we would list the documents we wanted photocopied and left us under the supervision of his colleague. She buried herself in a novel as we waded into the mountains of paper in front of us.

After five minutes we knew we had hit the motherlode. We didn't say anything to each other. We didn't need to.

After we'd been sifting through the documents for a while, the door opened. In walked big John Cahill, the manager of the Science Challenge programme. We had not been expecting him.

In that small room with the table covered by stacks of documents, we asked him a few questions about expenses and he told us about his 'passion' for the Science Challenge. When we pieced it all together, we saw that his 'passion' had cost the taxpayer €124,000 in travel to the US, South Africa and Japan.

We had been stalking FÁS for years – and for years FÁS officials had been fighting to keep us off their backs. Even in the distant nineties, chief executive John Lynch (now head of CIÉ) had complained to the top management of Independent Newspapers about the adverse coverage FÁS had received in the *Sunday Independent* business pages. Lynch was at a loss to see how a newspaper group that was closely involved in sponsoring FÁS's 'Opportunities' jobs fair could publish material critical of a colleague in a joint venture.

The same attitude persisted after Lynch departed from the agency. FÁS, with its massive advertising budget, constantly flexed its muscles in the media to ensure soft coverage. Significantly, the Comptroller & Auditor General's report in 2008 criticized FÁS for placing advertisements in print that 'did not appear to be conducive to the attainment of value for money'. When Greg Craig was asked about his practice of directly placing ads himself, rather than leaving this task to the agency's advertising firm, he referred to how 'the ability to be seen to have a media spend could potentially influence how FÁS was portrayed in the newspaper or magazine in question.'

FÁS expected good publicity, and FÁS usually got it. The powerful employment agency used advertising as the stick to beat media bosses, and it used junkets as the carrot to keep the hacks happy. Politicians too were well looked after. Employment schemes were placed in politically sensitive locations and local political warlords were allowed to take the credit.

After a hard-hitting article in the *Sunday Independent* in 1996, letters of protest about the wonderful work of FÁS were sent to the editor; they had the tone of an orchestrated campaign. Well-directed invitations to visit FÁS centres, including disability projects, kept arriving.

After several years of sustained probing of the FÁS finances, we started to receive anonymous letters, from a single source, alleging serious malpractices in the agency. Initially they pinpointed slovenly training practices and cronyism. Later they alleged massive waste. We checked up on each one. Nearly all were independently confirmed by other sources.

After a while we had built up a formidable dossier from our anonymous source. We were certain we knew the identity of our informant and rang him, but he refused to confirm that it was he or to speak to us face to face. Even to this day we are in little doubt that we know who was feeding us the information, but we have never had a conversation with him on that basis.

One of the anonymous letters had allowed us to publish an

embarrassing report about the utterly chaotic state of training at the agency, but we lacked the hard evidence we needed to confirm our deep suspicions about FÁS's culture of waste.

In the tiny room on the fifth floor, on that November day in 2008, the hard evidence was staring us in the face.

During the summer of that year, our anonymous informant had directed us to seek information about the antics of the FÁS bosses' jaunts to the US as part of the FÁS Science Challenge programme. It suggested that we would need to use the Freedom of Information Act. The Act had been – up to that stage – a bit of a waste of time. When it was introduced in 1998, there had been a splurge of journalists lashing in all kinds of requests for files and government documents. Most of the time they got back piles of photocopied documents with black lines obliterating the text; the information had been 'redacted' by civil servants hiding behind those provisions in the Act that prevented the release of 'sensitive' information. There had been some successes: we now know how much Bertie Ahern spent on make-up during his time in office. But most of the information that had come out was less than spectacular. We weren't hugely confident that using the Act would produce anything valuable.

The FÁS Freedom of Information Department left its response till the last legal minute to give us an answer. We weren't surprised – delay was a FÁS trademark. But when the answer finally came back, we were pleasantly surprised: the response was 'Yes'. The information would be released.

There was a slight catch. FÁS said that it would cost nearly a thousand euro to prepare the information for our inspection. We saw this as a play for a delay and told FÁS that the cheque was on its way – which seemed to surprise them.

Soon after that, they changed their minds. The charge would be only four hundred euro. The FÁS bluff had been called. We wondered about the reduction in price, but concluded that they had expected us to back off once we had been quoted the initial amount. When we didn't, we reckoned, they began to fear that we would expose them for ripping us off over a relatively simple search.

We dispatched the cheque. A few weeks later, having heard nothing from FÁS, we contacted them to find out why they had failed to acknowledge it. We were told it had never arrived.

A fresh delay.

We found the failure of the cheque to travel the few hundred yards from Kildare Street to Baggot Street a trifle curious. After complaining to An Post, we dispatched another one. The second cheque landed. (The first one turned up a few days later.) The papers were released and FÁS made arrangements to allow us to inspect them.

The dazzling array of receipts we were shown on that day covered the travel-related expense claims of FÁS chief executive Rody Molloy and his wife, of FÁS chairman and IMPACT trade-union chief Peter McLoone and a host of FÁS senior managers. We did not know where to start. We sat at opposite ends of the table and began to work our way through the thirty-odd cardboard boxes on the table and the floor, filling notepads. Nick Webb spotted one receipt for $410 attached to a claim form with just the word 'presentation' scribbled on it. The receipt was from a place called Solutions in West Cocoa Beach, Florida. When Nick returned to the *Sunday Independent* offices, he googled Solutions and found a mention in a local directory: it wasn't a high-tech company doing research on space exploration, but a beauty parlour and nail salon. The bill was for none other than former Tánaiste Mary Harney, who had had responsibility for FÁS in her capacity as Minister for Enterprise between 1997 and 2004. She – and at least one other member of the travelling party – had arranged to have their hair styled and blow-dried at their Florida hotel by hairdressers from the salon.

Was that gem more sensational than the €900 tip in a top Dublin restaurant, or the $942 for Rody Molloy's round of golf? We knew that the documents in the room spelled the end of the road for Molloy. They raised serious questions for the board, for Mary Harney and for the Taoiseach.

When we left later that afternoon, Michael Bowden took a list of the papers we wanted to photocopy. He told us that he would like to inform Rody Molloy 'out of courtesy'.

As we left the premises, we spotted top-dollar public-relations spinner Jim Milton of Murray Consultants in the foyer. Milton was a

troubleshooter, often called in by commercial outfits in deep doo-
doo. His services did not come cheap, and his presence in the foyer
that afternoon suggested that FÁS already knew it was experiencing
major difficulties. In any case, whatever fees Jim charged to dig the
board and executives out of a hole would be paid for by taxpayers,
the same victims who had been stung for the cost of the Florida junkets. Almost two years later we discovered that Murray Consultants
had bagged a €54,000 fee from FÁS.

In the days before we published our exposé, we telephoned several
top FÁS officials about the story. They failed to respond. But we
were aware that calls had been made to the highest level in the *Sunday
Independent*, trying to get our story spiked or delayed. We guessed
that if there had been a delay of even one week, FÁS would have
been able to feed the information to friendly hacks in other newspapers or media groups, who might have downplayed the story and
ultimately buried it. Despite the influence of FÁS as a key advertiser,
our bosses did not yield to the pressure.

Two days after the story broke, Molloy was gone. The public
now knew that FÁS was a cesspool of waste and political cronyism.

It was not alone.

1. The Rise of the Semi-States

The phone rang at the *Sunday Independent* business desk; the voice at the other end of the line was a cabinet minister's. 'A bit of news for you,' the Fianna Fáiler whispered to Shane Ross. 'Two slots on the Aer Rianta board have been filled. One for Bertie and one for Mary.'

It was November 1997, a Friday afternoon – a point in the week when exclusive news is precious to journalists.

'Dermot O'Leary is Bertie's. Tadhg O'Donoghue is Mary's,' confided the caller. Albert Reynolds's man, Noel Hanlon, remained in the chair and Charlie Haughey's pal, Noel Fox, was still on the board.

'Board meetings at Aer Rianta will not take too long' the Fianna Fáiler quipped. The minister was a good source, and we happily published the story two days later.

The reappointment of Dermot O'Leary to the state airport authority was stunning. A Fianna Fáil loyalist on the semi-state directors' circuit, he had created untold bother a year earlier as chairman of CIÉ. Originally an apostle of Albert Reynolds, he had left the semi-state transport monopoly after a spat with Michael Lowry, the short-lived Fine Gael Minister for Transport, who had raised questions about O'Leary's proposed sale of a CIÉ property in Cork to the developer Owen O'Callaghan. Lowry had announced an inquiry into the sale, alleging a sweetheart deal and accusing O'Leary of disbanding the CIÉ property subcommittee in order to hasten the transaction. O'Leary denied the allegations, stating that the plan had been brought to him, as chairman of CIÉ, by top executives. (In the end O'Callaghan pulled out of the deal.)

O'Leary was not a man to be tackled lightly. Word in political circles was that the Fianna Fáil diehard – who had launched a legal action against Lowry – was now too hot to handle, and that Bertie Ahern's new government was quietly grateful to Lowry for removing him from the pitch. Now, according to the conventional wisdom,

O'Leary would vanish quietly from the Aer Rianta board when his time was up. So it came as a great surprise when his directorship was renewed – and at the insistence, according to our source, of the Taoiseach.

O'Leary was a member of Fianna Fáil's national executive and a former chairman of its Dublin South Central Comhairle Ceantair. His business, Crane Hire Ltd, had made him a millionaire. He was a typically brash, flashy specimen of the new Fianna Fáil, who liked fast cars, loud clothes and first-class travel.

After O'Leary's less than glorious exit from the CIÉ chair, the *Sunday Independent* reported that his successor, Eamon Walsh, believed that O'Leary had made trips to South Africa and Australia that had yielded not 'one bit of value' to CIÉ. O'Leary strongly defended his travels as CIÉ chairman after Lowry used Dáil privilege to quote Walsh's comments, thereby fuelling the allegations of misuse of public funds.

O'Leary's ten-year spell on the board of Aer Rianta was marked by a series of controversies. On one occasion when his friend Liam Lawlor was flying home from the United States to face a spell in Mountjoy Prison, O'Leary made a telephone call that enabled the disgraced TD to avoid the waiting press corps by slipping through a special exit at Dublin Airport. O'Leary successfully resisted calls for his resignation following this incident, probably because of his impeccable Fianna Fáil connections.

He was one of five recipients of a €9,000 Cartier watch that the departing Aer Rianta directors awarded to themselves when their terms ended in 2003. After the controversy surrounding the taxpayer-funded gifts broke, the red-faced directors returned the watches – except for O'Leary, who said he would pay for his.

The bizarre gift had been organized by the airport authority's chairman Noel Hanlon, a member of the cosy quartet of Fianna Fáil loyalists on the Aer Rianta board. Hanlon had run a successful ambulance business before it went into voluntary liquidation in 1988. Since then he had been hopping from one state board to another, mostly courtesy of fellow Longford man Albert Reynolds. As early as 1982 he had been made chairman of the state rescue agency, Foir Teoranta, followed by a spell as a director of Aer Lingus. To his credit, he frequently refused to accept director's fees at his semi-state fiefdoms.

Hanlon saw himself as a hands-on chairman at all his posts. As chairman of the VHI he became embroiled in a row about whether he or the chief executive was in charge. At Aer Rianta too he fiercely defended his patch, never yielding an inch to those who threatened his monopoly, winning a series of turf wars and keeping the competition at bay. He successfully opposed the efforts of the entrepreneurial McEvaddy brothers, Ulick and Des, to build a second terminal at Dublin Airport. He tried to quash the emergence of another rival when Aer Rianta sought a judicial review of a decision to allow a rival car park at the same airport. In the process he delayed the emergence of the cheaper competitor, John O'Sullivan's Quickpark, by several years.

Hanlon had an office and a big Merc out at Aer Rianta's headquarters and took any threat to its dominant position personally. He hated Ryanair, believing that the upstart airline had disturbed the status quo in the aviation industry. After years of jousting about landing charges and the number of passengers Ryanair could bring to Dublin Airport, Hanlon went in front of an Oireachtas committee in 1999 to accuse Ryanair boss Michael O'Leary of telling 'blatant lies' when he promised to bring one million extra passengers to Aer Rianta and then delivered only 179,000. O'Leary – who had been a long-standing thorn in the side of Hanlon's board at Aer Rianta, frequently denouncing the authority's monopoly – threatened to sue.

After ten years at the helm of Aer Rianta, Hanlon's loyalty to the airport empire he had defended began to take precedence over his party allegiance. He had always managed to keep on the right side of Fianna Fáil ministers by personally attending to their needs. Cabinet members travelling through Dublin Airport were regularly seen off at the tarmac by the chairman. Despite his dependence on Albert Reynolds, he managed to maintain excellent relations with Mary O'Rourke, Reynolds's internal party foe, when she was given the transport portfolio in 1997.

This cosiness with Fianna Fáil politicians ended suddenly in 2003, when the new Minister for Transport, Séamus Brennan, decided to break up Aer Rianta into separate companies, to be based at Cork, Shannon and Dublin airports. Hanlon and his board resisted Brennan's plans to the last, joining forces with the trade unions and using all their Fianna Fáil clout to frustrate the minister. Due to Hanlon's manoeuvres, Brennan found himself obstructed by Minister for Finance Charlie McCreevy and finally – to Hanlon's delight – demoted by Bertie Ahern to the department of Social and Family Affairs.

Hanlon was joined in his resistance to this split of the empire by Tadhg O'Donoghue, a fellow Fianna Fáiler on the board and another semi-state veteran. O'Donoghue, according to our cabinet source, was Mary O'Rourke's choice for the board in 1997. He had been a senior partner in the giant accountancy firm Pricewaterhouse-Coopers and carried the urbane sophistication generally associated with the highest echelons of that profession. In 2000 O'Rourke made him chairman of the ESB, an important semi-state post that even the most tribal Fianna Fáil ministers had always awarded to commercially competent businessmen. O'Donoghue met that criterion, but, as former Fianna Fáil director of elections for Dún Laoghaire, he passed the tribal loyalty test too.

O'Donoghue had filled an Aer Rianta vacancy left by an obscure board member named Pat Moylan. Moylan's story fits a familiar pattern. He hails from Offaly, and was a key figure in the local organization of Brian Cowen TD, destined to become Fianna Fáil leader and Taoiseach. Cowen, who served as Minister for Transport in 1993–4, appointed him to the board of Aer Rianta days before the Fianna Fáil–Labour government left office in 1994. Moylan had little, if any, experience of aviation. A farmer, with Cowen's help he was elected to Seanad Éireann on the Agricultural Panel in 1997, necessitating his immediate resignation from Aer Rianta. Today Moylan is Cowen's eyes and ears in the Seanad, and the Taoiseach's support helped him to sail into the position of Cathaoirleach of the Upper House. The post carries a salary of approximately €110,000 per annum.

Moylan's appointment to Aer Rianta was only one of ten made by Cowen in the eleventh hour of his dying ministry in 1994. Another was the elevation of Fianna Fáil fundraiser Jim Lacey to the chair at the Irish Aviation Authority soon after he quit as chief executive of National Irish Bank; he would resign the post in 1998 on foot of revelations about practices at the bank.

The last of the Fianna Fáil quartet in the Aer Rianta board's class of 1997 was Noel Fox. Fox had been appointed to several state boards by Charlie Haughey from as early as the seventies. Like Hanlon, he was also a director of the VHI. He starred in the McCracken Tribunal's investigation into payments to Haughey and to Michael Lowry, emerging as a link between Haughey's crooked bagman Des Traynor and supermarket supremo Ben Dunne: while Traynor was touting for money for the former Taoiseach, Fox – a senior partner in accountancy firm Oliver Freaney – was the conduit between Dunne, Traynor and Haughey. Both Fox and Freaneys were censured by a later accountants' inquiry, finding that Fox was effectively carrying out management functions at Dunnes while Freaneys was auditing the same company's books.

The Aer Rianta board of 1997, with four Fianna Fáil cronies among its eight members, was the one that took Ireland's airport authority into the third millennium. It was a far cry from the ideals of the founders of the semi-state companies. Aer Rianta had been created under the leadership of Seán Lemass; but by 1997 it was the creature of Haughey, Reynolds, Ahern and Cowen.

Lemass, had he lived to see it, would have been horrified at what became of his semi-state legacy. In a few short decades the companies set up to assist the fledgling state in vital areas of national economic interest had become playthings for the new rich. Aer Rianta was only one example of this decline.

Lemass was Minister for Industry and Commerce when Aer Rianta was set up in 1937. Lemass's first chairman of Aer Rianta was a legendary civil servant, John Leydon. Leydon was no political patsy. When Lemass asked him to become Secretary of the Department of Industry and Commerce after the creation of the first Fianna Fáil government in 1932, he is said to have accepted the post, but only conditionally. He warned Lemass that he was no 'yes man' and that

he was unhappy about certain of his policies. The minister replied
that Leydon need have no fears, that his opinions would not be an
obstacle to his progress. Lemass was true to his word, and eventually
made Leydon chairman of Aer Rianta and Aer Lingus.

In a paper delivered to the Institute of Public Administration (IPA)
in March 1959 – three months before he became Taoiseach – Lemass
spelled out the rationale behind the semi-states. He wasn't a socialist
with a blind belief in state ownership; rather, he was a pragmatist.
Semi-state enterprises had been formed where private enterprise had
feared to tread. If private capital would not take a long-term view,
the state would step in with more patient investment. Lemass ap-
plauded the profit motive, but where national policy demanded it, he
had set up semi-state companies.

Lemass outlined in the IPA paper the compelling reasons why the
state provided capital for the establishment of the ESB (1927), the
Industrial Credit Company (1933), The Irish Sugar Company (1933),
Aer Lingus (1936), Aer Rianta (1937), Irish Shipping (1941), CIÉ
(1944/50), Bord na Móna (1946) and other companies. According to
Lemass, the reasons were always strategic necessity, self-sufficiency
and jobs. He saw the new companies not only as vital to meet social
needs, but also as dynamic engines of the economy.

Yet even in 1959 he warned presciently of the pitfalls:

There is a danger that after the initial drive, to set up a new organisation
and to get it functioning properly, has expended itself the organisation may
settle down to routine operations characterised by excessive caution and
loss of initiative and flexibility. There is the danger that in the course of
time these organisations may be directed and administered with decreasing
regard for the national needs and increasing and undue concern for the
benefit and convenience of their staffs. There is a danger that bureaucratic
procedures may stifle efficiency and delay necessary or desirable innova-
tions and changes.

Wow. Was he anticipating the overmanning at Telecom Éireann or
the ESB, the featherbedding of the staffs at Aer Lingus or the chronic
inefficiencies at Aer Rianta? Could he have imagined the Employment

Share Ownership Trusts, the shares gifted to employees just before the semi-states were launched on to the stock exchanges? Is this what he meant by the 'decreasing regard for the national needs and increasing and undue concern for the benefit and convenience of their staffs'? The words are uncannily prophetic of the decay to come.

The father of Ireland's semi-state enterprises went on to warn of the necessity for constant vigilance:

In most instances in the case of these organisations, there is, apart from the spirit of public service, no automatic spur to efficiency. They lack the stimulus of private enterprise and competition. When it is possible that every rise in costs can be offset by higher charges, the danger is more acute and the need for some means to ensure continuing efficiency becomes clearer. The State-sponsored boards, if they are to fulfil their proper role in the national economy, require to be kept under continuous pressure, from inside and outside, to revise their procedures and costs in a continuous effort to maintain their efficiency.

In recent years the profligacy in semi-state bodies such as FÁS, CIÉ, the Health Service Executive (HSE), An Post and the Dublin Docklands Development Authority (DDDA) has demonstrated that Lemass's warnings weren't heeded.

Even as Lemass delivered his paper to the IPA in 1959, a bill setting up An Cheard Chomhairle (ANCO), the training agency that later became FÁS, was before the Dáil. Lemass had a clear vision of the importance of apprenticeship for the economy. ANCO was established as a lean, purposeful outfit. What would its creator think of FÁS, the bloated monster it had begotten, destined to become the shame of the state sector?

Lemass ended his paper by giving himself a pat on the back: 'By and large,' he declared, 'State boards and companies have been successful by every test and their contribution to the national economy has been a very important factor in the nation's growth.'

Perhaps he was right in 1959. Certainly the next speaker in the debate that day would have heartily endorsed the minister's favourable verdict on his own creation. C. S. 'Todd' Andrews, the colossus of the semi-states, rose to reply to Lemass. He insisted that 'without these companies the country would be little better than a cattle ranch' and went on to describe state companies as 'my interest and my life'.

It was probably understandable that Andrews should be more starry-eyed than Lemass about the semi-state enterprises. Having fought in the War of Independence and on the anti-Treaty side in the Civil War, he then worked for the Irish Tourist Association – later Bord Fáilte – and the fledgling ESB before Fianna Fáil took power in 1932 and appointed him to develop Ireland's turf industry. Later he moved from the bogs to the railways, taking charge at CIÉ in 1958.

Andrews's autobiography, *Man of No Property*, reveals a love of the unlovable semi-states unmatched in modern times. At one point he describes himself grandly as being not only a 'Jeffersonian democrat but a socialist' who 'regarded the semi-state industries as socialism in its practical form'. Lemass would have shunned such labels. He would happily have lived with the later privatizations of semi-state companies on a case-by-case basis, while Andrews would probably have opposed them on principle.

Todd Andrews's insights into the early days of the ESB are priceless. He describes the workforce as 'messianic in its enthusiasm' and insists: 'There were no labour problems. Hours worked counted for nothing with the technical or administrative staff.' He reveals that 'when emergencies occurred . . . total co-operation at all levels was assured. Even some members of the board chipped in.' He recalls seeing William Fay, a member of the board during the thirties, dressed like a skier, helping to restore the high-voltage lines in Kildare. It is hard to imagine the chairman of today's ESB, Lochlann Quinn, or his predecessor, Tadhg O'Donoghue, up an ESB pole in a storm. Writing in 1982, Andrews described the ESB as 'the finest industrial organisation in the country', citing its rural electrification scheme as evidence.

Andrews notes that in the early days of the state each side in the Civil War had promoted its own comrades. The anti-Treaty side – which would become Fianna Fáil – initially regarded the civil service as 'a crowd of Free State bastards'. After Fianna Fáil took power, he was exasperated by the nakedly political opposition of Cumann na nGaedheal to the development of the Irish bogs. As a result of this opposition, the Turf Development Board was politicized – and Andrews played the 'jobs for the boys' game pretty unapologetically himself. After receiving the nod from Lemass, he asked Robert Barton, a celebrated republican, to chair the Turf Development Board. Barton combined competence in the agriculture area with political acceptability.

Andrews goes on to admit that 'later at my request two other part-time members, both friends of mine . . . were added to the board.'

'Friends of mine'? The phrase was meant as an endorsement, a revealing justification of their appointment. The author's message is clear: if they were friends of his, they were, *ipso facto*, fine as directors.

When Andrews sought an accountant for the Turf Development Board, he looked no further than his 'intimate friend' Dermot Lawlor. Andrews said he 'persuaded him to apply for the accountant's post . . . to which he was duly appointed'. If that were to happen at executive level at Bord na Móna today, there would probably be political outrage; but then Dermot Lawlor's competence was never in question, unlike that of the party hacks stuffed on semi-state boards today.

Andrews served in Bord na Móna for twenty-five years. With an endearing lack of modesty, he claims that he was eager to leave in 1956, 'but I was identified so publicly with Bord na Móna and it was reflecting such credit on the government that their reluctance to sever my connection with the board was understandable'. Lemass eventually asked him to transfer his talents to the chair at CIÉ in 1958. According to Andrews, the minister's only problem was the 'difficulty that would arise in replacing me in Bord na Móna'.

Andrews hesitated because of his doubts about the proposed composition of the board. He took one look at CIÉ and decided that he needed to be both chairman and chief executive, and later wrote that 'a crash operation was needed which could not be successfully carried out unless . . . the chairman was chief executive; an operation of this kind required the virtually complete authority of one man.' (Such thinking is still alive and well at CIÉ, where the current supremo,

John Lynch, combines the roles of chairman and chief executive –
contrary to corporate-governance best practice.)

Writing in 1982, Andrews was outspoken on the boards of semi-
states, noting that their members 'are given their appointment for a
variety of reasons'.

The commonest of these is that they have participated in or supported the
activities of the political party in power, but frequently because they have
subscribed heavily to political funds. Some are appointed because they are
friends of particular ministers or TDs. A trade unionist is usually appointed
for cosmetic reasons. From time to time an academic is appointed to provide intellectual cachet or to reflect some cultural interest on the part of the
minister concerned. Sometimes the statutes require that the government
makes the appointment, sometimes a particular minister. It is not important. No appointment is ever made without the agreement of the Taoiseach
and the government whatever the statutes say.

Andrews's experience had led him to believe that an appointment
to a semi-state board should be seen as an honour, and that directors
should ideally not be paid. He tells us approvingly that the first directors of the Turf Development Board worked without payment and
did so 'with enthusiasm and success'.

His views on retired civil servants sitting on semi-state boards were
uncompromising, believing that those who had served in a department that had supervised the semi-state body should be excluded and
calling such appointments a 'depreciation of the currency of public
life'. He also judged it 'bad in principle that the secretary of the
Department of Finance should automatically become chairman or a
member of the board of the Central Bank' – a tradition that, with
regard to the chair, remained virtually unbroken until 2009, when
Minister for Finance Brian Lenihan appointed an academic economist, Patrick Honohan, as Central Bank Governor. By that time, of
course, the damage caused by the unhealthily close relationship
between the Department of Finance and the Regulator had already
been done.

Andrews viewed the directors of semi-state bodies as instruments of government policy. 'The basic function of the board of a state-sponsored body is to ensure that the chief executive is carrying out the policy of the government as laid down by statutes . . . they "direct" nothing.' What would he have thought of the Aer Rianta quartet of Noel Hanlon, Dermot O'Leary, Tadhg O'Donoghue and Freda Hayes (a Fianna Fáil supporter who had replaced Noel Fox in 2001) when, in 2003, they defiantly opposed transport minister Séamus Brennan's policy of breaking up the airport monopoly? He would probably have sacked Hanlon as chairman on the spot. Brennan contemplated the dismissal route, but Hanlon's Fianna Fáil connections were strong enough to stymie this. Aer Rianta had become the board's, not the state's, possession. Eventually government policy was implemented, though not before Brennan was humiliated.

Andrews's tenure at CIÉ was more difficult than his years with Bord na Móna, but his reorganization of the moribund transport body bore fruit. The 1958 Transport Act had given the transport company an annual subvention of £1.75 million; after that, it was expected to wash its face.

Andrews ruthlessly shut down railway routes – most controversially, the Harcourt Street line between Dublin and Bray – in his quest to break even, and by 1961 CIÉ was within a quarter of a million pounds of achieving this. But after nearly achieving solvency in 1961, CIÉ's fortunes fell into decline. Cursed by intransigent unions, expensive wage settlements and inefficiencies, it made bigger and bigger losses. Andrews retired from CIÉ in 1966, on his sixty-fifth birthday. Today, CIÉ makes losses of over €300 million a year, which are covered largely by a subvention from the taxpayer, and its name is synonymous with waste, cronyism and inefficiency.

Andrews's retirement from CIÉ should have marked the finish of his career as a public servant, but there was one semi-state left for his attention. His old patron Seán Lemass – now at the very end of his tenure as Taoiseach – offered him the job of part-time chairman of the RTÉ Authority. Andrews accepted but – in his typically puritan style – declined the offer of an office, a secretary and a chauffeur-driven car. Luxuries and perks were beginning to creep into the remuneration packages of semi-state chiefs, but he felt the enjoyment of such rewards by a part-time chairman could not be justified.

His tales of RTÉ Authority meetings do his colleagues of the day little credit. He asserts that the authority usually said 'yes' to the director-general's proposals, partly because 'some of the members never went to the trouble to read the supporting documentation and discreetly remained silent'. Many only opened their mouths when it came to discussing specific TV programmes. No meetings of the authority went beyond lunchtime because 'post-prandial meetings have many evident demerits'. Lunch appears to have been the main item of the day for some RTÉ bosses.

Andrews had been appointed because he was a safe pair of hands. He had succeeded his namesake Eamonn Andrews (no relation), the best known of a growing band of Irish-bred broadcasters who had achieved success in Britain at the BBC and at ABC Television. Eamonn had resigned as chairman, partly because of what he saw as RTÉ's excessive use of the Irish language and partly because of the state broadcaster's reluctance to employ foreigners. Eamonn's status as a celebrity chairman, meanwhile, had not suited Fianna Fáil.

Todd Andrews, by contrast, wanted more, not less, of the Irish language on the airwaves and was far more in tune with the nationalist mood of the day than Eamonn, the Irishman who had won so many accolades as the star Irish broadcaster in the United Kingdom. The government took advantage of Eamonn's departure to tighten its grip on RTÉ.

Todd Andrews relates how the Minister for Posts and Telegraphs, Erskine Childers, would relay cabinet grouses about RTÉ to him every Thursday. He says that he ignored nearly all of Childers's gripes, but there is little doubt that the government could rely on him to act in what they perceived as the national interest. After all, he had been a Fianna Fáil supporter all his life. Although his membership of the party had ended when he joined the civil service in 1933, he had been an undisguised Fianna Fáil 'sleeper' in the semi-states ever since. Yet by the time he retired for the last time in 1970 his infatuation with Fianna Fáil was fading.

Andrews makes a fleeting but significant reference in his autobiography to an ominous development in the Irish political world of the sixties. A Fianna Fáil fundraising organization called 'Taca' (the Irish word for 'support') had sprung up in November 1966. It involved businessmen and Fianna Fáil in a mutual back scratching exercise that hardly put the nation first – and that, for Andrews, 'diminished further any emotional interest' he had in the party.

His resignation was not unrelated to Taca's leading personalities and associated activities. By his own account, he resigned because his son David became chief whip of the Fianna Fáil parliamentary party and he did not wish to be faced with any conflicts of interest. Significantly, David Andrews had been appointed because of vacancies created by the fall of some of the best-known Taca enthusiasts: Charles Haughey, Neil Blaney and Kevin Boland had been sacked or resigned from the cabinet as a result of events leading up to the famous Arms Trial. The way was cleared for a fightback within Fianna Fáil by the opponents of the dubious activities of Taca.

While Andrews and Lemass had soldiered together in the IRA and in the semi-states, the next generation of their republican families parted ways. Lemass's son-in-law, Charles Haughey, led the wing of the party that cultivated the brash type of businessman typified by Taca. Andrews's son David, meanwhile, opposed the Haughey/Blaney/Boland wing of Fianna Fáil to the hilt. The party's former unity of purpose, seen as patriotism by Andrews and Lemass, did not survive into the succeeding generation. Haughey and many of his Fianna Fáil followers were mesmerized by the benefits politics could offer in terms of material wealth, and this ethos ultimately gained the ascendant in the party.

Lemass had been succeeded as Taoiseach by Jack Lynch in 1966. The new Taoiseach was hardly a wet week in office when Taca was born. The departure of Lemass, a strong man of integrity with Civil War roots, gave the green light to the brash mohair-suit brigade of Haughey, Blaney, Donogh O'Malley, et al. Their desire to plug Fianna Fáil into the business community was indulged by Lynch in a way that Lemass would never have tolerated.

Taca's methods were a sea change from the church-gate collections for the party in the era of de Valera and Lemass. The new industrialists, builders, bankers and architects of the sixties were approached with requests for donations of £100 a year to become members of this secretive organization. Members paid £100 a head for dinners in the Gresham and the Burlington, where they hobnobbed with ministers. Its activities attracted the interest of maybe as many as 500 businessmen and a lot of adverse media comment, with the opposition insisting that 'Tacateers' were buying favours from the government.

Taca was a two-way street. Some members were already in key business positions but saw membership as a means of influencing Fianna Fáil government policy. Others used it to secure prestigious posts in state bodies. The chairman of Taca was a high-flying surveyor named Desmond MacGreevy. His careful cultivation of political contacts won him valuable contracts, including the huge flats complex at Ballymun in North Dublin. MacGreevy was a friend of both Haughey and Donogh O'Malley – whom he succeeded as chairman of the national Building Advisory Council. When it was merged with the semi-state An Foras Forbartha (the National Institute for Physical Planning and Construction Research), he became a director. He secured a multitude of state contracts including the Central Bank headquarters in Dame Street, the expansion of RTÉ at Montrose, the engineering and agricultural faculties at Belfield, the new Dublin Airport Hotel, the National Currency Centre at Sandyford, and the Ireland Houses in London and Brussels.

Taca caused deep divisions within the party. George Colley, a leading member of the traditional wing, was understood to be talking about Haughey when he gave a celebrated speech in 1967 in which he deplored 'low standards in high places', but some also detected a swipe at Taca; and the following year he declared that 'under no circumstances can we allow big business to dominate Fianna Fáil'. Two years later, dogged by bad press, Taca was disbanded. But the love affair between Fianna Fáil and big business lived on; and party supporters continued to receive preferment in state appointments.

While Fianna Fáil led the way in placing its own members on state boards, it would be wrong to brand Haughey, Blaney, O'Malley and the rest as exclusive practitioners of the dark art of patronage. Fianna

Fáil, of course, had the advantage of being in power most of the time. When Fine Gael's Liam Cosgrave became Taoiseach in 1973, after sixteen years of Fianna Fáil rule, he led a government that claimed to be intent on cleaning up politics. In practice, Fianna Fáil patronage gave way to Fine Gael patronage. As vacancies occurred, Civil War politics determined many of the appointments; and just before he left office after losing the election of 1977, Cosgrave forever damaged his reputation with what historian Tim Pat Coogan dubbed an 'orgy of appointments'.

Less than a week before he dissolved the Dáil, in May 1977, he decided to promote his Attorney General, the Fine Gael TD Declan Costello, to the High Court. To replace Costello in the AG's office he named Professor John Kelly, a Fine Gael TD for Dublin South Central. He then incensed the Bar Council by instantly elevating Kelly's status to that of Senior Counsel, a title in the gift of the government.

A defeated Cosgraveite TD, Brendan Toal of Cavan–Monaghan, was compensated for the loss of his seat by being made a land commissioner in the short interim period between Cosgrave's humiliation at the polls on 16 June and the first sitting of the new Dáil and the election of a new Taoiseach on 5 July. In the same interregnum Cosgrave nominated four defeated Dáil candidates to fill vacancies created in the Senate by senators who had been elected to the new Dáil. This dubious manoeuvre, possible only because the old Senate is still sitting after the new Dáil is elected, is regularly practised by outgoing Taoisigh. Other Taoisigh have planted party loyalists in these brief Senate vacancies merely to give them parking in Leinster House for life.

In the Dáil a year later, George Colley, now serving as finance minister for the second time, was announcing some fresh appointments. Challenged over the party-political connections of the appointees, he told the House that 'during the period after the election and before the change of government', the outgoing Fine Gael–Labour coalition had made 'well over 100 appointments, in the main, to boards in every vacancy they could create or think up. This was done by a government who had been defeated by the people. If there is to be any question of raising the political affiliations of appointees of this kind, I do not think that any Deputy over there can afford to open his mouth.'

Paddy Moriarty was a 'Charlie' man, though not a Taca man. He came from a well-known Fianna Fáil family in Kerry. (His brother is the renowned GAA broadcaster Micheál Ó Muircheartaigh). He was deeply involved in the promotion of the Irish language, the GAA and horse racing.

Paddy Mo (as he was known) became chief executive of the ESB in 1981. In 1985 he came under fire in the Jansen Report on the ESB, which found that the semi-state was overstaffed to the tune of 3,000 workers. It had increased its staff numbers by 20 per cent between 1979 and 1983, a period during which consumption of electricity actually fell. In an interview with the *Irish Times* in the aftermath of the report he admitted that 'in 1979 and 1980' – just before he became chief executive – 'we recruited people for training and apprentice-ship to jobs that are not now there.'

One contemporary describes Moriarty at the time as having 'an undying loyalty to Kinsealy' – the sylvan corner of North Dublin that became synonymous with Haughey. Moriarty denied that the ESB had ever been in the 'employment-creating business', but the overstaffing fuelled the suspicion that it and other semi-states were being manipulated by politicians to reduce the numbers on the regis-ter of unemployed. Meanwhile, as Lemass had feared, the interests of the employees became more important than the interests of the state. More contented employees means fewer discontented voters. Tele-com Éireann, An Post, Aer Lingus, Aer Rianta and CIÉ all became chronically overmanned.

Des O'Malley, who was Minister for Industry, Commerce and Energy in the Fianna Fáil government of the late seventies, tells a story that illustrates the ESB's attitudes at the time. 'I tried to per-suade the ESB to explore the possibilities of wind power and other alternative forms of energy,' O'Malley says. 'The response from Paddy Moriarty was frosty. The ESB top guys insisted that wind power would never work.'

The minister eventually persuaded Paddy Mo to buy thirteen

wind generators as an experiment. The state monopoly installed them under ministerial duress in Wicklow and other rural areas. All thirteen broke down. When O'Malley made inquiries about what progress had been made in their repair, he was told by Moriarty that they were not worth fixing, that wind power was a nonsense.

Two years later O'Malley was surprised to hear that two wind generators had been installed and were working well – on the Kerry island of Inishvickillane, Charlie Haughey's holiday hideaway.

In the eighties and nineties a wave of privatizations of state utilities swept through Europe. The UK led the way: under Margaret Thatcher and John Major, billions were raised for Britain's empty Exchequer as the government sold off the railways, the airports, the airways and other utilities.

When Irish governments came to consider the possibility of privatizations in their own country, the obstacles were multiple. Few state companies were suitable for flotation on the stock market. They were overmanned and wasteful, and lacked commercial edge. Their reputation as political playthings was widespread. Privatizations would undoubtedly lead to heavy job losses as staffing was reduced to rational levels – a tricky prospect at a time of high unemployment.

Charles Haughey had set his mind against the privatization of semi-states when in opposition. Back in government in 1987 and again in 1989, he did a volte-face. Two thriving companies were selected to test the waters. The government decided to float Irish Sugar (to be renamed Greencore) and Irish Life, the state's insurance company. The privatization of Irish Life was smooth and successful; Greencore was a disaster.

The decision to float the Irish Sugar Company was driven by two men: its chairman, Bernie Cahill, and its chief executive, Chris Comerford. Cahill, a Fine Gael supporter, had been appointed by Fine Gael Minister for Agriculture Austin Deasy. Cahill and Comerford drove the company hard to prepare the way for a sale.

Cahill's allegiance to Fine Gael was not full-blooded, and when his enthusiasm for sailing brought him into contact with that celebrated sailor Charles Haughey, the two became as thick as thieves.

Michael O'Kennedy, the Minister for Agriculture (and consequently Irish Sugar's nominal boss at the time of flotation), told us: 'Bernie Cahill had reached Charlie. They were sailing companions. Real decisions were being taken by Charlie and [by] others outside government. I told Charlie so: "I either have a job or not." I was not comfortable with it. It was the most tense time I ever had as a minister.'

Despite his representations, O'Kennedy remained sidelined. The appointment of Haughey's personal solicitors, J. S. O'Connor, as joint legal advisers to the flotation and NCB, the Taoiseach's favourite brokers, as brokers to the privatization led to eruptions both in the Dáil and at a subsequent shareholders' meeting. Cahill was discovered to have held several hush-hush meetings with Haughey in his Kinsealy pile at crucial times during the flotation. Many of the lucrative appointments to the sale were believed to have been cooked up between the two men. The state's first privatization became mired in a welter of controversy as politics and cronyism took precedence over the interests of the taxpayer. The suspicion arose that Haughey viewed the sale of state assets as yet another way of enriching those who worshipped at his court.

Despite the political turmoil, the sale of Irish Sugar went ahead. But just a few months after the stock market launch, the journalist Sam Smyth broke a sensational story in the *Sunday Independent*. Chris Comerford was revealed to be taking legal action to recover a sum of £2.1 million that Irish Sugar allegedly owed to an unknown company, registered in Jersey, called Talmino; Comerford claimed to be its owner. The ownership of Talmino was in question, but what was not in dispute was the disturbing revelation that Comerford was seeking to benefit personally from Irish Sugar's pre-flotation purchase of a company in which he claimed an interest. As the boss at Irish Sugar he was on both sides of a mysterious deal. Worse still, the interest in Talmino that Comerford now claimed had not been spelled out to investors in the prospectus.

After Smyth's story was published, it became clear that the board had been kept in the dark about Comerford's legal action to establish his personal ownership of Talmino. Comerford was forced to resign, and other Greencore executives who were party to the deal followed him out of the door. Government-appointed inspectors later concluded that Comerford was 'an unfit person to be a director of a company in the State'. A year later the Minister for Finance, Bertie Ahern, told the Dáil that 'there appears to have been a failure or inability on the part of the board of directors of Siucre Éireann to exercise any proper and effective control over Mr Comerford in his capacity of managing director of that company.'

Despite this indictment of the directors, Bernie Cahill somehow survived in the chair for many years.

Further follies followed. Less than a year after the flotation, the government again disillusioned Greencore investors by suddenly selling its remaining 15 per cent shareholding without notice. Investors regarded this as a breach of faith, as the government had given previous undertakings to hold on to its remaining shareholding for far longer.

What came to be known as 'the curse of Greencore' also afflicted the blue-blooded stockbroking firm of Davy, after its directors were outed as major buyers in a share placing of Greencore stock carried out by their own firm. Bertie Ahern was vitriolic: 'You cannot sell to yourself and it appears to me that it got as near as selling to yourself in this case as to make me very unhappy.'

The fiasco at Greencore dampened enthusiasm for privatizations in Ireland for over a decade. Opposition from the trade unions and their powerful disciple, Bertie Ahern, created an additional political obstacle. Bertie was Minister for Finance from 1991 to 1994, and Taoiseach from 1997 to 2007. In the intervening period from 1994 to 1997, the finance portfolio was held by Labour's Ruairi Quinn. No socialist was ever going to sell state assets.

Bertie Ahern allowed the trade unions to clasp the ailing semi-state companies close to their bosoms and their beards. Obvious candidates for privatization like the ESB, Aer Rianta, Bord na Móna and An Post were so union-dominated that investors were bound to be put off by the sight of a militant workforce in the habit of issuing orders to the Taoiseach.

Bertie's first finance minister, Charlie McCreevy, was far more bullish about taking on the unions and privatizing state assets. Specifically, he wanted to sell Telecom Éireann. It should have been easy.

The economy was booming and employees of semi-states were enjoying its fruits. All the old moans about selling the family silver were softened by the nation's prosperity.

Telecom Éireann was privatized (as Eircom) in 1999. The pace of the privatization was dictated not by the management but by the workforce. Tortuous negotiations were held. The unions won a deal that gave the employees 15 per cent of the company. Management, meanwhile, gorged themselves on share options within a year of the launch. In preparation for the flotation, the Minister for Public Enterprise, Mary O'Rourke, moved to replace five of the six government-appointed directors, and promised those who stepped aside that other state appointments would be found for them.

When Eircom shares were floated, 575,000 citizens plunged into the shares, many in the hope of windfall gains. Unrealistic expectations about Eircom's share prospects were encouraged by a massive public-relations campaign. After an initial spike, the price gradually drifted well below the offer level. The vast majority of small shareholders lost heavily. Naturally, they blamed the government. Confronted by massive public anger, the Eircom directors panicked and rapidly sold the mobile division and the fixed-line business separately. Eircom was to change hands five times in the next ten years. The losses sustained by the small investors on the shares all but guaranteed that the general public would not subscribe to future Irish privatizations.

The legacy of the Eircom fiasco hung heavily over efforts to privatize Aer Lingus, the national airline. Aer Lingus needed capital for a new fleet, and a stock-market flotation was originally targeted for 2001. The events of 9/11 changed everything – in its aftermath, airlines were folding and merging, not raising capital. Aer Lingus was in deep trouble when a young man by the name of Willie Walsh rescued it from oblivion.

Walsh was a most unlikely saviour, having started his career as a pilot before jumping over the wall to Aer Lingus management. He was chief operations officer when he was picked from relative obscurity for the hottest job in the semi-states.

Only thirty-nine when he took over, he set about cutting costs with a ruthlessness never before seen in Aer Lingus. He even sold the airline's collection of Jack B. Yeats and Louis le Brocquy paintings while imposing a low-cost model and achieving 2,000 redundancies. In 2004, impatient with continued union intransigence and a lack of capital at the airline, he attempted an audacious management buyout. He was blocked by none other than the Taoiseach, Bertie Ahern.

Ahern showed his true colours when responding to Walsh's move, describing it as 'a time when management wanted to steal the assets for themselves . . . shafting staff interests'. Ahern was in the pocket of the unions that represented Aer Lingus workers and terrified of job losses that might cost Fianna Fáil votes in North Dublin. He managed to duck and weave, delaying the flotation until 2006. By then Walsh had departed in frustration. Ireland's semi-state disease had defeated him. He was immediately headhunted and made boss of British Airways, a global giant many times the size of Aer Lingus. The semi-state culture, the unions and the Taoiseach had driven him away; Ireland was the loser.

The Aer Lingus flotation was finally forced on Ahern because of the airline's critical need for capital. The shareholding structure was a farce. The government retained 25 per cent and, as with Eircom, the unions were handed 15 per cent on a plate. Aer Lingus became a publicly quoted company, but it had hardly emerged from the semi-state infirmary. Even after Walsh's cuts it remained overstaffed – and the overmanning was allowed to continue because of the efforts of Bertie and the unions. Large institutional shareholders mostly spurned it as a political/trade-union hybrid.

So that was Ireland's record: three out of four privatizations botched. The workforce, not the public interest, dictated the shape of the flotations; the government held on to too big a share of the companies for too long; politics interfered at every point; restrictive work practices and waste persisted.

While the state was making heavy weather of privatizing four companies in the 1990–2006 period, there emerged a contradictory development: an explosion of state bodies. Just as the state appeared to have taken the tentative leap into dismantling the semi-state

apparatus and increasing efficiency, it was indulging itself in a prolif-
eration of unnecessary agencies.

Back in 1927 there were fewer than a dozen state agencies or
semi-state bodies. The 1970 Devlin Report identified eighty. By
2008, according to a policy paper prepared by Fine Gael TD Leo Varadkar, there were 445 national state agencies. If all the other task
forces, boards and agencies set up at local-authority level were to be
included, the number would approach four figures. As Varadkar puts
it, 'the island of saints and scholars had become the land of a thousand quangos.'

Varadkar found that no fewer than 207 state agencies had been created between 1997 and 2007, and that there were huge overlaps in a
number of areas, including drugs, scientific research and corporate
law. Such obscure quangos as the Ireland Newfoundland Partnership
Board, the Dormant Accounts Board and the Irish Expert Body on
Fluorides and Health are among the new outfits. It is difficult to see
why any vital work they may have been charged with doing on behalf
of the state cannot be done in the appropriate departments.

Varadkar determined that there were 2,416 people sitting on the
boards of these quangos, all at the whim of their political masters.
That figure does not include nominations made by ministers on the
advice of other insiders, such as the Irish Congress of Trade Unions
(ICTU) or the slovenly Irish Business and Employers Confederation
(IBEC). At the time of Varadkar's report, the Minister for Justice
could land 325 of his favourites on to various quangos, while the
Minister for Health and Children held 472 positions of patronage in
her gift. All in all, by 2008 nearly 6,000 directors had been appointed
to Ireland's state bodies, the vast majority of the lucky boys and girls
drawing juicy fees.

Todd Andrews must be turning in his grave. His opinion in his
autobiography – that those who serve on state boards should do it for
nothing – rings hollow in the ears of Ireland's gluttons for patronage,
while his belief that those who volunteered pro bono would do a better job than those so generously rewarded today remains true.

The snouts-in-the-trough culture provided the breeding ground
for the scandals of FÁS, CIÉ, the HSE, the Dublin Docklands

Development Authority and dozens of others, including many surely still to emerge. This was the culture that allowed politicians to run riot with rewards for their pals. This was the culture that gave us the Charlie Haughey industry and the Bertie Ahern industry. This was the culture that gave birth to a whole industry of waste.

2. The Bertie Industry (and Other Tales of Political Patronage)

There is a tall tale told about Bertie Ahern from 2004, when Ireland held the presidency of the European Council. One Saturday morning the Taoiseach was due to meet his army of canvassers at 11 a.m. on the corner of Dublin's Griffith Avenue near his Drumcondra stronghold. Some of his loyal door-knockers were puzzled. They had heard on the news late on Friday evening that the Taoiseach was spending the night in Finland and was meeting the Finnish Prime Minister the next day.

They concluded that there was a change of plan. Bertie the EU statesman had taken over from Bertie the constituency warlord. The next morning it was lashing rain. So with their hero safely in Scandinavia, they decided to play truant for the day. Some of them even stayed in bed.

Bertie had other ideas. His breakfast meeting with the Finnish Prime Minister took place at the airport. He pleaded an important engagement in Ireland, curtailed the encounter to forty-five minutes, hopped on to the waiting government jet and headed for Dublin. He landed at Dublin airport at 10.45. The state car was waiting to speed him to Griffith Avenue to keep his 11 a.m. appointment canvassing with the Drumcondra troops. Bertie is said to have been gobsmacked when none of the party workers appeared, leaving the leader of the nation, the president of the European Council, standing lamely alone at the corner of the leafiest avenue in his Dublin Central constituency.

Fianna Fáil insiders tell another, possibly embellished, tale of his devotion to his Drumcondra base. While Taoiseach he accepted a dinner invitation to the County Down mansion of one of his nominated senators, Eddie Haughey, a.k.a. Baron Ballyedmond of Mourne, one of the richest men in Northern Ireland. Among those invited to the dinner was Princess Michael of Kent, often unkindly known as 'Princess Pushy', and certainly one of the raciest of the British

Royals. (After Prince Michael married her he lost his place in the royal pecking order because she is a Roman Catholic.)

Haughey (no relation of the former Taoiseach) sent his chopper down from Newry to collect Bertie and two sidekicks, Fianna Fáil general secretary Pat Farrell and long-time Ahern confidant Des Richardson. As they hovered over Newry, Ahern is said to have turned to Richardson and instructed him to point to his watch at 10 p.m. and tell the Taoiseach that he had to keep an important engagement with an ambassador in Dublin that evening.

His fellow travellers reminded the Taoiseach that Princess Michael was royalty and that the protocol at such outings was never to leave before those with blue blood. Bertie blew a fuse. He would put up with the princess and indulge Eddie Haughey's weakness for British royalty for a couple of hours, but there was no way he was going to miss a few pints in Fagan's of Drumcondra.

The Taoiseach won the day. At 10 p.m. the Fianna Fáil group breached royal protocol, apologized to Haughey's guests and left three empty seats at the banquet in the plutocrat's ostentatious pile. The chopper delivered them safely to Dublin airport in good time for a couple of pints in Fagan's. Princess Michael was dumbstruck, and Eddie Haughey far from pleased.

That is Bertie Ahern. No lover of royalty, no prisoner of prime ministers, princesses or protocol. The centre of Bertie's world is Drumcondra. And Drumcondra is only fifteen minutes away from one of Bertie's most vital protectorates, Dublin Airport.

Through his heyday, Bertie had neither confidants in Leinster House nor any real friends within his own cabinet. Members of the Fianna Fáil parliamentary party loved his accessibility, but none knew him well personally. While his cabinet colleagues hatched plots in the members' bar and restaurants of Leinster House, Bertie was rarely seen in either. The nerve centre of Ireland's government for the ten years of Bertie's premiership rested not in Government Buildings but in three North Dublin watering holes: Fagan's, the Beaumont House and the Goose. His comfort zone began and ended in his Dublin Central constituency, where he could enjoy the company of selected cronies, preferably over a few pints.

Bertie may have had no friends in Leinster House, but his group of local lieutenants, known as the 'Drumcondra Mafia', provided ample compensation. They ran an electoral machine without parallel in Ireland. They looked after him personally and politically. Whatever his needs, the Drumcondra gang catered for them, making Bertie's base the envy of other politicians.

He repaid their loyalty in spades; patronage was his tool. He used it skilfully to reward his friends and to protect his own political interests. Nowhere was his exercise of patronage more evident than in his treatment of Aer Lingus.

Dublin Airport was not in Bertie's constituency, but any threat to Aer Lingus was a dagger pointing at the heart of his wider political landscape: the four constituencies in North Dublin where thousands of employees of Aer Lingus or its sister semi-state, Aer Rianta, lived. In the constituency of Dublin North at the 2002 general election Fianna Fáil won two out of four seats; in Dublin North Central two out of four; in Dublin North East two out of three; and in Dublin North West two out of three (one of which went to Bertie's own brother, Noel). This was territory Fianna Fáil needed to hold.

During the eighties, nineties and noughties, Aer Lingus stumbled from crisis to crisis. Its monopoly was gone. The EU no longer allowed endless government subsidies. The aviation world was changing, with national airlines having to adapt to global considerations. Aer Lingus, so long protected, was now under fire. In order to compete, it had to cut costs, which meant reductions in staff. Aer Rianta, meanwhile, remained a monopoly, unaffected by competition. Although its slovenly ways were coming under parallel scrutiny, it did not have to endure the same compelling commercial pressures as Aer Lingus.

Government ministers exercised unfettered powers of patronage over the boards of the two companies. While they were officially the preserve of the Minister for Transport, the holder of the ministry knew that he or she must never make a move affecting such sensitive flashpoints without first alerting Bertie.

Bertie had no vision for Aer Lingus. The great controversies at the airline, such as the endless row over the Shannon stopover, hardly registered with him. He could barely distinguish between an Airbus and an Airedale. Bertie's mentor, Charlie Haughey – whose own North Dublin constituency was even more reliant on employment from Dublin Airport than Bertie's – had set an example for his protégé by promoting people to the board of Aer Lingus with his own and Fianna Fáil's interests in mind. His appointments included a number of Fianna Fáil loyalists and cronies – including the notorious Des Traynor, who set up the Ansbacher-account scam and who became an Aer Lingus director in 1982.

The Aer Lingus board was the biggest prize in the semi-state sector because of the free travel for directors and their families that came with the job. Not everyone on the board was suspected of being in it for the perks, but no political party was willing to waste such a gift on people whose loyalties were in doubt.

Bertie's lack of a grand plan for Aer Lingus became blindingly obvious when he put two members of his Drumcondra Mafia on the board of the national airline. In 2001, when chief executive Michael Foley was facing allegations of sexual harassment, the Aer Lingus disciplinary committee consisted of Paddy Wright – who came from a staunch Fianna Fáil family and had been appointed to the board by Charles Haughey – and two members of Bertie's Drumcondra gang, Des Richardson and Chris Wall.

Bertie's tentacles extended far. One government minister told us that when Bertie was at cabinet meetings he would suddenly spit out detailed knowledge of individual semi-states that he could have got only from members of the boards. 'I would be sitting there and Bertie would suddenly state facts about the internal problems of a state body under my department that I knew nothing about. I would feel a fool, but Bertie was being fed information from elsewhere. I was being bypassed. He knew that information was power. His men were crawling all over the quangos by 2006 and he could pick up the telephone to find out exactly what was happening on any of them.'

Richardson and Wall were Bertie's eyes and ears on the Aer Lingus board. One fellow director observed to us that both men were 'third-division players in the league of commerce', but this may be a little unfair. Richardson had made plenty of money by the time he was appointed to the board of Aer Lingus in November 1997, a few months after Bertie was first elected Taoiseach. Besides being Fianna Fáil's Mr Moneybags, he was reported to have made a mint in a controversial company called A1 Waste, which was prosecuted for illegal dumping in County Wicklow.

Aer Lingus was not Richardson's only dip into quango-land. He had been a director of a FÁS offshoot, FÁS International Consulting, through Bertie's good offices, and had served a term on the Health and Safety Authority. But both paled into insignificance, in terms of status, fees, perks and importance, compared with the Aer Lingus gig.

Beside him on the Aer Lingus board for a few years sat Chris Wall, Bertie's closest political ally in Dublin Central. Wall had known Bertie since the early eighties, when he had been involved in athletics with Bertie's brother Maurice. He was often spoken of as a 'consultant', and had enough of a business pedigree to justify his addition to the Aer Lingus board, but his principal role in life was that of Bertie's constituency lieutenant. As a man with his finger on the constituency button, Wall was priceless to Bertie on the board of Aer Lingus. Nothing moved in either the airline's or the voters' patch without Wall knowing about it. He served as a director for a record eleven years until 2008, not exiting until his patron had left the Taoiseach's office. He somehow survived the privatization purge in 2006 when other political nominees were eased out.

Wall was even more generously rewarded by Ahern in 2007, when he was made a senator for a few weeks. Bertie made use of the gambit employed by all victorious parties following a Dáil election: after four of his eleven Senate nominees from 2002 were elected to the Dáil in the 2007 general election, Bertie decided to fill the four temporary Senate vacancies for the few weeks until the 2007 elections were completed. Four Bertie loyalists swaggered into Leinster House to take their seats, entitled to claim pay and privileges during this brief lacuna. After four weeks they were out of office, but Chris Wall, among others, now has the right to park in Leinster House for life and enjoys access to the members' restaurant and bar.

Aer Lingus, Wall and Richardson were only the tip of the iceberg when it came to Bertie's patronage. Happily for him, his other obsession, Aer Rianta, was still in safe Fianna Fáil hands when he was elected Taoiseach in 1997, as hardly any board vacancies had opened up during the brief Fine Gael–Labour coalition government. As related in Chapter 1, he ensured that the vacancies that arose in the autumn of 1997 were filled with party sympathizers.

Once he had stuffed the Aer Lingus and Aer Rianta boards with his appointees, he turned his gaze seawards to protect the other flank of his constituency.

Dublin Port was a vital part of Bertie's protectorate. It already provided employment, but it had the potential to buzz, and he wanted a tighter hold on it. As property values began to boom, its huge land bank assumed a new importance: at one point the property portfolio was valued at €1.246 billion. Speculation abounded in business circles about the port being too small for the traffic. Rumours circulated that a move to Bremore on the Dublin–Meath border was on the cards. Such an idea was unlikely to find favour with Bertie.

A keen eye needed to be kept on this asset, which had the potential to enrich or impoverish the constituency. In 2002 Bertie's Minister for Marine, Frank Fahey, appointed one of Bertie's oldest pals, Joe Burke – a one-time building-site foreman from Donegal who had run a crash-repairs business in North Dublin – to the chair of the Dublin Port Company. Burke's appointment to the €22,000-a-year post was confirmed just before the general election of 2002. There was a minor political rumpus, but no noisier than was usual among politicians now battle-hardened by decades of outrageous political promotions. Burke's appointment was – equally controversially – renewed just before the 2007 election for another five-year term.

According to Michael Clifford and Shane Coleman in their riveting book *Bertie Ahern and the Drumcondra Mafia*, Ahern made a lame attempt to justify the appointment in the Dáil, asserting that Burke had 'a number of attributes' including the fact that his wife's family was 'very involved in the port, is from the port and lived in the port'. In truth, the lucky Burke had little knowledge of ports or shipping.

Burke was also accident-prone. His pub refurbishment company went belly-up, leading to a court finding that he had behaved irresponsibly in not preparing final accounts and in allowing the company to build up debts to the Revenue while insolvent. The judge found that he had behaved honestly, but he restricted his role as a company director for five years unless he fulfilled certain conditions.

Burke resigned as chairman of the Dublin Port Company in early 2009. By then Bertie was out of office, and Wall and Richardson were out of Aer Lingus. The Drumcondra Mafia's influence in the semi-states was waning. But Bertie had already managed to infect most of the vital organs of the state. Plenty of his protégés survive in situ today.

Paul Kiely, a dark horse from the Drumcondra retinue, is one of the survivors. He was part of a powerful trio – with Bertie and the late Tony Kett – who started their working life in the Mater Hospital back in the seventies. They formed a political alliance that spread its wings wide in the succeeding decades.

According to Clifford and Coleman, Kiely was 'the brains' behind Bertie's Drumcondra operation. He was quieter than Burke or Richardson, but he carried huge clout in the inner circle. Kiely even allowed his name to go forward as a 'dummy' candidate at a Fianna Fáil nominating convention for a by-election in 1983. In his autobiography, Bertie Ahern explains: 'We had to play cute to get what we wanted. We put Paul Kiely's name in as a potential candidate and everyone assumed he was "my" man. But just before the vote was taken we withdrew Paul and threw our weight behind Tom Leonard.' Kiely's name had been put into the contest to stop another candidate, a Haughey protégé named John Stafford, whom Bertie appeared to regard as a threat to his supremacy in the constituency. The ploy worked. Leonard inherited all of Kiely's votes at the convention, was duly nominated and later elected.

Kiely was appointed to the board of CIÉ in 1998 – a plum job that carried a fee of £5,000 at the time. It was not demanding work, but it carried prestige. Kiely ended up as the chairman of the transport company's powerful audit committee, its finance committee and its remuneration committee. Only the CIÉ property committee was entrusted to the tender care of another board member.

It is difficult to fathom how Kiely merited such a responsible position in a sick semi-state outfit that loses hundreds of millions every year. But CIÉ was another tinderbox where political or industrial trouble could have upset Bertie's applecart at any time, and Kiely was an ultra-reliable pair of hands. Even more importantly, one of Dublin's busiest rail depots, Connolly Station, was in the heart of Bertie's constituency. Bertie was now carefully covered in his local bailiwick – not only in the air, but also on the sea and the railways.

Kiely's credentials hardly qualified him for the task of saving a semi-state, but he did have one intriguing line in his CV. Since 1988 he had been chief executive of the Central Remedial Clinic (CRC) in Clontarf, North Dublin.

The CRC has a proud history. It was founded in 1951 by Lady Valerie Goulding for polio victims. A member of the British nobility who married the Irish fertilizer magnate and art collector Sir Basil Goulding, she worked selflessly for invalids struck down with paralysis by polio. She constantly sought state aid for the clinic, and struck up an unlikely alliance with Charles Haughey soon after his acquittal in the Arms Trial. The British aristocrat asked the Irish republican to head up the clinic's fundraising committee. It was an initiative of genius: no one knew how to raise funds like Haughey. Years later, in 1987, she said, 'But for Charlie, we'd have no centre today.' She helped with his political rehabilitation, while he helped her to save the clinic.

During the seventies Lady Goulding joined Fianna Fáil. She stood for the Senate in 1977 but failed to be elected; a few weeks later Jack Lynch gave her a Taoiseach's nomination. Her dedication to the CRC had been recognized in a tangible form. Fianna Fáil generosity to her creation still survives in the form of an annual Exchequer grant.

Lady Goulding died in 2003. Her well-respected son Hamilton sits on the board of the clinic but otherwise its membership reads like a North Dublin 'Friends of Fianna Fáil' pressure group. In the chair sits Des Peelo, an accountant who represented both Charlie Haughey and Bertie Ahern at the height of their tribunal problems. Alongside Peelo on the clinic's board sits James Nugent, one of the most prominent of Bertie's supporters during his financial travails. Nugent told the Mahon Tribunal that he gave Bertie £2,500 as part of a whip-round organized by Des Richardson and Bertie's now-deceased solicitor Gerry Brennan; other donors included the colourful publican Charlie Chawke, Pádraic O'Connor of NCB stockbrokers, auctioneer Fintan Gunne and Paddy 'the Plasterer' Reilly.

Nugent received tangible rewards for his efforts: not only did he serve three terms as chairman of CERT, the state tourism training agency, but from 1998 to 2003 he sat on the board of the Central Bank. Nugent, a friend for thirty-seven years, was a diehard, remaining loyal to Ahern to the last. He even showed up at the count in the 2009 Dublin Central by-election to offer support to Bertie's lost cause when his brother Maurice was humiliated at the polls.

Another Fianna Fáil veteran on the CRC board is Vincent Brady, former Haugheyite cabinet minister and one-time Fianna Fáil chief whip. So there they are, Bertie's pals shoring up a worthy North Dublin charity: Kiely his constituency strategist, Peelo his accountant, Nugent his financial guardian angel and Brady his former fellow cabinet minister – all singing from the same Fianna Fáil hymn sheet. There are a few others with likely Fianna Fáil links. Certainly there is not an identifiable Fine Gael sympathizer in sight.

Back in 1956 the CRC won the coveted right to nominate a candidate for the Senate. In one election it nominated founder Lady Goulding; but in the 1997, 2002 and 2007 elections the CRC nominated Tony Kett, one of its own employees. Once nominated to the Senate by the clinic and backed by Bertie, he was sure to be elected on all three occasions. From time to time he would advocate the cause of the clinic on the floor of the Upper House. In his autobiography the former Taoiseach described Kett as his 'closest friend'.

It paid to be a close friend of Bertie. In a desperate bid for survival in September 2006, after facts about his bizarre personal financial arrangements had been leaked to the media, he admitted to RTÉ's Bryan Dobson on the six o'clock news that he had appointed people to semi-state jobs 'not because of anything they had given me' but 'because they were friends'.

It was a sensational admission. Bertie was using the defence of cronyism. And the admission did not damage him politically; if anything, it seemed to help. Bertie's popularity spiked in the next opinion poll.

Bertie's approach to state appointments was never more outrageous than in the case of his former life partner, Celia Larkin. She was a semi-detached member of the Drumcondra Mafia – semi-detached because there were tensions between her and some in the Fagan's/Beaumont House crowd. She was resented by the activists because she was seen to have cast more of a spell over Bertie than the rest of them.

Bertie's relationship with Celia – who became his partner after he separated from his wife – had always been controversial. She often travelled abroad with him on official visits, and from time to time they encountered protocol problems because they were not married. On one occasion their lifestyle provoked heavy criticism from the Church of Ireland Dean of St Patrick's Cathedral, Robert MacCarthy. The outspoken dean refused an invitation from the couple, accusing Bertie of portraying his relationship with Celia as 'quasi-marital'. The Roman Catholic Archbishop of Dublin, Desmond Connell, turned up at the reception but was greeted by Bertie and Tánaiste Mary Harney, rather than by the official host and hostess, Bertie and Celia.

Breaches of protocol were of little interest to an Irish public now mostly indifferent to the domestic arrangements of their political leaders. But in 2005 – after their relationship had ended – the Minister for Enterprise, Trade and Employment, Micheál Martin, dropped a bombshell: Celia Larkin was to be appointed to the board of the fledgling National Consumer Agency (NCA). Although Martin was officially making the appointment, there was no doubt that the instruction came from above. Typically, Bertie had slipped her name in under the radar at the eleventh hour, six weeks after the original twelve directors' names had been agreed.

Bertie's decision to arrange the job for his former partner was stunning. While she undoubtedly had political skills, her consumer-protection credentials were virtually nil. She had set up a beauty salon in Drumcondra, just a stone's throw from Bertie's St Luke's headquarters; but her practical business experience was minimal. She was hardly qualified to sit in judgement on consumer cases or to launch inquiries into malpractice. The Consumers Association of

Ireland broke cover and condemned the appointment, claiming that it had been made at the expense of one of its own nominees.

There was uproar in the Dáil. A Taoiseach nominating his former partner to a state board was seen as a new low in cronyism. One member of the Drumcondra Mafia told us that Celia must have demanded it: 'And what Celia wanted, Celia got.'

Bertie's former lover continued to attract controversy in her new role. In May 2009 consumer champion Eddie Hobbs resigned from the board of the National Consumer Agency after learning that a €40,000 loan to Larkin from the Irish Nationwide Building Society had been fast-tracked by its boss, Michael Fingleton. It seemed wrong to Hobbs that a member of the agency's board, with political connections, should be given such preferential treatment. He told the *Irish Times* that the disclosure 'reinforced perceptions of cronyism'.

Hobbs had already been concerned at Larkin's presence on the board, taking the view that her testimony to the Mahon Tribunal about payments to her former partner were damaging to the public's perception of the agency. He also clashed with her over his insistence on questioning whether consumers were receiving value for money from state services; Larkin, he told us, felt that he wanted to 'bite the hand that fed' the agency. By the date of Hobbs's resignation, Larkin had received more than €55,000 in fees and expenses for her work on the board.

As a result of Celia Larkin's appointment, the National Consumer Agency was stillborn, becoming yet another in the long list of pointless quangos, abused by politicians for their own ends. In 2009 Minister for Finance Brian Lenihan passed a death sentence: the short-lived NCA would be merged with the Competition Authority.

Hobbs was right. All the indications were that the agency was feathering the Fianna Fáil nest. In February 2009 the *Irish Independent* reported that Celia had proposed that the public-relations account for the National Consumer Agency be given to a company called Q4 – seen in business circles as a Fianna Fáil outpost. It was founded by Martin Mackin, former general secretary of Fianna Fáil, and Jackie Gallagher, an adviser to none other than Bertie Ahern. Several government departments favoured Q4 for their public-relations work. In 2007 and 2008 it secured contracts worth €236,000 from the departments of Justice, Enterprise, and Arts, Sports and Tourism. It even won the contract to publicize the disastrous e-voting machines.

Back in 1988, when he was Minister for Labour, Bertie Ahern appointed Paddy Duffy to the board of the training agency FÁS. Duffy had known Bertie since 1975, when the two had joined forces to plot his successful election to the Dáil in the Fianna Fáil landslide of 1977. Well educated and a spoiled priest, Duffy was in a good position to observe Bertie's influence over the board of FÁS. As Minister for Labour, Bertie made the announcements about appointments and Bertie signed on the dotted line.

'Directors of FÁS,' Duffy says, 'always saw their appointments as personal ones from Bertie. He would come along to one meeting per annum or a board dinner or reception. He would think it important that they speak to one another and they did.' The appointees felt in Bertie's debt.

When Bertie was appointed Minister for Finance, Duffy became his adviser, and eventually he followed his boss to the Taoiseach's office. Unlike many others on the semi-state merry-go-round, who, enjoying political patronage, would move happily from the board of a place like FÁS to the boards of Aer Lingus, Dublin Port or CIÉ, Duffy was a true grafter. He was eventually involved in a conflict-of-interest controversy that forced his departure from Bertie's team in 1999. After Duffy was outed as having been the director of a company that had advised NTL on the purchase of Cablelink from two state companies, his position in government was no longer tenable, despite his protestations of a series of 'misunderstandings'.

Paddy was not one of the 'dig-out' boys – the guys who had supposedly put their hands in their pockets to bail out Bertie when he hit the financial rocks – and, perhaps as a result, he missed out on the easy pickings. Nearly all those who were named as contributors to Bertie's dig-outs were rewarded. Des Richardson's great pal Dave McKenna was one of those. McKenna, whose shareholding in Marlborough Recruitment was at one time valued as high as €60 million, was an affable entrepreneur, a risk-taker. Originally a plumber, McKenna had emigrated to the UK building sites in the eighties but returned to Ireland in the nineties, hitting the business scene with a bang. He floated Marlborough on the Irish stock exchange in 1997 and made a mint before the company went belly-up. In its dying days Marlborough relied heavily on two former Fianna Fáil fundraisers: Des Richardson became executive chairman, while Paul Kavanagh agreed to take a seat on the board.

As a member of Ógra Fianna Fáil, McKenna had known Bertie before emigrating, and the two attended Manchester United matches together. McKenna happily handed €2,500 to Richardson for the first Bertie dig-out in 1993. In 1999 McKenna was made a director of Enterprise Ireland – a potentially important organization that was constantly devalued through the padding of its board with favourites of ministers and Taoisigh. (The most recent chairman, Hugh Cooney, was a donor to Brian Cowen's last re-election campaign.)

A year before McKenna's appointment yet another of Bertie's pals, Tim Collins, had been slotted into a board vacancy at Enterprise Ireland. The announcement was made by the Minister for Enterprise and Tánaiste, Mary Harney, but she was at pains to point out that the appointment had been made 'at the behest of the Taoiseach'. Collins resigned suddenly in 1999, citing health reasons.

Collins was a trustee of Bertie's constituency office in Drumcondra. He was also a beneficiary of the sale of the historic site of the Battle of the Boyne to the state. He told the Mahon Tribunal that the sale had been clean and that he had never discussed the transaction – which yielded a £5 million profit to a consortium – with the Taoiseach. He was a 5 per cent holder in the selling consortium, trousering £250,000 from the deal. Collins went on to tell the tribunal that a bank account he controlled, denominated 'B/T', from which £30,000 found its way into Celia Larkin's pocket, was not the 'Bertie/Tim' account, as had been suggested. He insisted that the initials 'B/T' stood for 'Building Trust' and that the account was a sinking fund for a rainy day, so that if anything happened to Bertie no liabilities would be attached to the trustees of his constituency office. However, four staff members at the bank testified that the account was in fact for the benefit of Bertie and Tim.

Collins told the tribunal that the money paid to Celia Larkin was a loan, needed because she wanted to buy a house for her ageing aunts, who were being put out of their rented home. Larkin bought the property with the loan. Collins said the loan had been granted for 'humanitarian' reasons. So humanitarian was it that no repayments were made for fifteen years, not until the matter attracted the attention of the tribunal.

Although the list of Bertie's local friends who featured on the boards of Ireland's quangos is almost endless, his own autobiography gives them hardly any credit for the great work they've done for the state. Tim Collins's name never features in the book. Neither Dave McKenna nor Jim Nugent features there. Des Richardson, his most powerful back-room boy, gets just a single mention (the same number as Tina Turner). No members of the Drumcondra Mafia appear in the book's photo section. Celia Larkin merits a small picture, as does his wife, Miriam. But the rest of the illustrations are of Bertie mixing with the Pope, Edward Kennedy, Nicolas Sarkozy, George Bush, Tony Blair and other heads of state. It is as though he is turning his back on his cronies, hoping to relegate them to the background while he struts upon the world stage.

The book is full of other strange omissions. For example, he rarely mentions his siblings and the way he advanced their careers. He unexpectedly promoted his likeable brother Noel to a junior ministry at the Department of the Environment in 2002, and in 2007 promoted him again, this time to a prestigious junior post in the Department of Finance. Noel was knocking on the door of the cabinet when Bertie resigned as Taoiseach and party leader in 2008; his name did not feature on Brian Cowen's list of seniors or juniors.

Bertie's elder brother, Maurice, became a Dublin city councillor in 1999 with his support. In the run-up to the 2009 Dublin Central by-election after the death of Tony Gregory, Bertie still had enough clout within the local Fianna Fáil organization to ensure that Maurice was nominated as the party's candidate; but the electorate, loyal for so long to the Ahern name, sent him a clear message: the Ahern magic was over. Maurice trailed the field, finishing in fifth place.

Although Bertie never built up a lasting political dynasty, it was hardly a disadvantage to be a member of the Ahern clan. Another protégé whom he failed to mention in the book was Ronan Kelly. In 1992 Bertie appointed Kelly to the post of tax appeals commissioner. This was a politically sensitive post meant for competent, objective, qualified people. Ronan Kelly was all of those things. He was also Bertie's brother-in-law.

In 1998 Kelly was the presiding tax commissioner at Charlie Haughey's appeal against a Revenue assessment of £2 million that was linked to a cash gift of £1.3 million from supermarket million-aire Ben Dunne. Haughey's counsel claimed that Dunne had given the money to someone overseas, who then made the gift to Haughey; and that because the donor was domiciled overseas, Haughey was not liable for any tax. The entire case, therefore, hinged on the domicile of the donor.

According to Kelly, the Revenue had failed to establish a direct link between Haughey and Dunne, partly because the money had been transferred from the Cayman Islands. Haughey won his case, and all hell broke loose, with Bertie coming under serious attack in the Dáil.

The irony is that expert opinion backed up Kelly's ruling. But the optics were awful. Kelly's decision released his brother-in-law's crooked mentor from paying €2 million in taxes after Haughey's acceptance of large sums of money from Ben Dunne and others.

Others in Bertie's government were also accused of shamelessly promoting their relations. In 2000 Tánaiste Mary Harney elevated her future husband, Brian Geoghegan, to the chair of FÁS. Geoghegan had already been in contention for the chair as an IBEC nominee: the lucrative position normally rotated between top bosses at IBEC and ICTU, and Geoghegan was an IBEC apparatchik. Although the pair were married within a year of the appointment, sources close to Harney insist that the first green shoots of love sprouted only after the job announcement. Trade-union sources at the time were reported to have been unhappy with Geoghegan's appointment, as his predecessor had also been an employers' nominee. They felt it was their turn.

The chair of FÁS was the softest of sinecures, with little accountability, a good salary and minimum stress. A po-faced Harney made the announcement in November 2000: 'I am delighted that Mr Geoghegan has accepted my invitation to become chairman of FÁS. He fills this important post at a time of great change in the Irish labour market and I have no doubt that his vast experience within the Irish business community will be of great assistance to the organisation.'

Although Harney's Progressive Democrats enjoyed a reputation as the moral guardians of the first two Ahern governments, they played the patronage game as well as the rest of them when it came to their own party people. Under an informal arrangement, a share of appointments was awarded to each arm of the coalition, vaguely in proportion to its size. Most of the spoils were small beer, served to quench the thirst of minor players; but in 2003 the PDs had an awkward problem. Their former party leader, Des O'Malley, had retired from the Dáil in 2002. Still only sixty-four, he had a lot to offer outside politics. Astonishingly, no multinational or big bank had come knocking on O'Malley's door. He would have made a superb Governor of the Central Bank of Ireland or chairman of AIB. Indeed, had he been offered either position, recent events in the shameful history of Irish banking might have unfolded differently.

The reason O'Malley was cold-shouldered by Irish business was obvious: he was challenging, cranky, nit-picking, knowledgeable, independent and brilliant. Those were the last qualities that any of Ireland's banks were seeking. If ever a man deserved a soft reward for his record of independent service to the state, it was O'Malley; but he was far too straight to be let loose in the semi-states. He would have caused holy war in the incestuous worlds of CIÉ, the HSE or FÁS.

The PDs, and PD-friendly Minister for Finance, Charlie McCreevy, rode to the rescue. The word was out in Leinster House that it was time to 'fix up' Des. A lucrative job as alternate director of the European Bank for Reconstruction and Development (EBRD) passed across McCreevy's desk. It was a post well hidden from Irish politics, based in London, ideal for a man who ruffled feathers wherever he went at home. Ireland shared a seat on the EBRD board with Denmark, rotating the full board place every three years and thereby splitting the workload. O'Malley, as always, made a big impression and became a full board member by the time he left.

The EBRD had been established in 1991 to help rebuild the devastated economies of Central and Eastern Europe after the collapse of the Soviet Union. Although it was not a bank that came under much media scrutiny, the attention that it did receive was unwelcome. It made a bad start when the press revealed that the EBRD had spent more than €300 million on plush offices, parties and jet travel in its first two years of existence. Its London headquarters boasted gold-plated door handles, Italian marble floors and lift frames costing €1 million.

A directorship with a wasteful European quango was not a post equal to O'Malley's talents. But the former PD leader, unrewarded at home, accepted the €116,000-a-year job. A row broke out in the Dáil when the opposition discovered that the salary was tax-free. The PDs had to endure jibes from Fine Gael for behaving in a way that they would surely have disdained in the heady days of their foundation as a liberal, anti-corruption party in 1985.

(Seven years later, in 2010, the EBRD was again used as a soother for a loser. Fianna Fáil MEP Eoin Ryan had lost his seat the previous year. Ryan, a good pal of Taoiseach Brian Cowen, had optimistically lobbied for the ultimate prize of European Commissioner, but Cowen baulked at giving the best-paid gift in his bag of goodies to a man who could not hold his seat in the European Parliament. The EBRD was just the business for Ryan. It restored status and money to a fallen Fianna Fáil tribal chief, whose family had held political office since the state was founded.)

Today the Progressive Democrats have disbanded, but hardly a sinner has not been 'fixed up'. One of its first TDs, Anne Colley, was rewarded for loyalty to the party with the chair of the Legal Aid Board – a gift from a Minister for Justice, none other than Progressive Democrat Michael McDowell. Other founders of the party of purity were given lesser retirement rewards. Peadar Clohessy, a farmer elected twice as O'Malley's running mate in Limerick East, found his talents recognized with a place on the Shelton Abbey Place of Detention Visiting Committee. The prison is in Arklow, a long way from Clohessy's Limerick base. It is unclear what Clohessy knows about prison conditions or why his expertise in this special-ized field would be of particular value in County Wicklow. But then, in some prison visitor committee's books, the further away the prisons were from home the better. The travelling expenses were generous. Visiting committees became a gravy train for retired councillors or party workers. The late TD Pearse Wyse, another early convert to the Progressive Democrats, was put on the Mountjoy Prison Visiting Committee when he retired from the Dáil. Wyse lived in Cork; Mountjoy is in Dublin.

In 2000 Mary Harney gave deposed PD Senator Cathy Honan a seat on the Crafts Council that carried a per diem payment. She was reappointed in 2003. In 2008, before the party was formally dis-banded, its chairman John Dardis was compensated with the chair of the board of the quango Safefood, at a salary of over €10,000 a year.

Paul Mackay, a founder and trustee of the party, managed to land on the boards of the ICC Bank and Eircom, and was appointed to the Industrial Development Agency (IDA) by Harney. In 1998 Mackay refused to vacate the Eircom position prior to the flotation, eyeballing the Minister, Mary O'Rourke, when she asked him to make way.

Stephen O'Byrnes, a former PD policy director and assistant gov-ernment press secretary, won a seat on the RTÉ Authority as the Progressive Democrat nominee. O'Byrnes managed to have his term renewed to this key post, a role that cannot do a professional spinner any harm.

During the Bertie Ahern era – he was in ministerial office for all but two and a half years between 1987 and 2007, and was Taoiseach for eleven years – stuffing the quangos became a competitive disease. The opposition had little time to compete with Bertie – just the thirty months the Fine Gael/Labour/Democratic Left 'Rainbow Coalition' was in power, from the end of 1994 until June 1997 – but they did their best. They had grown well practised at hollow protests against the patronage given to Fianna Fáil supporters, but when they held the levers of power themselves they inserted their own favour-ites with a vengeance.

Liam Cosgrave, whose parting appointments back in 1977 caused

such a stir, would have been proud of the enthusiasm with which his
Fine Gael successors ruthlessly installed their own people in the state
bodies. Fine Gael played the prison visiting committees game to per-
fection in the 1994–7 period. Councillors and party workers from all
parts of the country were given jobs in corners of the island that they
had never previously set eyes on. The generous mileage allowances
kept them sweet. Naturally they played the semi-state game too,
replacing nearly all Fianna Fáil vacancies as they arose with their own
nominees. Aer Lingus was, as ever, the most coveted prize. The coalition put economist Jim O'Leary and businessman David Austin – both
of whom had recognized Fine Gael sympathies – on the board of the
airline.

Gary Joyce was given the chair of the ACCBank in gratitude for
saving John Bruton's political hide. She had written a blueprint for
the revival of Fine Gael after the disastrous election defeat of 1992
that had bought just enough time for Bruton to hold off the discontented forces within the party. Joyce knew little about banking,
however. She later added to her portfolio when she surfaced at the
top table at the Irish Museum of Modern Art.

One predictable consequence of the patronage system was that
state bodies were often at loggerheads with the new government after
an election. Mary O'Rourke tells an amusing story about Brian Joyce,
one of Michael Lowry's more controversial appointments to the chair
of CIÉ when he was Minister for Transport in the Rainbow Coalition. CIÉ had become a party-political quagmire, as old Fianna
Fáilers on the board resisted Lowry's plans; and after a series of resig-
nations Lowry installed Brian Joyce in the chair. Joyce outlived the
Rainbow Coalition and remained in the CIÉ hot seat, but found
relations with the new Fianna Fáil transport minister – O'Rourke –
stressful. In early 2000 Joyce resigned, pleading that the government
was interfering in industrial relations and breaching the autonomy of
CIÉ. For a week the minister and Joyce were at war.

One evening O'Rourke was due to slug it out on RTÉ's *Prime Time*
with the opposition spokesman on transport, Ivan Yates. A few hours
before the programme her telephone rang. At the other end of the
line, to her surprise, was a rather excitable Brian Joyce. He obviously

thought he had dialled Yates's number. Without pausing to listen to the voice at the other end, Joyce barked out suggestions about how Yates should deal with O'Rourke that evening. She let him go on for a few moments before revealing herself to a much embarrassed Joyce.

Fine Gael had lost a great deal of support from within the business community during its long period in opposition, so only a small pool of corporate supporters needed to be rewarded for financial or material help in the lean years. Few were of genuinely high calibre.

One of those who had been predictably steadfast in support of the party was Mark FitzGerald, son of former Taoiseach Garret Fitz-Gerald. Mark, a successful estate agent not noted for his fishing prowess, found himself planted in the chair at Bord Iascaigh Mhara, the Sea Fisheries Board.

The VHI was a rare board on which the Rainbow Coalition was able to establish a meaningful presence. Vacancies fell at the right time. Former Fine Gael trustee Derry Hussey (husband of former cabinet minister Gemma Hussey) took the chair, while Paul Coulson – a Fine Gael supporter who had made a mint in the leasing business – became a director. Gemma Hussey herself was slotted into the board of the Abbey Theatre in 1995.

Even Garret FitzGerald was not above accepting a reward for services to the state: in 1995 the former Taoiseach brought some gravitas to Montrose when he was made a member of the RTÉ Authority. He probably needed the money. Only two years earlier FitzGerald had settled a spot of financial bother with AIB. It transpired that the former Taoiseach had borrowed £170,000 to buy shares in aircraft leasing company GPA, of which he was a director. The shares tanked. AIB settled the debt for £40,000 in 1993. RTÉ paid members of the authority generously.

The RTÉ Authority changed personnel en masse during that government. Labour's Michael D. Higgins, Minister for Arts, Culture and the Gaeltacht with responsibility for broadcasting, cleaned out the board and installed Professor Farrel Corcoran, an academic from Dublin City University, in the chair, replacing Fianna Fáil's nominee John Sorohan. Connemara film maker Bob Quinn joined trade unionist Billy Attley to give the station's ruling body a completely new political complexion. Des Geraghty, a former Democratic Left MEP who had become president of the country's largest trade union, the Services, Industrial, Professional and Technical Union (SIPTU), was added to satisfy the needs of the third party in government.

The Labour Party would live to regret several promotions given to the brethren. In 1997, after a brief spell in exile, the emperor returned to steal Labour's clothes. When Bertie gained power he muscled in on the long-established link between the Labour Party and the trade unions by opening a second front in his patronage offensive. As we shall see in Chapter 6, new quangos in the social-partnership industry were created and then filled by trade-union oligarchs of Bertie's choosing. A fresh layer of waste was born.

3. Behind the Scenes at FÁS

One day on, and our scoop in the *Sunday Independent* about FÁS squandering taxpayers' money on fine wines, business-class tickets, golf three-balls and fancy hotels in Florida and elsewhere seemed to have sunk without a trace. Monday's broadsheets looked elsewhere for news. The *Irish Independent* led with a story about VAT rates being lowered in the North. The *Irish Times* had a particularly boring piece about education cuts based on quotes from the Taoiseach at a trade mission in China. It's a mystery to Sunday newspaper journalists why daily newspapers don't usually pick up their stories until a Tuesday at the earliest.

But RTÉ wasn't asleep. Early that Monday morning producers from RTÉ Radio One's *Today with Pat Kenny* asked if one of us could go on the show to shoot it out with FÁS director-general Rody Molloy. Clashing appointments meant that we weren't able to do it. As it happened, we weren't needed: Rody Molloy committed career suicide on the programme all by himself. Pat Kenny, just a week after the conclusion of his bitter court case with his neighbour in Dalkey, had had his Weetabix that day. He was ready for Molloy and his waffle.

Kenny asked Molloy about that $942.53 bill for a three-ball at Orlando's Grand Cypress Resort Golf Club in January 2005 – the same hotel where Ben Dunne had had his infamous cocaine-and-escort meltdown in 1993. 'I've already explained to you, Pat, that people aren't volunteering to come here to look for our students to go to these major scientific events,' Molloy replied. 'We are out there developing relationships. I had an opportunity to work with some people as part of building that relationship and I took that opportunity. If that is a major sin, then I hold my hands up and say very sorry.'

Then there was the $410 bill from Solutions hair salon in West Cocoa Beach, which was paid with the corporate credit card of FÁS

Corporate Affairs chief Greg Craig. 'Again, the amount of money, in terms of the total package, is very, very small,' Molloy said.

Kenny moved on to the sticky subject of the pay-per-view movies top male executives from FÁS had watched in their US hotel rooms. These ranged in price from $12.71 to $34.40. We don't know what kind of movies these were: they could have been action blockbusters, tearjerkers or comedies. Or they could have been films with lots and lots of kissing and groaning. 'Ah well, the amount for pay-per-view movies, with all due respect, Pat, it's chicken feed,' Molloy guffed. 'What, $10 for a movie?'

Kenny told him that pay-per-view movies weren't part of RTÉ's expenses regime. The director-general must then have realized that 'chicken feed' wasn't an appropriate term. 'Maybe that was an oversight on our part, but the bill was paid as a communal bill for a number of people who were there at a time when we were trying to develop relationships with senior people.'

Our revelations had also included details of a bumper jolly taken by former assistant director-general Gerry Pyke and his wife: a three-week, around-the-world trip to Frankfurt, Tokyo, Honolulu, San Francisco and back to Dublin via Frankfurt. The business-class tickets cost €12,021, courtesy of you and me. Pat Kenny wanted to know whether Molloy had signed off on this lengthy expedition, and Molloy confirmed that he had.

The sheer volume of travel undertaken by FÁS – often at the plush, pointy end of the plane, often with spouses in tow – was next on Kenny's agenda. 'Well, it wasn't first-class travel, it was business-class travel,' Molloy responded. 'It is hellishly expensive, but any time that a spouse travelled, it was because there were reasons for the spouse to travel, to do with the kind of activities that were involved there. One which comes to mind was a dinner which involved President McAleese and her husband. All I can say to you on that, when a spouse travels with FÁS, they travel at no additional expense to the organization – unless there's a very specific reason for it. There are occasions when it is appropriate for my spouse to be with me. But any time she has been with me, there was no additional expense to

FÁS because I traded down my travel entitlement to allow her to travel so it comes in at less expense to the organization.'

In response to probing from Kenny about his 'travel entitlement', Molloy stated directly that he was 'entitled' to travel first class.

November 2008 was one heck of a time for a public servant, earning €203,000 per year, to be going on about his 'entitlement' to first-class travel. The Finance Bill the previous week had stipulated that most families would see their tax burden rise by an average of €2,000 per year because of new levy thresholds. The grim realization that the banks would go bust unless the taxpayer coughed up billions in bailout money was sinking in. Jobs were being lost, companies were going under, Poland had just beaten us at home in a soccer friendly and Munster's 'B' team had been robbed of a famous victory over the All Blacks. Molloy's interview was like flicking the switch on a vast political, economic and social Hadron Collider: everything milled around, then smashed together. It wasn't quite clear what was produced by this pile-up, but anger, real anger, was a very large part of it. Switchboards at RTÉ lit up. It wasn't just taxi drivers either; it was everyone.

The newspapers led with the interview the following day, and further revelations about FÁS spending emerged. Taoiseach Brian Cowen gave Molloy a vote of confidence, describing his fellow Offaly man as an 'excellent public servant'. Incredibly, Cowen was probably the only person in the country who hadn't realized that the FÁS boss was in the wrong. Molloy went to ground, consulting friends and at least one journalist with whom he was close. The message was clear: he was toast. On the Tuesday night, about thirty-six hours after the Pat Kelly interview, Molloy resigned. In later testimony to the Public Accounts Committee (PAC), Molloy described the interview as 'ill-advised' – one of the understatements of the century.

But in the final hours of his reign, Molloy had fought for the deal of his life. It was a secret arrangement, one that didn't emerge for nearly a year. Initially it was reported that Molloy would get a 'golden-handshake' package of about €500,000. But that was well wide of the mark. More than a year later, revelations of Molloy's hush-hush kiss-off emerged, following a series of reports by Danny McConnell in the *Sunday Independent*. The full details of this extraordinary deal were later published in full by the Comptroller & Auditor General (C&AG). It was miles more favourable than what any comparable public servant taking early retirement would have received: the overall cost of the package to taxpayers, according to the C&AG's calculations, will be almost €900,000 in excess of what it ought to have been. He also got to keep his company car, an Audi A6.

The board of FÁS approved Molloy's severance deal, which had been hammered out with officials from the Department of Enterprise and sanctioned by the then enterprise minister, Mary Coughlan – Molloy's boss – without any legal sign-off. It was an appalling arrangement, a payment for failure. This wasn't transparent government; this was a ropy pact to get rid of someone whose dismal management skills and taste for the high life had cost the taxpayer millions. And he was going to go on costing us even more.

The following weekend we published further details about the lavish expenditure at FÁS on things like surfboard rental, limousines and seven children's spacesuits that had been posted home from Cape Canaveral. With these revelations appearing in the country's biggest-selling newspaper and, now, in other newspapers too, it was inevitable that both the PAC and the C&AG would delve even deeper into FÁS's shoddy spending habits and practices. In February 2009 the PAC released its first report on the gravy train at FÁS. It wasn't pretty reading, especially as it came just after Dell announced that it was shuttering its Limerick factory, with the loss of 1,900 top-end jobs. It found that FÁS had spent €1.7 million on hotels, lunches, limos and other perks over the seven-year period. These included golf fundraising events, concert tickets, match tickets and hospitality, and limousine services 'when more economical forms of transport would have been more appropriate'. One receipt showed that €240 was spent on a limo to ferry Greg Craig from his home in Terenure to his kids' school and then into Kildare Street. The PAC also found that €6,900 was spent on golf classics in which there was 'no evidence' of any benefit to FÁS. John Cahill, manager of the Science Challenge, spent

€474 on duty-free shopping in Dublin and €147 on items from British Isles Inc. in Houston before buying a €100 bag at Macy's to carry the presents around.

A subsequent report by the C&AG in January 2010 found that there was 'a lack of regard for economy on some occasions' and that there was 'some evidence of extravagant expenditure that seems to have gone unchallenged'. That was putting it mildly. FÁS executives and their guests were painting the town red in some of Dublin's finest restaurants at our expense. In one case it was discovered that when three FÁS executives went out to lunch to discuss the One Step Up programme, a training scheme, nearly two thirds of the bill was accounted for by booze.

FÁS had coughed up €43,100 for four ten-year premium-level tickets at Croke Park. (They were given back after Rody Molloy resigned.) It had also spent another €7,000 on tickets for All-Ireland football and hurling finals from 2002 to 2008, as well as €4,640 on rugby tickets and another €1,960 on soccer matches. An extraordinary €8,299 was spent on booze and canapés at these matches. All but one of these vast outlays were approved by Molloy.

What on earth was a state vocational training organization doing at Croke Park? Were they bringing unemployed people to matches to cheer them up? No chance – the unemployed were far too grubby for the top suits at FÁS – but the details of who actually got the tickets have proved exceptionally hard to find. Records simply do not exist for most of the matches or concerts – except for a Robbie Williams gig in 2006. This was the concert where FÁS also spent €2,255 on beer and nibbles for the guests. Sean Gorman, secretary general of the Department of Enterprise, Trade and Employment – the department that signed off on Molloy's subsequent golden-parachute payment – was one of the twenty-eight people who attended at the taxpayers' expense. Gorman, a former FÁS director himself, attended with Pádraig Cullinane, a former principal officer of the department. He was joined by the top two executives at the Labour Relations Commission (LRC): chief executive Kieran Mulvey and his number two, Tom Pomphrett. Ark Life boss Billy Finn and two journalists were also there, as were FÁS's own Rody Molloy, Gerry Pyke, Greg

Craig, assistant director-general (and future GAA president) Christy Cooney and assistant director-general Oliver Egan. The €2,255 bill might have been worth it if we could have seen them all dancing to Robbie.

Between 2002 and 2008 FÁS spent €4.7 million on foreign travel. Over this period an extraordinary 4,400 flights were paid for, of which about 1,000 were long-haul jollies. The bean-counters at the C&AG's office calculated that about 27 per cent of the long-haul flights were business class or first class. Contrary to Rody Molloy's claim on Pat Kenny's programme, 'The Committee has established that there is no entitlement to first-class travel and that any down-grading of a ticket should result in the saving being returned to the State.' In April 2008, as quarterly unemployment figures showed a 21.1 per cent jump compared with the same period in 2007, Rody Molloy and two other travellers boarded a plane to Orlando and turned left into the first-class lounge. The three return flights cost a total of €27,000 – or the salary of a special-needs primary-school teacher for the best part of a year.

Taxpayers spent €124,000 so that John Cahill, manager of the Science Challenge, could fly a remarkable twenty-four times to the States, as well as twice to South Africa and once to Japan. Greg Craig clocked up eighteen trips to the States with another three to the UK or Europe – at a cost of €95,000. Rody Molloy was a champion traveller: despite having a 'a problem' with flying, as he told the PAC, he took twenty-nine trips overseas between 2002 and 2008, including the infamous trip to Florida with Mary Harney and their respective spouses on the government jet. His other twenty-eight junkets cost a total of €93,000. Gerry Pyke, the assistant director-general, took twenty-four trips during the same period, at a grand total of €60,000. The wives of Molloy and Pyke travelled at a cost to the taxpayer of €32,000.

FÁS, originally set up in hard times to train Irish workers and match them up with employers, took on a new brief during the boom: helping Irish employers, particularly in the construction sector, recruit workers from other countries. The PAC's report acknowledged that a degree of foreign travel was necessary and appropriate in connection with this agenda. The committee also found that, in order to develop the Science Challenge programme in 2003, there was a need for top FÁS executives to travel to the US. 'However,' the PAC report stated, 'it appears to the Committee that the programme was used to justify extensive foreign travel that is unsustainable. In addition to FÁS executives, spouses of senior executives, board members, former board members, journalists and ministerial delegations were brought to Florida.'

The Department of Enterprise publishes details of the nationalities of those granted work permits each year. In 2005 some 242 new work permits were given to people from New Zealand, with 272 a year later. Chinese people were granted 282 new work permits in 2006 and 372 the following year. Australians got 436 new permits in 2007 and 445 a year earlier. South Africans were awarded 686 work permits in 2007. At a time when the vast bulk of foreign workers in Ireland were coming from Eastern Europe, jaunts to more exotic climes could not be justified in terms of the needs of Irish employers.

The gravy train should have been stopped. But the people who could have stopped it were in many cases glugging from the gravy boat themselves.

The rampant waste and junketeering at FÁS came to public view only after our stories appeared in the *Sunday Independent*, but it had been a live issue within the organization for at least four years before that. Some months after Mary Harney had returned from her lavish Florida trip funded by FÁS – or rather the taxpayer – she received an anonymous letter that made a number of serious allegations about her hosts in Florida and about the FÁS Corporate Affairs Department, headed up by Greg Craig. All of the allegations contained in the letter would eventually prove to be completely untrue, but the letter's arrival set off a series of events that was in itself highly revealing about how FÁS operated.

By the time she received the letter, Harney was no longer in charge at the Department of Enterprise, having moved to the Department of Health, so she passed the letter on to FÁS. Her husband, Brian Geoghegan, who was then FÁS chairman, was among those who saw it.

An investigation into the allegations contained in the anonymous letter was started by the FÁS Internal Audit team in November 2004. Most of the detective work was initially done by Joe Roe, manager of IT Audit and Support, and Tony Killeen, director of Corporate Governance and Internal Audit. After Killeen retired in mid December 2005, FÁS policy adviser Terry Corcoran took up the baton as the new head of Internal Audit.

The probe was substantially complete by June 2005, but the board did not get sight of it until 6 December 2007 – two and a half years later. Details of this investigation – and of how its findings were kept from reaching the board for so long – emerged in an explosive nine-page letter written by Corcoran to the PAC in February 2010. Corcoran revealed that his department had been on the receiving end of massive interference from the top echelons of FÁS. 'The level of interest from and contact with senior management (mainly the ADG corporate services [Gerry Pyke] but also from time to time the Director General) experienced by Internal Audit in relation to the investigation was unprecedented . . . Internal Audit had to be aware that any adverse findings from the investigation might therefore reflect unfavourably on the ADG and DG.'

Indeed, all of the travel that wasn't arranged through FÁS's designated travel agent, Club Travel, consisted of trips by Rody Molloy, Gerry Pyke or members of the Corporate Affairs Department. (Procurement regulations specified that departments and organizations with large travel budgets needed to use a designated travel agent to avoid duplication or waste of money.) Virtually all the credit-card expenditure probed centred on Molloy, Pyke and Corporate Affairs, and all of the expenditure on events had been approved by Molloy or Pyke. This was enough to sink a career – even in a safe, pensionable job in the public sector.

'The investigation was initially constrained in a number of ways at senior management's behest – notably, Internal Audit restricted its initial work to examination of records and interviews only with a limited number of staff in Corporate Affairs,' Corcoran wrote. 'This represented a major restriction on the investigation, given that all of the allegations related to relationships and interactions with external parties.'

Despite this, Internal Audit did approach people outside FÁS, such as contractors, suppliers and other business partners. It was a brave move, and it led to their knuckles being rapped. 'Senior management objected strenuously to Internal Audit having interviewed another external party. This complaint came via the ADG [Pyke], who expressed the opinion in May/June 2005 that the DG was very upset about the contact made by IA as it was a source of embarrassment for FÁS.'

Once the investigation was effectively completed in June 2005, senior management were briefed 'on the main emerging findings'. Then the lawyers got involved. A draft report was completed in August 2005. After discussions and meetings with some of the third parties named in the report, it was revised and another draft completed and sent to Molloy and Pyke in January 2006. Three meetings were held between management, Internal Audit (how headed by Corcoran) and legal advisers before the findings were sent to Greg Craig. On 19 May the finalized report was sent to Molloy and Pyke, who were given fifteen days to respond – standard practice. The fifteen-day deadline passed. On 23 June a memo was sent to Pyke and Molloy asking for a response, as the report needed to be sent to the C&AG. (All internal audits are supplied to the C&AG on a quarterly basis.)

Molloy and Pyke decided that they would not respond to the report unless it was split into two parts: one that dealt with the anonymous allegations and one that covered various procedural breaches. Corcoran fired off a letter to Molloy on Bastille Day, 14 July – an apt day to challenge the rotten *ancien régime* at FÁS. 'I do not think it would be appropriate to withdraw this report as issued on 19 May. Rather I think it would now be best for management to respond to the findings and recommendations in the already issued report, along the lines set out in the covering memorandum that accompanies it.' Molloy responded that he would deal with the issues raised in the report only at a full meeting of the FÁS audit committee. It took three months to arrange a suitable date when everyone could attend.

FÁS had received legal advice not to let the report – which became known as 'INV 137' – enter 'inappropriate circulation', and on this basis it did not include the report in the quarterly batch of internal audits forwarded to the C&AG's office. But a covering letter with the other Internal Audit documents let the C&AG know that another report was waiting for a management green light. The file was also given to Niall Saul, chairman of the audit committee, 'to allow him to consider the impasse that had arisen between the DG and the Director of Internal Audit' in advance of the audit-committee meeting. Saul, an IBEC representative on the board, had recently left Irish Life & Permanent for Bernard McNamara's property business. (That was seen as a good move back in those pre-crash days.) The audit committee received an abridged version of the report. Molloy attended the audit-committee meeting and repeated his demand that the report be split in two. He believed that the report would be leaked and the public wouldn't be able to tell the difference between the criminal and procedural breaches – 'leading to severe and unnecessary damage to the public perception of FÁS'.

The meeting was adjourned to consider Molloy's views and to engage further legal advice. Despite the seriousness of the findings, it would be four months before the audit committee met again. However, in January 2007 the audit committee informed Molloy that it was siding with Corcoran and that a single report would be absolutely fine. He was told in no uncertain terms to respond to its findings. On 6 February 2007 he replied in a letter that absolutely hammered Corcoran and his audit. He made eleven critical allegations about the conduct of the investigation and the subsequent report. One of the key criticisms concerned 'the long delay in concluding the report', which was a bit rich, given that Molloy had received the full report over a year before and been informed of the key findings as early as mid 2005.

Corcoran rebutted Molloy's criticisms and was backed up by the audit committee, which wrote to Molloy rejecting all of his allegations on 15 March 2007. The report was finally forwarded to the C&AG, starting the process that would ultimately expose the wild spending practices at Greg Craig's department and result in a series of high-profile barbecues in front of the PAC the following year.

A fortnight after receiving the audit committee's letter, Molloy removed Corcoran from his position as the head of Internal Audit.

In his letter to the PAC in February 2010, Corcoran gave his version of these events. 'On 30th March 2007, I was informed that I was to be removed from Internal Audit and to take up an appointment in the employment services division of FÁS. I met with the DG [Rody Molloy] to seek to know the reasons for this decision. At this meeting, two weeks after the date of the audit committee's letter to him, he informed me that my removal was entirely unrelated to the events surrounding INV 137 but rather reflected his desire to modernise Internal Audit and give it more of a supportive and consulting role in relation to FÁS management.'

Nearly eighteen months later, in October 2008, Molloy wrote to the PAC about Corcoran's removal. 'Based on legal advice, we are not currently in a position to answer the committee's query as to the fact that three different directors of Internal Audit dealt with the investigation of Corporate Affairs and in particular the current status of the second head of Internal Audit and the reason that individual was moved from his post to another position in FÁS.' To recap, Rody Molloy told Corcoran that he was being bumped out of Internal Audit in order to modernize the division. The following year, he said that he couldn't answer any questions about Corcoran's move for legal reasons.

Corcoran's work wasn't in vain. His 2006 report formed the basis of swathes of other reports and reviews. The C&AG was first out of the traps with a report published in May 2008. FÁS featured in just a short part of the document, which also covered issues at the Abbey Theatre and the Vocational Education Committees. After this report was digested by the PAC, it grilled key FÁS players in the saga, then produced its own interim report in February 2009. This in turn boomeranged back to the C&AG, which produced a report on advertising and promotion at FÁS in September 2009 as well as a report on corporate governance and internal control at the agency in January 2010.

The last of these reports got Corcoran's dander up. He felt that punches were being pulled. 'What is left out of the C&AG's account of these events is remarkable,' notes Corcoran's February 2010 letter to the PAC. 'The facts are that a properly constituted audit committee, a statutory subcommittee of the board of a non-commercial semi-state body with a budget of almost €1 billion, was faced by a refusal by the chief executive to respond to a major investigation report. As far as I am aware, this was an unprecedented event in the governance of the Irish public sector.'

The C&AG's office responded to newspaper queries arising from Corcoran's claims about omissions from the report by issuing a statement saying there was 'essentially no conflict' between the C&AG report and the contents of Corcoran's letter. (Niall Saul, chairman of the FÁS audit committee, later rowed into the debate, lashing the performance of the C&AG, which, he said, had completely missed all the overspending and waste despite its auditing of FÁS's books annually.)

When details emerged of high-level obstruction of the Internal Audit investigation, the PAC really stuck it to FÁS management. The committee was especially critical of management's dealings with Greg Craig during the probe: 'senior management gave certain assurances to the Director of Corporate Affairs during the course of the investigation to the effect that the matters being investigated by Internal Audit were procedural and, by implication, not of a serious nature; this should not have happened.'

Craig's four interviews by the FÁS audit team were convoluted at best. 'It has been the experience of Internal Audit that in response to a number of critical matters of fact, Greg Craig has changed his statement when presented with additional material which had become available to Internal Audit,' the FÁS Internal Audit document noted. On six separate occasions Craig changed his tune, on matters ranging from how certain people won contracts or jobs to whether he had asked newspapers for tickets to sporting matches after booking ads. He amended his statements when presented with emails from his computer about these incidents.

It's hard to know what you'd have to do in order to get the flick from FÁS. Craig remained in his post until June 2008 before going out on sick leave. He later returned to FÁS but was moved to different posts, including a stint managing the agency's response to a potential swine flu outbreak.

For someone who played such a pivotal role in the calamity at FÁS, Craig is an unremarkable individual. He often wears a beige trench coat, which appears to be several inches too short for him.

He's Fianna Fáil through and through, which may explain a few things. In the nineties he ran unsuccessfully for a council seat in Ballyfermot, part of the late Brian Lenihan Senior's power base in Dublin County West. Craig had been close to the late Fianna Fáil heavyweight, the father of finance minister Brian Lenihan and junior minister Conor Lenihan.

Craig's bosses at FÁS allowed him to stray well off the plantation, with disastrous effects. Craig was a fixer. He was known in the business as a man who looked after journalists. Back in 2000, when Nick Webb was working in the business section of the *Sunday Tribune*, he was chasing up a relatively innocuous lead about FÁS and whether one of its programmes was actually having any sort of impact. If the story had been true, it wouldn't have reflected well on FÁS; but the economy was in full roar and people weren't very interested in the state employment agency. Nick rang Craig at FÁS HQ. Within minutes, Craig asked Nick if he'd like to go to South Africa: FÁS was arranging a trip and some journalists were to be brought along, all expenses paid. Nick told him he'd think about it, but never called back. By all accounts the South Africa trip was a spectacular jolly – it was the one where a classical pianist was brought in to play at Mary Harney's hotel suite at massive cost to the taxpayer.

Craig's Corporate Affairs Department, with a staff of nine, looked after public relations, advertising and events. It also became a glorified concierge service for the top floor at FÁS HQ on Baggot Street, arranging travel, wining and dining and assorted junkets for the hard-pressed chiefs. There was little control over what Craig could or couldn't do. Financial structures were weak. (Craig would later claim to have asked for a financial controller to help run his unit and to have been turned down.)

FÁS was not only guilty of wasteful spending; it also took a dodgy approach to awarding contracts and assessing tenders. The organization had apparently learned nothing from one of Craig's earliest mistakes in this area.

In late 2000 Craig and his Corporate Affairs team decided that FÁS needed another website to promote Ireland as a place full of jobs for skilled and semi-skilled workers. The website would have enabled employers to advertise vacancies and potential workers to register their details. Bizarrely, the Corporate Affairs team didn't discuss the idea with FÁS's own IT department; instead, they went off on a solo run.

The contract was given to a company called Ultimate Communications, which had been incorporated just ten working days earlier. The website, unsurprisingly, was a turkey. When the site was shut down, all the vacancy and client details were lost.

In July 2001 FÁS received twenty invoices from Ultimate Communications for a total of €687,000. All hell broke loose. The board – then led by current CIÉ chairman John Lynch – had been unaware of the contract agreed by Craig. Extricating itself early from this entanglement wasn't possible, and FÁS eventually agreed to pay all but six months of the three-year contract. Between hosting, administration and other maintenance costs, a total of some €3.55 million was paid out to external contractors for a website that was shut down after just one year.

Craig finally faced disciplinary proceedings in June 2007 after the completion of Corcoran's internal audit. FÁS clammed up when questioned by the PAC in November 2008 over Craig's punishment. FÁS assistant director-general Christy Cooney, who was in charge of HR, would say only that Craig had not been suspended. FÁS insisted that 'legal reasons' prevented it from telling the Oireachtas committee exactly how it had dealt with this issue. Although we don't know what measures were taken to discipline Craig, we do know that his career didn't suffer as a result: he was shortlisted for promotion in December 2007.

Craig rode roughshod over safeguards designed to protect taxpayers' interests and disobeyed procurement regulations. 'It is hard to avoid the conclusion that the budget, in certain respects, was misused in that contracts appeared to have benefited a restricted number of suppliers,' the PAC found. Close to €1.8 million had been wasted on useless or unnecessary services, suppliers or contracts, while proper procurement rules had not been followed when granting another €6.8 million in contracts to certain suppliers. One North Dublin business consultancy and accountancy firm, OSK, was 'consistently successful when applying for work' and had been given 'unusually generous' conditions in their contracts, in some cases being paid up front. In 2003 the fee paid to OSK for a consultancy review of various internal financial controls within Craig's Corporate Affairs unit simply doubled 'without any reasonable explanation'. The auditors found that 'the output from this work did not appear to match the cost'.

FÁS Corporate Affairs discussed consultancy tenders with OSK even before putting them out for public bids. In one extraordinary case, OSK suggested a number of companies that could tender against it for the contract to produce a review of the Science Challenge in late 2004. Unsurprisingly, OSK landed the contract. Internal Audit took the view that 'the process of tendering via FÁS procurement and advertising agencies was flawed and in some cases contracts were awarded in the absence of genuinely competitive tenders.'

This cavalier attitude to competitive tendering and correct procurement is sadly widespread in the public sector. However, there is another element that is crucial to these breaches at FÁS: Greg Craig had a conflict of interest. The report compiled by the FÁS Internal Audit unit found that OSK tax partner Terry Oliver was a close friend of Craig and had been 'providing financial advice to him on personal matters'. In 2005 Craig told Internal Audit that he had discussed the allegations made against him with Oliver. (Incredibly, despite the internal investigation into his activities, Craig was awarded a €10,000 'special merit' bonus for an 'exceptional' performance in June 2005. This was the very same month that the investigation was substantially complete and management had been apprised of the key emerging findings. FÁS looked after its own, regardless of what was going on.)

The money FÁS spent on advertising and promotion was quite astounding: more than €48 million from 2002 to 2008, more than €13 million over budget for the period, according to a special C&AG report in June 2009.

The FÁS auditors could not explain why FÁS had spent taxpayers' money 'to place considerable advertising' in the *Lucan and Blanchardstown Gazette* — the only local paper that FÁS 'regularly' used for advertising. When questioned about this, Craig indicated that he had been directed to place the ads by Rody Molloy. (No evidence was found to back this up.)

But FÁS didn't get much bang for its buck. In April 2005 it commissioned an external media consultancy firm to gauge how effective its advertising had been; the subsequent report found that 'advertising and promotional activities lacked strategic direction and that much of the advertising was ineffective in increasing awareness of services provided by FÁS.'

A €140,000 TV campaign to promote the Science Challenge in October 2005 had almost no effect on increasing the number of primary schools applying for the programme. The €150,000 campaign for 'Opportunities 2007', the FÁS jobs fair, was another dud: it was supposed to be seen at least five times over a short period by 976,000 people aged fifteen to thirty-five, but fell short because of an 'over-reliance on poorly performing TV stations and poor management when the campaign was live'.

Investigative journalism wouldn't be the first thing you'd associate with RTÉ's filthy-minded puppets Podge and Rodge. But the proprietors of Ballydung's Stickitt Inn landed quite a coup when they got their hands on copies of four ads made by FÁS. These had cost the agency €600,000 but were never aired because – in a recessionary break from its usual practice of ignoring its promotional budgets – it didn't have the money to pay for broadcast costs. The ads were aired on the show almost a year to the day after the *Sunday Independent* blew the lid off the can of worms at the state agency. After the ads were shown, Podge and Rodge told the *Evening Herald*: 'The ads seem to suggest that blue-collar work is criminal and that 60 per cent of the Irish working population should be deeply ashamed of their jobs. If FÁS had their way there'd be no cleaners, storemen or secretaries left in the country, and we'd all be PowerPoint-touting marketeers spouting jargon in totally manky offices.'

The annual FÁS 'Opportunities' jobs fairs were the centrepiece of the agency's promotional strategy. They would, however, lead to one of the most bizarre cases of taxpayers' money simply vanishing. A €9,200 Toyota Yaris was to be given away as a raffle prize during the FÁS fair in 2000, with large numbers of visitors entering the competition. But it was soon discovered that the car could not be given away because FÁS had not obtained a gaming licence for the raffle. A subsequent invoice submitted for the car was paid. But the car could not be found, according to a FÁS internal audit.

In November 2008 Patrick Kivlehan, part of the FÁS Internal Audit team, told the PAC that the company that issued the invoice had been subsequently taken over by another firm, and inquiries with Toyota had proved fruitless because records were kept for only seven years. The Internal Audit squad said that Craig believed that FÁS 'must have' got the money back as a credit, but a trawl by the C&AG could find no evidence of this. It had entirely disappeared.

For 'Opportunities 2007', FÁS made a star of Assets model Georgia Salpa, who did wonders for the backs of buses and became something of an internet sensation. The promotional budgeting for these events was haphazard at best. Over €2 million was spent advertising the 2007 fair – more than double the previous year – but an internal survey found that fewer people had become aware of the event through advertising than had been the case in 2006. Between 2002 and 2008 FÁS overspent its budgets for the jobs fairs by 45 per cent.

One of the heaviest costs for these jobs fairs was the construction of exhibitor stands: the C&AG found that about €2.3 million was spent on stands between 2002 and 2008. There was a common thread among the successful tenders. Display Contract International won the contracts for five years during this period before being replaced by O'Brien Expo Services. The C&AG noted that 'the principal in O'Brien Expo Services formerly worked in Display Contract International.' The contracts were awarded 'on the basis of familiarity', according to Corcoran's audit team.

Craig's approach to doling out major contracts was further highlighted in 2002 by a €250,000 agreement awarded to external event manager Deirdre Lynam to sell exhibition space at the jobs fair. The sum agreed was extremely high compared with other years, and it later emerged that she had bagged the contract before she had even tendered for it.

It wasn't just Craig who steamrolled through the regulations designed to protect the taxpayers' interests. Expenditure of over

€250,000 on any one item had to be cleared by the board of FÁS. However, in January 2008 Rody Molloy and Gerry Pyke inked a deal with the GAA to host the jobs fair at Croke Park that year; a fee of €590,000 was agreed, with 50 per cent paid up front as a deposit. This deal should have gone to the board for approval, but it did not. The bill finished up being even nastier, with FÁS ultimately paying €640,000 for the venue.

The high-profile move of the lucrative jobs fair from the RDS in Ballsbridge across the Liffey to Croke Park had caused enormous controversy, mostly because many of those involved in the event, including Craig, were vehemently opposed to the switch. 'In my opinion, and this is in no way critical of the excellent facilities in Croke Park, the RDS was a more suitable venue for an exhibition of the type and size of Opportunities,' Craig wrote in a subsequent submission to the PAC. 'At the request of FÁS management, FÁS Corporate Affairs was obliged to make the exhibition work in Croke Park.' In order words, Get on with it, boyo! When the C&AG delved into the reasons for the switch, it discovered 'no file on the background to the decision to the move could be found.'

'Opportunities 2004' went ahead in Croke Park. It was not well received. The Institute of Guidance Counsellors fired off a missive to Molloy after the event to complain about the facilities, describing Croke Park as 'totally inappropriate'. The letter noted that members of the institute were adamant that under 'no circumstances' would they return. Molloy wrote back to say that a review of the facilities was under way – and then promptly announced that the event would be held in Croke Park again. Molloy was questioned by the board about hosting 'Opportunities 2005' at Croke Park but he pushed it through by saying that the RDS was booked out on the proposed dates.

The Guidance Counsellors wrote to Molloy again in October 2008, expressing their dissatisfaction with the venue. They were fobbed off with vague promises. But Croke Park's days were numbered. In late 2008 the planned event for March 2009 was cancelled. The massive annual jobs fair has now been scrapped for the foreseeable future, with FÁS planning on running smaller regional events instead. It wasn't all bad news for the GAA, which pocketed €25,000 in cancellation fees. The GAA benefited from another major exhibition when the FÁS Munster jobs fair was moved from Cork City Hall to GAA club Nemo Rangers.

'The choice of venue for the Opportunities exhibitions was not the subject of a competitive process in any year,' the C&AG noted.

The links between the GAA and FÁS were probed by the PAC. FÁS assistant director-general Christy Cooney had served on the Cork County board of the GAA for most of the nineties. He had narrowly missed out on becoming GAA president in 2005, when Nickey Brennan topped the poll by a mere seventeen votes. Cooney was finally elected president in August 2008, with his term running until 2012. His positions in FÁS and the GAA led to his being questioned by the PAC in November 2008, days after Molloy's resignation, about the jobs fair being held at Croke Park. Cooney declared he 'had no hand, act, or part' in awarding the contracts to the GAA. But whether or not Cooney had anything to do with it, it was quite clear that the GAA and FÁS were well beyond the stage of just holding hands, and not necessarily to the benefit of FÁS's agenda or the public interest.

While FÁS was close to Rody Molloy's GAA hobby, it was also close to his roots. Molloy grew up in a local authority house in Crinkle, on the outskirts of Birr in County Offaly. The county did well out of FÁS during Molloy's tenure at the helm. Under the government's barmy decentralization wheeze, Birr was chosen as the location for the organization's new headquarters. Bypassing the Office of Public Works, which normally handles land deals for the state, FÁS spent more than €3 million buying land from a developer and fitting out temporary accommodation in Birr. However, before construction of the new headquarters went ahead, the government's decentralization programme imploded: the FÁS move to Birr was one of some fifty decentralization projects chopped by Brian Lenihan in late 2009.

The €3 million-plus wasted on the abortive Birr move was dwarfed by another piece of FÁS largesse in County Offaly: the agency splashed out €6.7 million on the grandly titled FÁS National Construction Centre, which opened in Edenderry in early 2009. The centre already looks like a white elephant: twelve trainees completed two courses in 2009, and at the time of writing just one course was scheduled for 2010. It emerged that the centre had more employees than trainees, with the total cost of training the twelve students in 2009 coming in at close to €466,000. In effect, taxpayers paid more to train one of these students than they would have paid to put someone through a year in medical school or the King's Inns. At the time FÁS indicated that the new centre would play 'a pivotal role in construction and safety training for the country as a whole in coming years' – this despite the fact that there is not likely to be much construction in Ireland for the next decade or so. 'The centre has not been able to open with the level of activity planned,' FÁS said. It was 'pursuing alternative strategies'. It is purely a coincidence of birth that both Rody Molloy and Brian Cowen are from Offaly.

In October 2009 FÁS film producer James Brooke-Tyrrell was charged with forty-six counts of deception by manufacturing false tenders between 2002 and 2008. A court heard allegations that he'd created a false tendering process that led to cheques worth €612,950 being issued to accounts held by companies he controlled.

The C&AG's finding on the Brooke-Tyrrell affair was that 'The non-effective payments appear to have been facilitated by shortcomings in the procedures for altering the recorded details of suppliers in the FÁS records.' This was a common theme at an agency where financial management was extremely lax. Nobody seemed to be in charge. The ultimate responsibility for that must fall squarely at the door of Rody Molloy, who was appointed director-general by Mary Harney in August 2000, replacing the CIÉ-bound John Lynch. The board, made of social-partnership worthies and top civil servants, was also asleep at the wheel.

During the years when Molloy was at the helm of FÁS, Ireland had abnormally low unemployment rates. Despite this, successive Fianna Fáil allocations saw the agency's budget grow and grow. The long-term unemployed accounted for around one third of our jobless total. Meanwhile, close to 400,000 young workers from places such as Poland, Latvia, other EU accession states and further afield flocked to the country, efficiently filling vacancies in service industries, retail and construction. FÁS, jostling for position, desperately tried to reinvent itself as a vehicle for sourcing talent from abroad. The quango went increasingly global, hosting jobs fairs and other employment exhibitions in Eastern Europe and the US.

Like the government, the banks and the property developers, FÁS bet the house on the construction sector. The builders and developers must have been pinching themselves in the tent at the Galway Races: here was a state agency willing to groom thousands of young people for their business – and saving them millions in the process.

In August 2008 it emerged that registrations for FÁS's building-related apprenticeships had fallen off a cliff. And yet even at that stage – over a year on from the beginning of the credit crunch – construction-related courses still accounted for 80 per cent of trades intake into FÁS. While the employment conditions in Ireland had changed utterly, FÁS just stood rooted to the spot, paralysed by either indecision or blindness.

When unemployment returned to Ireland with a vengeance, the sheer inadequacy of FÁS quickly became clear. In August 2009 Department of Enterprise, Trade and Employment figures revealed that almost half of the places on its jobs schemes and training programmes were empty. FÁS had thirteen courses with the capacity to train and upskill 132,601 people. But, with unemployment heading for half a million, just 73,682 people had been taken on. The Return to Work scheme, which had 855 places, was hosting only 480 people. A short-course programme aimed at upskilling had 15,710 places but only 3,930 registered participants. The audit provided a morale-sapping snapshot of the mismatch between the country's needs and FÁS's offerings.

The rather unimaginatively named Job Training programme, aimed at getting the long-term unemployed back to work, cost €29 million in 2008. Just forty-six people completed the course, at a cost of about €890,000 per person, and, according to a Forfás review, not one of the participants got a job that year. Each of the participants could have just been given almost €45,000 a year for the next twenty years instead. It might have been of more use.

A report by state advisory board Forfás, which was leaked to the media in March 2010, recommended that the programme be culled immediately, as there was no evidence that anyone was actually benefiting from the scheme. More broadly, Forfás found that the state had absolutely no idea how effective its €970 million spending on various training and jobs schemes was because of a 'significant information deficit'. In other words, it couldn't figure out whether FÁS was doing what it said on the tin.

The report was long on management-speak and jargon – it was produced by Forfás after all – but beneath the waffle was a strong message: FÁS jobs and training schemes were a mess and they badly needed to be overhauled. The Community Employment (CE) scheme is one of the biggest in the country, offering the long-term unemployed temporary placements in jobs in the community. It has a budget of €392 million per year, divided among staff, allowances, training and other costs. The report found that the state needed to decide whether the CE scheme was a jobs programme designed to get people back to work (in which case it was clearly not succeeding) or just a device to boost communities through the cash payments made to participants. Forfás said that these payments should be examined to ensure that they were not acting as a disincentive: in some instances it was more lucrative to be on the CE scheme than to hold down a real job. When the figures were crunched, it emerged that 7,736 people had completed the scheme, at a cost per person of almost €127,000. Just over 3,000 of these obtained jobs or went into further education.

FÁS was also making a dog's dinner of retraining workers for the so-called 'smart economy', Forfás found: the programmes were 'not well aligned to deliver the strategic policy response required for the new labour market environment'.

In February 2010 another scathing report, produced by a working group from the Department of Employment, Science Foundation Ireland, FÁS and Forfás, asserted that the controversial Science Challenge programme, which cost €8.36 million, was of no real value. 'There were no measurable or quantifiable targets or goals set,' according to the report. 'It is therefore difficult to establish any benefits arising directly from the Science Challenge programme.' There was no evidence that the programme was independently reviewed, and it had been allowed to grow in an ad hoc manner. The Science Challenge 'did not quantifiably contribute' to the government's strategy for science, technology and innovation. In other words, it was a complete waste of time and money.

But while some courses and jobs programmes were ineptly run or just pointless, others turned out to be genuinely dangerous. In early September 2008 we came into possession of an explosive FÁS report written by management consultant Tony Spollen, the former AIB auditor who had helped blast open the DIRT scandal. The report, which had been written in 2003 and buried, revealed that FÁS had been rife with internal hostilities after allegations that several of its approved construction-sector tutors and assessors were not qualified to teach the required skills. This meant that the state training agency had been sending out hundreds of unprepared workers to dangerous building sites. It was quietly forced to retrain hundreds.

Serious misgivings by a senior FÁS employee about the safety of these courses prompted Spollen's probe and subsequent report. His inquiry focused on the FÁS construction skills and Safe Pass schemes. He found that there was 'an absence of trust, poor communication and breakdowns' at the top level of the organization. Thirty 'serious problems' in FÁS training and assessment procedures in the construction and building sector were identified. It was discovered that an assessor had been appointed who wasn't even qualified to operate the required machinery. Spollen also uncovered the falsification of dates by a training company and the use of a non-approved tutor on a safety course.

'All the issues have been dealt with and there is now a procedures and quality assurance system in place to ensure that those issues cannot recur again,' said a FÁS statement after we reported on the findings of the Spollen report. 'All tutors have to undergo regular assessment and briefing sessions to ensure this quality assurance standard is maintained.'

But clearly that wasn't the case. In October 2009 it emerged that exam results in some FÁS computer courses in the north-east had been fiddled by the outside contractors running the courses. Certain companies had falsified results in order to boost the numbers, which meant that a percentage of students received certifications that they did not merit. A FÁS internal audit had uncovered the irregularities in April 2007 after having been tipped off by SIPTU, which had claimed that one of its members was being leaned on to pass trainees. Ashfield Computer Training Ltd, one of the outside contractors involved, had trained 1,049 people on FÁS courses and received over €2 million in fees from 2002 to 2007. The company blamed a 'rogue trainer'. But the students still had to be retrained and reassessed at further cost to the taxpayer. Despite putting its hand up and admitting to the irregularities, Ashfield was permitted to tender for other courses before FÁS called a halt in early 2009. The agency subsequently sought the return of €190,000 in fees, but Ashfield went into liquidation in early 2010. A review of all 257 training courses run by outside contractors was ordered by the hapless enterprise minister, Mary Coughlan.

Two other courses run by another company – which had received over €1 million in fees from FÁS – have been associated with similar problems. Fine Gael TD Fergus O'Dowd raised the issue in the Dáil. 'It is a disgrace that the system has been abused so much. It is an appalling situation where people in need of training at such a difficult time are having question marks raised about their qualifications through no fault of their own.' He went on to say that 'We need a full-scale inquiry into all FÁS courses run by outside contractors and also the further subcontracting of courses.'

It has also emerged that FÁS apprentices were being used as cheap labour by tutors. A leaked FÁS monitoring report in November 2009 showed that students at a FÁS-funded Waterford Youth Training and Education Centre (WYTEC) had carried out construction work on a tutor's property as part of their course. Work on a wall, roof trusses, plasterwork and a unit for a loo were partially completed in a shed on a tutor's property. The chairperson of WYTEC, Nora Walls, accepted the findings of the report but insisted that no one had acted for personal gain. 'On this occasion we made a mistake. It seemed like a good idea at the time but in hindsight things should have been done differently. It was a once-off arrangement. We didn't have the facilities on site and at the time we were delighted when they were offered to us. The centre was trying to make sure the youngsters got instruction in practical skills.'

FÁS has spent over €140 million on its Competency Development Programme, a scheme designed to 'upskill' workers for the changing workplace. The Department of Enterprise commissioned a major report into the efficiency of the scheme and then buried it, causing the chairman of the review group to resign in frustration. The report is sealed in lead, encased in concrete and buried several hundred feet underground. Or at least the department must hope so.

In 2008 some €38 million was spent on the programme but that was cut to €15 million in 2009. Large blocks of the funding come from the EU – and here lies the problem. If the money isn't spent, it gets taken away. The budget for the programme rocketed from €8 million in 2004 to €44.4 million in 2008, putting serious pressure on FÁS to spend it. So the vast, bloated, spending machine recruited its buddies in IBEC and ICTU to help it eat through the cash mountain and had them devise and run a range of outsourced training schemes and programmes for FÁS.

The government allocated FÁS extra money to spend on another programme, a €19 million 'in-company training scheme', with fourteen external organizations – including ICTU and IBEC. Many of these bodies were given substantial advances. But an Internal Audit report from June 2007 found that the programme was 'out of control financially'. 'It is difficult to see any operational requirement for these substantial advances,' the audit stated. 'The front-loading of these contractors with advances involved substantial risk to the funder, FÁS, in the event that projected training volumes were not substantially achieved. This did in fact turn out to be the case in a number of instances.' A FÁS executive responded in an internal memo to the audit report, claiming it had 'effectively taken a number of minor issues and exaggerated them out of all proportion' and adding that there was little real risk to FÁS, as most of the advances had been made to ICTU, IBEC and Chambers Ireland.

Of course, both IBEC and ICTU were represented on the board

of FÁS, so this was a conflict of interest of a spectacular order. IBEC and ICTU helped govern FÁS through its boardroom, but at the same time they were both big clients of the organization, providing large numbers of places on training schemes in return for big FÁS handouts. When the state money was divided up among all of FÁS's external contractors and training providers, IBEC got €2 million and ICTU €889,336 in 2007 alone, with Chambers Ireland, the Construction Industry Federation, the Small Firms Association and the Irish Management Institute also bagging cash for the employers.

The FÁS board of €14,000-per-year insiders (with €24,000 for chairman Peter McLoone) may have been dozing while the agency was splurging taxpayers' money on first-class flights, plush hotel rooms, games of golf and pay-per-view movies. They slept soundly. But when it came to carving up the taxpayers' money for their own pet organizations, the representatives of IBEC and the trade unions didn't muck around. In many ways, it was symptomatic of the FÁS mentality. Get as much money as you can and burn through it as fast as humanly possible.

4. The Sickness of the HSE

In late September 2009 Nick Webb made a request under the Free-dom of Information Act for data on the credit-card usage of Brendan Drumm, the chief executive of the HSE, and his praetorian guard of advisers. After a couple of weeks we received two envelopes jammed with documents. One was a ring binder labelled 'Visa Card state-ments of CEO of HSE Professor Brendan Drumm for the period August 2006 to August 2009'. An awful lot of work had gone into putting a positive slant on the contents of the binder. The other files were photocopies of credit-card statements for IT chief Damien McCallion, human resources executive Martin McDonald and prop-erty chief Brian Gilroy.

The documents reached us on Friday, 30 October. Within hours, the HSE launched an operation intended to limit the damage that would be caused by publication of this information. Towards 5 p.m. that day, as our deadline approached, the HSE emailed a press release to newsrooms across the country. It was publishing details of its managers' credit-card use to promote 'greater transparency and ac-countability in the organisation'. The information was to be uploaded on to its website on a quarterly basis. The HSE was trying to kill our story by pretending it had initiated the disclosure. The credit-card details for the first six months of 2009 were put up on the website late that evening.

The HSE had already become synonymous with mismanagement, but its PR team were playing a stormer. Cleverly they had released the headline figures and bulked them up with boring statistics and percentages. 'Most of the money was spent on hotels (36 per cent), followed by travel, parking costs (16 per cent), as well as publications and education courses (2 per cent), according to the organisation,' the following day's piece in the *Irish Times* noted. It was a 'so what' story, too dull for anyone even to bother reading to the end.

Our story had been dented but not totalled. 'HSE Chiefs in Credit Card Binge' was the best headline we could come up with, having discarded 'HSE Chiefs Living the High Life', which was a bit too similar to our FÁS headline from 2008. The strapline on the piece was 'Top brass blow thousands on golf fees, clamping fines, Michelin-starred restaurants and flights'. By 10 p.m. that night the pages were ready to go and had been cleared by the *Sunday Independent* lawyers.

Even at a time when public-sector waste was being uncovered almost every week, the scale and sheer extravagance of the HSE executives' spending was obscene. This was a body that pleaded the poor mouth as it closed children's hospital wards, cutting back on care for the elderly and infirm. But it was able to cover its executives' greens fees. One of our revelations was that in July 2007 Brian Gilroy claimed €82 for a round at the Paradise Golf Club in Malahide for the appropriately named John Wedge, a visiting Canadian orthopaedic surgeon who had been one of the advisers on the proposed new National Children's Hospital.

Visiting Canadians were expensive that summer: in June, Gilroy spent €1,296 on dinner for some consultants from Toronto in Ross Lewis's Michelin-starred restaurant Chapter One in Parnell Square, Dublin. Gilroy obviously liked the restaurant, having spent €313 there a week earlier. The taxpayer also forked out for a €919.01 'working dinner' at Chapter One for Brendan Drumm and diplomats from the Caribbean island of Grenada in November 2006. HSE national director Tommie Martin used his company credit card to pay for a retirement knees-up at Giorgio Casari's swish Unicorn Restaurant on Dublin's Merrion Row in January 2006. Laverne McGuinness, national director of Primary Community and Continuing Care, splashed out a staggering €1,285.55 on a meal at Shanahan's steak house on St Stephen's Green in the summer of that year. As patients lay on hospital trolleys due to a shortage of beds, HSE chiefs also billed the public for boozy lunches and dinners in salubrious joints such as Peploe's on St Stephen's Green, once favoured by Anglo Irish Bank executives and their spivvy property clients; Rhodes D7, the short-lived eatery set up in Dublin by the spiky-haired TV chef Gary Rhodes; the Merrion Hotel; One Pico; the Winding Stair; and the

Mint Bar in the Westin Hotel, among others. How exactly the HSE or the Irish public might have benefited from these expensive feasts is hard to fathom.

The organization's taste for luxury extended beyond the culinary realm. The plebs were avoided even on trains. Gilroy spent €360 for two train tickets from Dublin to Belfast to visit his NHS counterpart, John Cole. (A standard return to Belfast costs €28 when booked online.) Gilroy was used to the better seats on trains, having spent $372 (around €275) for two return tickets from New York's Pennsylvania Station to Philadelphia in March 2007. The journey time for the trip is around one hour and thirteen minutes, with standard fares less than a quarter of what Gilroy paid.

Brendan Drumm and his lieutenants amassed enormous bills from travel around the globe, flying business class and staying in luxurious hotels. Jaunts to Beverly Hills, New York, Boston, Chicago and Toronto in 2006, 2007 and 2008 saw Drumm spend €4,200 on hotel bills. On Drumm's eight-night trip across the Atlantic in May 2008 he slept in the five-star Toronto Le Royal Meridien and the Westin in Chicago. The journey also included a stay in May 2008 at the €360-per-night Helmsley Hotel in Manhattan, once owned by the so-called 'Queen of Mean', Leona Helmsley, who left a $12 million chunk of her fortune to her dog Trouble. There was nothing mean about the travel or accommodation arrangements.

Drumm's transatlantic journeys were comfy business-class flights – although the HSE points out that he flies economy for European travel. Receipts for Drumm's AIB Executive Visa corporate card – which had an annual fee of €200 – show he spent €5,834 with Trailfinders on flights to Toronto and Los Angeles as part of a business trip in mid 2006. Drumm also coughed up $108 on an Aer Lingus flight to buy a present for his hosts, and paid for corporate lounges at Cork, Dublin and the US. Over a three-year period, other HSE executives travelled further than swine flu, clocking up bills of more than €4,800 in hotels from Sydney to Seattle, from Barcelona to Budapest.

If some important person failed to put enough money into a parking meter, the taxpayer was there to cover the fine. Drumm's card was used to pay a €95 clamping fee for an unnamed 'VIP guest', and the HSE spent €80 on a clamping fee for Brian Gilroy before he'd even joined the organization – Gilroy was clamped as he was being interviewed for the job. Even when the top health officials travelled abroad with Minister Mary Harney, they took the taxpayer for a ride. On one trip to Milan in February 2007, an unnamed member of Harney's delegation, staying with her at the Park Hyatt Milano Hotel, let the taxpayer pick up a room-service bill for €4.10 for tobacco.

It wasn't supposed to be like this. The HSE was set up to create efficiencies and improve the lot of patients. It came into being on 1 January 2005, after a two-year planning and transition process to merge more than a dozen regional health boards and state bodies into a single national body tasked with providing healthcare and social services across the country. But it was a shambles from day one, and things haven't improved. In just a few years the HSE – whose annual budget is roughly equivalent to the state's annual take from income tax, and whose staff is larger than the total population of Tonga or Andorra – has ratcheted inefficiency up to a brand-new level. The money it squanders is money that could be used to pay for new artificial hips, vaccinations to prevent cervical cancer or life-saving operations.

Brendan Drumm was a UCD professor and a paediatric expert at Our Lady's Children's Hospital in Crumlin before he was hired to run the HSE. He had also chaired Comhairle na nOspidéal, a quango that appoints consultants and advises on the running of hospitals. Drumm wasn't the first choice for the job: in September 2004 the HSE announced that it had appointed Dr Aidan Halligan, an Irishman who had risen to the post of Deputy Chief Medical Officer for England and Director of Clinical Governance in the UK's National Health Service. But in November, before taking up the position, Halligan changed his mind, citing 'family reasons'. He dodged a bullet. Rather than offer the job to one of the other supposedly brilliant candidates on its shortlist, the HSE started the recruitment process from scratch. Drumm was eventually appointed in June 2005, eight months after Halligan had withdrawn.

This early setback would have lasting implications. Other than an interim board, there was no hand on the tiller for the crucial early months of the HSE's existence; the biggest transformation of the health service in the history of the state was launched without a full-time chief executive in place. The government, the Department of Health and their phalanxes of advisers had already decided how the HSE was going to look and what it would do long before Drumm came on the scene.

Drumm received a basic salary of around €371,000, plus pension and car allowance, bringing his package to over €430,000. There was also a bonus provision, which would become a political hand grenade. Drumm's deal saw him paid far, far more than his counterpart in the NHS, Sir David Nicholson, whose salary is €312,000 according to the latest figures in June 2010. For Drumm there was the added attraction of a guaranteed job – worth about €280,000 – back in academia when his five-year term expired. He couldn't lose.

The HSE was hamstrung by the politicians who presided over its establishment. The government of Bertie Ahern – never one to grasp a nettle when some folksy obfuscation would do – gave assurances to the managers and employees of the different health boards that not only would they not lose their jobs through the merging of operations, but they also wouldn't have to change jobs. This single decision set the HSE back by at least a decade. The whole point of creating a single body to run all the hospitals and healthcare services was to create efficiencies by merging the ten regional health boards, the Eastern Regional Health Authority and a clutch of smaller health-related quangos. Any rational observer could see that there were going to be massive overlaps. It made no sense to keep eleven separate accounting or legal teams, eleven separate HR or public-relations units and eleven separate procurement and IT departments. But that's effectively what happened.

The initial HSE board was first put together by the then Minister for Health Micheál Martin in November 2003. It was composed of insiders, people who had served time on state boards, agencies and assorted quangos, and it paid well: normal board members received annual fees of €17,500, with the chairman receiving €35,000.

Former AIB executive Kevin Kelly, who also sat on the boards of other state-controlled agencies including the Economic and Social Research Institute (ESRI), the Irish Museum of Modern Art and the National Children's Hospital, was the interim chairman of the body, tasked with getting the organization up and running before handing over the baton to more operationally skilled types. His former colleague from AIB, Donal de Buitléir, also signed on the dotted line. Nursing professor P. Anne Scott and NUI Cork Dean of Medicine Dr Michael Murphy – from Minister Martin's Cork South constituency – provided the medical smarts, and academic heft was provided by John Murray of TCD Business School and UCD corporate-governance expert Niamh Brennan. Former Beaumont Hospital and Blood Transfusion Board chief Michael McLoone – brother of jet-setting FÁS chairman Peter – was also a member. The board was completed by Dr Maureen Gaffney, chair of the National Economic and Social Forum; Eugene McCague, former Dublin Institute of Technology chairman and partner with law firm Arthur Cox; P. J. Fitzpatrick, the one-time head of the Eastern Health Board and subsequently boss of the Court Service; and Liam Downey, the former chief executive of medical devices firm Becton Dickinson Ireland and an IBEC-linked member of the Labour Relations Commission. All of the board members had served on other state boards or agencies or commissions over the previous decade. The make-up of the board represented conservative, old-school thinking; at a time when the Irish health service was failing on many fronts, there was nobody who seemed likely to challenge the established ways of doing things.

Under the legislation setting up the HSE, five of the twelve original directors would have to stand down three years after the organization came into existence in January 2005. None of the board members offered to step down when their time ran out, and board minutes from October 2007 show that a lottery was held. The names of the unlucky board members – Michael McLoone and John Murray – were drawn out of a hat. They were replaced by former Fianna Fáil party secretary Pat Farrell and retired Department of Finance civil servant Joe Mooney. Solid, well-connected people but hardly boardroom A-listers.

Taking the helm six months after the HSE had set sail, Drumm set about creating a team to help him shape the unshapeable. Money, it appeared, was no object. One of the first in the door was his communications adviser, Karl Anderson, who has been paid over €955,000 since joining the HSE on a five-year contract back in 2005. (In July 2008 Anderson broke his arm in a fracas involving HSE national director Tommie Martin outside Nancy Hand's pub and restaurant on Parkgate Street in Dublin after a farewell party for press officer Alex Connolly. In April of 2009 Anderson said that it was 'inappropriate' to discuss whether there had been a settlement with Martin over the episode. The HSE described it as 'a private matter'.) Backing up Anderson is a central in-house press operation that costs the taxpayer €1 million a year: in 2008, besides Anderson's €227,000 salary, it spent €500,000 on four special advisers and €241,000 on the salaries of five press officers.

Carlow general practitioner Sean McGuire was another of Drumm's early hires to his so-called 'kitchen cabinet' of advisers, on a contract worth a cool €1,500 per day. McGuire's expertise was in setting up community clinics for primary care. Having co-founded Britain's first major out-of-hours GP co-op, Medway Doctors, in 1989, McGuire returned to Ireland and set up Caredoc in Carlow in 1999. The HSE intended to shift much of the burden of non-acute services from overstretched hospitals to local health centres run by GPs. It was slow work. In 2007 McGuire jumped ship for the private sector, joining Unicare multimillionaire Fergus Hoban's Touchstone group, which is setting up private healthcare clinics around the country. This was another major setback for the HSE and prompted Labour TD Jan O'Sullivan to call for a conflict-of-interest code to be introduced into the HSE. 'Under the code of behaviour for civil servants, senior staff intending to switch to jobs in the private sector are required to take a year's career break to avoid a conflict of interest,' she said. 'The HSE should be treated the same way.'

Another key player in Drumm's kitchen cabinet was his Mayo-born performance manager Maureen Lynott, the former chairman of the National Treatment Purchase Fund. It was her role to achieve 'value for money' within the HSE, and she set up the HealthStat performance-monitoring system, which gives the HSE up-to-date data on how all the bits of the behemoth are performing.

Drumm's team also included former Comhairle na nOspidéal chief Tommie Martin, who was seconded from the Department of Health. Martin left his €190,000-per-year job at the HSE in late 2008. John O'Brien, former chief executive of St James's Hospital, rounded off Drumm's original team, retiring in November 2009. Despite the high pay, among the highest in the public sector, the HSE has a devil of a job trying to hang on to key personnel. With Drumm's departure at the end of his contract in August 2010 came the break-up of much of his remaining 'reform team' team. After earning almost €1 million over five years as Drumm's personal PR adviser, Karl Anderson left in October, with performance manager Maureen Lynott also leaving after earning €1.1 million over the same period.

In January 2010 Minister for Health Mary Harney appointed new members to the HSE board to replace those whose terms were up. Among the new appointees was Joe Lavelle, a manager with the giant accounting and consultancy firm Deloitte & Touche. The significance of Lavelle's appointment was completely missed. He may be a very pleasant and able chap, but his employer's dealings with the health service have been nothing short of catastrophic.

Years before the creation of the HSE, the Department of Health engaged Deloitte to consult on the development of software systems. The Personnel, Payroll and Related Systems (PPARS) project was due to deliver a payroll system for 140,000 staff in the health sector, and the Financial Information System Project (FISP) was to handle financial management.

When first promoted in 1998, PPARS was costed at €9 million. But new bits kept being added to the original specification and the scale of the project grew and grew. By 2002 the cost had risen to €17 million, and by the following year it was up to €30 million. In 2004 the bill was estimated at €100 million. By the autumn of 2005, with the costs well over €150 million, the HSE was forced to call a stop on both PPARS and FISP. A major review of IT spending and projects was undertaken, as it tried to find out why everything had gone so spectacularly wrong. In June 2007 the HSE announced that no new work would be done to roll out PPARS, but it would continue to be used in the areas where it had already been installed. Maintenance and running costs were over €7 million in 2008 but are believed to have fallen since.

Quantifying the overspending and mess caused by PPARS was too hard even for the trained bean-counters at the C&AG's office, who estimated that between €180 million and €220 million was wasted on PPARS. At the time it was suggested by external consultants that if work hadn't been halted on PPARS and FISP, the total bill could have surged past €400 million.

Taoiseach Bertie Ahern and Minister for Health Mary Harney described the consultancy costs on the software projects as 'excessive'. The scandal caused the government to initiate new systems for monitoring major IT projects. Under the present rules, ministers must now justify the use of outside consultants, and civil servants are being given a greater role in procurement. There have been quiet rumblings over a new system to replace PPARS but to date nothing has been progressed. Even without the prospect of a 'son of PPARS', hopes are high for the Nationwide Credit Management System (NCMS), a new IT system that is being introduced to track the estimated €200 million in unpaid patient fees clocked up by recipients of the HSE's services. Taxpayers may have to watch the roll-out of this through their fingers. But at least Deloitte isn't involved.

Consultants are clearly a crucial part of any functioning health service – the kind of consultants who poke around inside people or look at CAT scans, rather than the ones that devise new strategies or promise 'integrated solutions'. Both types of consultants drive expensive cars but only the medical ones will make you feel better. Even so, the HSE has also contrived to splash out over €51 million on management and technical consultants, advisers and other assorted wonks since it was set up. That would be enough to pay for about 1,200 staff nurses for a year.

More than a dozen different PR and marketing companies or advisers have received payments from the HSE since 2005, despite the existence of a well-staffed and resourced internal press and communications bureau. One of the most extraordinary bits of spending occurred in 2008, when the HSE coughed up €318,000 for what it described as 'STI/pregnancy leaflet design consultancy'. Not a book. Not a report. A leaflet.

Roddy Guiney's PR, media and lobbying group Wilson Hartnell, which produced this leaflet, has made a hatful of money from the HSE, bagging €464,000 in fees in 2007 alone. Another big PR company, Drury Communications, pocketed an extraordinary €55,000 for the 'formulation of a communications strategy' and the launch of the 2007 HSE annual report. Mary Harney's former deputy press secretary Iarla Mongey runs the public affairs unit at the firm.

Phil Flynn, the former Sinn Féin vice-president and labour-relations whiz, was paid €52,000 in 2008 to mediate with trade unions. Flynn resigned from his job as chairman of Bank of Scotland (Ireland) when it emerged that he was a shareholder and director of a company run by Ted Cunningham, who was involved in laundering some of the proceeds of the £26 million Northern Bank robbery in 2004.

Mark Moran – the former EBS chairman who banked over €40 million when private equity firm CapVest bought his stake in the private hospital group Mater Private – is also a backer of Bankhawk Banking Advisors, which earned more than €70,000 from the HSE for its 'analysis of banking services'.

Arthur Cox solicitors received €102,558 from the HSE for 'agency/consultancy services' in connection with the PPARS project. Its former managing partner Eugene McCague is a board member of the HSE, first appointed in November 2003.

Some of the firms that won big consultancy contracts have strong links to the Department of Health or to the HSE. One of these, Prospectus Strategy Consultants, was paid €581,000 for six projects, including a review of maternity services. The company is headed by Vincent Barton, a former high-ranking civil servant within the Department of Health.

With such a huge amount of money being shovelled out to all these advisers and contractors, sometimes the HSE isn't able to keep track of who it is actually doing business with. Close to 400 payments were made to various consultancy outfits between 2005 and

2007, according to figures we've been able to obtain; and the HSE actually spent €5,940 on what it described as a 'consultant cataloguer' to keep track of all the outside advisers.

But it still wasn't able to keep tabs on all its external consultants. In late 2005 it emerged that the HSE had shelled out €1.97 million to an offshore shelf company called Blackmore Group Assets, without performing proper checks on its credentials. The British Virgin Islands-registered company, administered through Guernsey, was paid by HSE North West for providing eight IT specialists to work on the disastrous PPARS project. Official procurement policies and appropriate tax-clearance procedures were not followed. This revelation caused an outcry, especially coming as it did hot on the heels of the Dublin Waterworld scandal in 2005, when it emerged that the €61 million contract to run the national aquatic centre in Blanchardstown had been given to a British shelf company.

Small forests have been felled to produce the mountains of reports the HSE commissions each year, and yet the usefulness of these reports may be questioned. In 2009 the HSE lashed out €871,000 on a report by McKinsey called 'Organising to Deliver Integrated Care'. A key part of this report suggested that healthcare should be delivered in 'six to ten regions with a catchment population of between 500,000 to 700,000'. The HSE opted for a four-region model. Essentially the advice in the report was about as useful as a chocolate teapot. Another report, costing €280,000 and produced by Howarth Consultants, recommended that Cork University Hospital become the sole provider of acute treatment in the Cork and Kerry region. This advice was ignored and it was decided that Kerry General Hospital would retain all these services instead.

Brendan Drumm has defended the spending on consultants, telling an Oireachtas committee, 'It would be difficult to find any organization with so large a budget that spends such a small amount of it on consultancies.' It may be the case that the bill for €51 million spent by the HSE to date on external consultants is, as Drumm claims, relatively small. But, given that Our Lady's Children's Hospital in Crumlin was forced to close a ward because of a €9 million shortfall in funding, perhaps it's not that small.

Remarkably, there were payments to forty different HR consultants between 2005 and 2007 – this, even though the HSE has its own very well-staffed Human Resources Department. Documents obtained under the Freedom of Information Act revealed that the organization had spent over €900,000 between 2005 and early 2008 on payments to Maura McGrath's human-resources consultancy, McGrath Associates. McGrath was one of Drumm's key advisers as he grappled with how to trim the 110,000-strong workforce and implement new working practices. But she was a stopgap, albeit a very expensive one. At the time the HSE was having difficulty hiring a HR chief. Eventually it tapped up National Irish Bank's Sean McGrath – no relation to Maura – to become its new HR chief in 2008, smashing through standard civil service salary levels to give him a basic pay package of €205,000 plus pension and bonuses.

Human resources, staffing and wage costs are the major structural problems faced by the HSE, which is by far Ireland's biggest employer, with over 111,000 staff at the end of 2009. (That's more than the total number of people who work in agriculture in this country.) The HSE's response to its ongoing financial difficulties has been brutal and badly targeted. Cost-cutting was introduced across the board. It wasn't a precise bit of keyhole surgery; a big hefty axe was used instead. Top-performing parts of the organization felt the same pressure as the more wasteful and less useful units. The primary approach to cost-cutting was to stop replacing staff who had left. This moratorium on filling jobs has left some services dangerously low on staff, according to an internal financial report leaked to the *Irish Independent* in June 2010.

Some of the cuts created quite ludicrous situations. In November 2009 it emerged that Peter O'Rourke, a senior consultant surgeon at Letterkenny General Hospital, and two of his colleagues, who were paid a total of €670,000 per year, were being forced to sit on their hands after the hospital cancelled all elective surgical procedures in order to combat a €2.7 million budget deficit. 'The government is paying me large sums of money to sit around doing nothing,' he told the *Irish Daily Mail*. 'I'm sitting here in my office looking out my window at a digger piling up clay on the site of a new emergency department, when I should be at work in my operating theatre.'

It's not just executive bungling and out-of-control spending that cause problems. Unions and some staff are clearly taking the mickey too. Work practices at HSE operations are from another planet. In the spring of 2007 Cork University Hospital shuddered to a halt when a row broke out between electricians and service staff and the hospital over new work practices. One of the issues in dispute was who should be allowed to change light bulbs at the hospital. The HSE suspended thirty-eight electricians, members of the Technical Engineering and Electrical Union (TEEU), from their jobs at Cork University Hospital, St Finbarr's Hospital, Kerry General Hospital and Mallow General Hospital after they refused to implement a labour-court recommendation permitting workers other than electricians to change light bulbs. A wildcat strike ensued.

The strike spread fast to other hospitals in the south and west. Eleven operations were cancelled at Kerry General. In the Mid-Western Regional Hospital in Limerick, the parents of a sick child and a hospital manager were forced to wheel the patient to the operating theatre after a porter was prevented from doing so by a union official.

Ultimately, the matter was resolved through mediation. Now anyone can change a bedside light bulb.

Another equally bizarre dispute erupted the same year. The National Hospital Hygiene audit unit issued a directive that ward curtains – the curtains that close around hospital beds to give patients privacy – needed to be changed twice a year to cut down the spread of infections. SIPTU objected to this directive being implemented at Mallow General Hospital because, it argued, there weren't enough staff to change the ninety-odd curtains twice a year and the workers weren't insured to change curtains. The curtains hang from rails six feet off the ground, and it seems SIPTU was concerned that stumpier members might have to use a stepladder to unhook them. The union told the labour court that it wanted extra staff – or else overtime to be paid to existing staff – before it would agree to allow its members to change the curtains. In its own submission to the labour court, the HSE said that it had bought brand-new safety ladders,

introduced dedicated training on how to unhook curtains and
changed the design of the curtains to make them easier to remove.
The labour court displayed extraordinary patience in listening to this
rubbish, ruling that the removal and the rehanging of these curtains
was a job for 'multitask' operatives and not just for support-services
workers. It also found that the workers were insured. It urged that
the curtains be changed as soon as possible.

The implications of the trade unions' ridiculous inflexibility on
work practices in the health sector were highlighted in UCD economist Colm McCarthy's 'An Bord Snip Nua' report of July 2009,
which recommended a range of public-sector spending cuts. 'The
Group observes that restrictive agreements and work practices,
involving trade unions and professional staff organisations, have been
a major inhibitor to staffing and pay efficiencies in the Health sector,
and a block to good-quality patient-focused care. The Group considers that such practices have no place in an efficient, modern health
system that is operating under severe budgetary constraints, and in
which the needs of patients should be a paramount consideration.'

In the summer of 2010 the HSE revealed that it had lost €2.35 million through its involvement with the trade union SIPTU. The
money was channelled through the HSE to a bank account called
'SIPTU national health and local authority levy fund' as part of a
programme to train lower-paid staff. However, SIPTU emphatically
denied ever having received the money. It later emerged that the
account, for which two union members were signatories, was not an
official union one. An HSE audit found that some of the money paid
into it had been used to fund thirty-one foreign trips undertaken by
civil servants, trade-union representatives and HSE staff, including
visits to Australia, Hong Kong, Britain and the US. In the absence of
a paper trail, it appears the money has vanished in a puff of smoke.

One of the most common criticisms levied at the HSE is that it has
far too many pencil-pushers. The Department of Health believes that
16.2 per cent of the HSE's staff are 'administrators' – a higher percentage than the notoriously top-heavy NHS in Britain. At the end
of 2008 the HSE employed 17,967 administrative staff – which means

that it has more administrators than it does health and social-care professionals such as physiotherapists, occupational therapists, dieticians, and speech and language specialists, who number roughly 15,000.

In the past ten years the ranks of managers and administrators have expanded rapidly. 'At the outset of the HSE [in 2003] there were something like six grade eight [civil servants] – these are highly paid individuals. Today there's over 760 of them,' according to Fine Gael TD Dr James Reilly. 'They are engaged in industrious futility, running around filling out very extensive reports that are terribly important in their own minds but which don't result in an iota of improvement in care or a single new service.'

Many of these numerous managers and administrators haven't been up to the job. Less than two years after the HSE was set up, the National Treasury Management Agency (NTMA) was parachuted in by the Department of Finance to review the organization's sprawling financial systems, in particular its banking and cash arrangements. What they found was a shambles of mismanagement, overlapping systems and downright waste. The HSE was operating 254 separate bank accounts in seven different banks, paying close to €2 million a year in bank charges alone. Over €14 million in funds were lodged in bank accounts that paid no interest, costing the organization around €700,000 per year in forgone interest. Some 1,000 people were employed by the HSE to manage its finances, but a number of these were in duplicate roles. Invoices cost between €75 and €100 to process – often more than the amount being billed for. In its report to the PAC, the NTMA found that a unified finance system should be created in the HSE as an 'immediate priority'.

The report identified €19.6 million in potential savings, including the reduction of bank charges and the electronic payment of money to patient accounts. Two years after the report was delivered, just nine of its twenty-five recommendations had been implemented.

For an organization that is so desperately strapped for cash, the HSE has also proved extraordinarily blasé about getting paid by insurance companies. The C&AG's annual report of 2008 highlighted this failing and blamed outmoded paper-based administration systems and delays in sign-offs by consultants for the high number of bills outstanding from privately insured patients in the twenty-four hospitals reviewed, suggesting that 'the State is facilitating private medicine without getting the related income for the service it provides.' About half of private in-patients are not charged for their accommodation, the report found.

The HSE's haphazard billing arrangements were symptomatic of a wider malaise, of which the calamitous financial mismanagement of 2007 was a particularly dramatic recent example. In November 2006 the HSE was told that it would have €13.98 billion to spend the following year. This was €341 million less than it figured it needed for the year ahead. A few sums on the back of a beer mat would have shown that something would have to be cut, but this did not happen. 'Despite its initial assessment of the financial position the HSE senior management team did not direct any specific action at this point to achieve the savings that were likely to be needed to stay within budget,' a subsequent C&AG report found. 'In rolling out the budget it did warn managers that the budgetary position was tight but, for example, it did not ask for specific plans to achieve quantifiable savings.'

The HSE just stuck its head in the sand. By February 2007 the HSE's control group, which is made up of top executives, knew that budgets were hurtling out of control and that the organization would encounter significant financial difficulties if spending wasn't cut. A full two months later it decided that savings targets should be set for each unit of the HSE, and by June of that year it demanded that each unit submit its savings plans. 'As the financial situation continued to deteriorate, it prepared a break-even plan in July that was designed to address the €341 million shortfall which had first been identified in November 2006,' the C&AG found.

The break-even plan was completely ineffective. By October the HSE control group found that the savings weren't materializing fast enough and took out a bigger, sharper axe. These cuts were vicious. Services to older people were chopped by €74 million, disability services took a €31 million hit, and €53 million was cut from primary-care and mental-health services. Despite these desperate measures, the HSE still failed to get within an ass's roar of its actual budget.

The C&AG is not widely known for its grasp of psychology, but its report on the fiasco appeared to hit the nail on the head. It described a widely held belief – inherited from the days of the old health boards – that budgets didn't really matter because the government would always step in with funds when things got tight: 'past experience had shown that further money would become available during the year, that if budgets were exceeded the hospital would not be penalised and that by adhering to the budget the hospital would lose out to other parts of the system which ignored the rules.'

Almost always, the waste of public money by the HSE goes hand in hand with a failure to deliver services to patients. For example, the HSE has approved spending on top-of-the-range equipment but then failed to provide the staff necessary to man these new machines. This situation has been exacerbated by the economic crisis and the implosion of the public finances. But even before the financial crisis the HSE was buying equipment that it couldn't afford to operate. In 2006 the HSE was allocated a €555 million budget for capital expenditure. The policy at the time was to create a small number of centres of excellence, where top-of-the-range equipment and specialist doctors would be gathered together, rather than scattered all across the country. Despite this policy, the HSE spent money hand over fist tooling up some of the smaller provincial hospitals. Pressure for such expenditure, which often went against the grain of HSE policy, came from local politicians and from central government alike.

The affair of the scanner at Mallow General Hospital, which sat mostly unused for two years, was a shameful example of waste arising from a lack of co-ordination. The situation came about because of dismal planning and substandard resource management. In October 2004 the purchase of a €1.5 million CAT scanner was given the green light. Mallow General Hospital had seventy-six beds and catered for a catchment area populated by 90,000-odd people in north Cork. Because of the time involved in getting planning and regulatory approval, building a new facility, and installing and fine-tuning the machine, the scanner wasn't ready to roll until the summer of 2007. Even at that point – nearly three years after the project had received the go-ahead – the HSE and the hospital were still in discussions over

staffing for the new facility, and nothing had been approved. The
PAC examined this shambles in mid 2008. It was told by the HSE
that because Mallow had 'sufficient staffing complement to manage a
CAT scanner', it had decided not to rubber-stamp the appointment
of two new radiographers. The committee found that 'a scanner to
the value of €1.5 million was purchased and a competition was held
to appoint radiographers, and it appears that these two decisions were
taken in a vacuum, when issues relating to staffing levels should have
been sorted out before this expenditure was sanctioned.'

It wasn't until September 2008 that the HSE cleared the creation
of a new radiologist position, with the selection of candidates taking
place the following month. The successful radiologist was set to start
tweaking knobs from July 2009. But then the doctor to whom the
job had been offered decided to turn it down in May 2009; the second-
choice candidate did the same. In August 2009 a part-time locum was
brought in to operate the machine, ending a two-year period during
which it was largely unused and almost 200 scans were done in a private hospital in Cork instead – at a cost of €151,000 and of untold
discomfort and inconvenience to patients in the Mallow catchment
area, who had to travel to Cork. After the locum was in place in Mallow, the scans were sent the thirty miles to Cork by taxi or ambulance
for examination by consultants in the private hospital.

Despite the outrage over the Mallow scanner debacle, lessons were
not learned. In late 2008 Cork University Hospital took delivery of
its very own €3.8 million PET scanner. A new facility was constructed and the machine installed in mid 2009. It has yet to be used.
A consultant radiologist cannot be recruited because of the hiring
freeze instituted by the Department of Finance before the scanner
was even turned on. So the machine remains idle and patients in the
south of the country have to be referred up to Dublin for PET scans.
The cost of this is enormous. Latest figures show that 108 sick HSE
South patients were sent up to Dublin for PET scans in 2008 – before
the scanner was operational – at their own expense. Cork University
Hospital paid the Dublin hospitals €251,000 for the scans in 2008.
The figures for 2009 are believed to be broadly similar. With the HSE
not expecting to fill the radiology post in 2010, if the figures remain

flat it will have spent €500,000 on sending patients the 300-mile round trip to Dublin for scans, with its very own €3.8 million scanner lying unused.

There were other cases of brand-new facilities and equipment being mothballed because of the embargo on hiring staff. A new CAT scanner sat in a cardboard box for months in the laundry room of Louth General Hospital; the opening of the new €80 million Tullamore Hospital was delayed because of staffing shortages; a €5 million accident-and-emergency unit at Cork's Mercy Hospital gathered dust while a search was made for doctors, nurses and orderlies.

The HSE's failure to think in a joined-up way when splashing out big money was disastrous for patients; and so was its failure to formulate a cohesive programme of investment. In June 2010 the newspapers were full of the shocking scandal at Our Lady of Lourdes Hospital in Drogheda, where it emerged that staff operating dilapidated foetal-scanning machines had wrongly told expectant mothers that their babies were dead. Apart from the emotional turmoil visited on these poor women, it was a catastrophic blow to the HSE's reputation.

The Drogheda scanner debacle of June 2010 came weeks after the HSE refused to provide an Oireachtas committee with details of the number of children who had died in its care; it reversed its position only under enormous pressure. Minister for Health Mary Harney gave an extraordinary interview to the *Irish Examiner* in which she admitted that if the HSE were a private company, its executives would be sacked over the serial bungling. 'It's an issue across the public service and it's one that hugely antagonises and annoys the public, and if it was a private sector organisation when serious errors happen, yes people would lose their job, but that's not exclusive to the HSE and it is a matter for the board of the HSE ultimately or the CEO of the HSE to decide,' she said.

One of the biggest reasons for waste and mismanagement at the HSE is the lack of effective accounting and spending controls. Some €377,038 was spent on 34,800 standard crutches in 2008, the HSE told Fine Gael TD Charles Flanagan in a response to a Dáil question in June 2009; but more striking than the figures was the HSE's own acknowledgment, in its letter to Flanagan, of just how badly it is run.

'In the absence of a single finance and procurement system for capturing this information HSE does not currently have data collated in respect of years 2005 to 2007,' the letter states. So the HSE has absolutely no idea what it has spent on crutches because it doesn't have a tracking system.

Crutches, according to the HSE, are 'single use' items. It doesn't expect to get them back when they are issued to patients, and it has no records to show what proportion of them it does get back. But crutches make up only a small part of the temporary equipment that the HSE buys, gives away and forgets about. In 2009 it emerged that HSE West had spent €16.24 million on wheelchairs, crutches and walking aids. While the HSE noted that some of these would be disinfected if returned, health-and-safety regulations meant that crutches and zimmer frames cannot be reused. In a response to a Dáil question posed by Labour TD Jan O'Sullivan in April 2009, the HSE indicated that crutches could not be reused, as 'the manufacturers will not guarantee them if recycled.' 'When the HSE is facing cuts of over €1 billion affecting frontline services, surely the executive can see sense and stop this crazy policy of using crutches only once. We cannot afford such waste now or in the future,' said Green Party councillor Brian Meaney, a member of the HSE West forum, a regional advisory group made up of local politicians.

Despite having Eugene McCague, a partner (and former managing partner) of the giant law firm Arthur Cox, on its board, the HSE has proved unbelievably wasteful when it comes to legal bills. It is the biggest spender on lawyers in the state, with an annual cost of €20 million. For its first four years in existence, the HSE paid its lawyers – engaged at regional level – an hourly rate. In November 2009 the HSE announced that it would modernize its legal-procurement practices by tendering for legal advice. Under the new centralized system, legal services will be charged at an annual fixed rate. The HSE estimates that this new approach will save it €5 million per year. It's almost five years too late.

If the HSE's management of staff, equipment and services has been dire, its handling of bricks and mortar has been even worse. The HSE owns properties across the country valued at €10 billion – or at least they were valued at €10 billion before the market collapsed. It is a vast portfolio, and one that the HSE struggles to keep tabs on. The estates division is headed up by former ESB and Diageo executive Brian Gilroy, who joined the HSE from the private sector in 2005. In mid 2008 an HSE audit of its properties revealed that it owned 2,632 buildings and offices around the country. Some of these were unused and lay empty. At the same time the HSE was paying €15 million per year in rent. Early in 2010 it emerged that the HSE had forty-three empty properties around the country; half of these had been vacant for more than nine months.

Some of these vacancies can be attributed to the HSE's cack-handed approach to property purchases while the market was booming. In 2005 it shelled out €1.7 million to buy Carriage House in Lusk. Although earmarked to become a residential centre for people with learning disabilities, it soon emerged that the building would need expensive refurbishment to make it fit for residential patients. These plans for refurbishment, however, were zapped after a sixty-bed bungalow development for patients in St Ita's in nearby Portrane was approved by the HSE as an alternative measure. The state-of-the-art residential unit was completed in December 2008 at a cost of just over €16.5 million; but the staff embargo meant that the forty additional staff nurses needed to run the new complex could not be recruited, and the sixty patients due to be housed in this new accommodation were forced to remain in dilapidated conditions at St Ita's. In May 2010 John Moloney, the Minister of State with responsibility for Equality, Disability and Mental Health, announced that the facility would open on a phased basis 'in coming months'. Carriage House was boarded up as the HSE searched in vain for a buyer in a bombed-out market. The site is now overgrown with weeds.

The Dáil's PAC has slated the HSE for its persistent failure to keep track of its property assets. In one particularly wasteful case, the PAC investigated the lack of planning associated with the purchase of houses in County Westmeath. In 2001 the local health board (which was subsumed into the HSE) completed the purchase of three properties at St Peter's Hospital in Castlepollard for around €640,000. Another €510,000 was spent on these houses to make them suitable for up to seventeen psychiatric patients moving from hospitals into community-based care. The properties lay empty for seven years, mothballed due to budgetary wrangles. Labour TD Róisín Shortall described the situation as a 'disgraceful waste of taxpayers' money'. In mid 2008 the PAC probed this deal, which had first been raised by the C&AG's annual report back in 2006. 'When the Committee investigated this issue, it found that the Midland Health Board entered into an arrangement to purchase the houses without a plan for moving the residents from St Peter's and without a budget to do so,' the report found. The HSE estimated that it would need €1.5 million to get the homes up and running. 'The Committee noted that, while the taxpayer ended up paying for something that was not used for seven years, the real losers in this case were the residents of St Peter's, whose quality of life would have been greatly improved over the past seven years had they been moved to community houses where they would have enjoyed a more independent lifestyle.' Following the PAC hearings in 2008, the HSE said that it was looking at opening the homes on a 'phased basis'. However, the embargo on hiring new staff means that the centre cannot operate at full capacity.

Even when it comes to disposals, the HSE moves like treacle. Our Lady's Hospital in Cork was a sprawling psychiatric hospital on the banks of the Lee. The complex, which opened in 1852, comprised Victorian hospital buildings, churches and various factory premises for the patients. From the early eighties onward, when there were 1,000 inmates in Our Lady's, the health authorities gradually began to scale down operations at the hospital, moving patients to newer facilities around the country. The last patients left in 1988, and apart from a few offices the hospital was closed down. The 140-acre site was valued at around €100 million during the boom. Between 2002 and 2007, while it was deciding what to do with the complex, the HSE spent almost €1.6 million on security to guard the site. Cork TD Bernard Allen, describing the affair as a case of 'neglect' and 'mismanagement', pointed out that some of the top administrators in the HSE were getting performance-related bonuses.

The issue of bonuses is not one the HSE is comfortable with. This is understandable. In September 2009 it emerged that Brendan

Drumm was to receive a €70,000 bonus, related to his performance in 2007. That's right, 2007: the year that the HSE completely cocked up its budgets and spent far too much at the beginning of the year before being forced to make sudden, damaging cuts to services towards the end of the year. The bonus for a year in which his organization had failed so spectacularly would have sent Drumm's overall pay in 2009 past the €500,000 mark – more than Taoiseach Brian Cowen is paid, or the cost of nearly a hundred potentially life-saving CAT scans. The bonus was approved by the HSE board and paid after Drumm made a submission to the board outlining various 'service targets' that had been achieved. The precise details of Drumm's targets and bonus structure are confidential. But the targets can't have had much to do with keeping the organization within budget.

There was political uproar at the idea that Drumm should be paid a bonus even as health budgets were being carved up and cuts of €1 billion in services proposed. (It is a curious side note that Drumm attended Summerhill College in Sligo – where the curriculum evidently included a course in how to secure a bonus despite poor performance. Around the same time Drumm was under fire for his bonus, it emerged that Summerhill old boy Dermot Mannion – who was utterly unable to make progress in rationalizing Aer Lingus during his time as chief executive of the airline – had negotiated a €2.8 million payment that would kick in if the airline was taken over. Or perhaps credit for this should go not to Summerhill College but to something in the County Sligo water supply: former Irish Nationwide Building Society boss Michael Fingleton, a native of Tubbercurry, also got in trouble in 2009 over his €1 million bonus, which he refused to pay back even as his bank was being rescued by the taxpayer.)

Health minister Mary Harney ducked the issue of Drumm's bonus, claiming she did not have the power to force the HSE to withdraw the award. 'A €70,000 bonus, twice the average industrial wage, on top of a €320,000 salary for the head of our broken health service is outrageous at a time when 300 patients were lying on trolleys around the country yesterday, 9,000 operations were cancelled in the first half of the year and there has been a 70 per cent increase in delayed discharges,' roared Fine Gael's James Reilly in the Dáil – but it made no difference.

Drumm himself remained quiet on the matter for nearly a month as public anger grew. He would later appear on *The Marian Finucane Show* on RTÉ Radio 1, telling the broadcaster that, in fact, he had given away the €80,000 bonus he had received for 2006 and that he was planning to do the same with the one for 2007.

While Drumm was giving away at least €150,000 of the €180,000 in bonuses he had received from the HSE, his top managers were also benefiting from the HSE's generosity. Close to €1.4 million in bonuses was paid out to them in 2008, based on Drumm's recommendations. His board did not react well, expressing concern over the level of payments. It suggested that in future bonuses should be lower. But the worsening economic conditions meant that all extra payments would be chopped and bonuses phased out in line with government policy.

At the time of writing, the country is shattered, with a budget deficit that would do Robert Mugabe proud. Savings will have to be made as we readjust to a world without frills and pointless spending. This begs a €500 million question: if the HSE is in charge of the hospitals, doctors, nurses, drug programmes, crutches and light bulbs, what exactly does the Department of Health and Children do? According to the blurb on its website, the department's role 'is to support the Minister in the formulation and evaluation of policies for the health services'. The supremo at Hawkins House is secretary general Michael Scanlan, a career civil servant who earns about €220,000 per year and was one of the key architects in the creation of the HSE. He presides over a staggeringly expensive operation.

The taxpayer handed over €498 million for the department to spend in 2009. Much of this was doled out to various agencies and quangos, with €138 million allocated to compensation schemes for victims of state cock-ups. That left €45 million for the 475 staff working in the department.

Much of the department's time is spent providing support to health minister Mary Harney and the three junior Fianna Fáil ministers,

Chris Andrews (children), John Moloney (equality, disability and mental health) and Aine Brady (older people and health promotion). It also liaises with the entire slew of health-related quangos, such as the Health Information and Quality Authority, the VHI, the Irish Medicines Board, the Irish Blood Transfusion Service, the Food Safety Authority, the Health Research Board, the National Treatment Purchase Fund and the various professional regulatory bodies.

In his opening statement to the PAC in 2009, Scanlan tried to explain the differences between the department and the HSE. 'Understandably, there remains some confusion about the respective roles of the Department and the HSE. Our ultimate customers are the same – the people who need and use the Irish health-care system – and we work together on a daily basis to try to ensure that the best possible services are provided to the people of Ireland. This does not mean that the work of the HSE is being duplicated in the Department or vice versa. We each have our own roles and responsibilities. The Department's primary role is to help the Minister for Health & Children fulfil her political accountability for the overall performance of the health system through our parliamentary work.'

We're still not quite clear what it actually does, but it looks and smells like a really big PR, research and lobbying group with a bit of policy thrown in. It's not a lot for €45 million – you'd get 180 hospital consultants for that kind of dough. In February 2010 a leaked Organizational Review Programme report on the department found that some staff had little or nothing to do, while others were swamped with work. The report found that morale was low and that senior management were out of step with the rest of staff. The report, compiled for the Taoiseach's department as part of a public-service modernization initiative, found that, while the organization was supposed to focus on policy-making, it actually spent most of its time handling crises and media issues.

But it's not all grim in 'Angola', as former health minister Brian Cowen once dubbed the department. There's plenty of money for a bit of an old party in Hawkins House. The Department of Health had a forecast €100,000 'entertainment' bill in 2009. Remarkably, this was the fourth biggest tab in the state, after €691,000 for Foreign Affairs,

€452,000 for the Gardaí and €110,000 for the Department of An Taoiseach. Amazingly, the government budget estimates for 2010 forecast
that the Department of Health bill would actually double, to €200,000.
We questioned the Department of Finance about this allocation: what
was the civil service doing with a big fat entertainment budget bang in
the middle of the worst recession ever to hit Ireland? And why was it
being doubled? 'An allocation is usually made under that heading for
most departments to cover incidental expenses, usually visits of foreign dignitaries,' the department told us, unhelpfully.

In May 2010 it was announced that former Eircom executive Cathal
Magee would take over from Drumm when the latter's five-year term
expired on 1 September 2010. Magee would earn €322,000 per annum
under his five-year deal – €100,000 more than originally forecast.
Like Drumm five years earlier, Magee was not the HSE's first choice.
The organization had wooed cancer expert Professor Tom Keane for
a number of months, but he pulled out of the race in March 2010
amid suggestions that he failed to receive assurances from the HSE
board on budget guarantees and the recruitment moratorium.

Magee worked at Eircom for fifteen years, serving as its head of
retail. He was briefly the company's interim chief executive but failed
to land the job on a permanent basis. The Cavan man also played a
role in the country's banking crisis, having sat on the board of the
EBS from 2002, all the way through the lending and property booms.
A disastrous move into lending to property developers saw the EBS
implode because of its bad debts, leading the government to bail it
out with €875 million of taxpayers' money. In 2005 Magee was
appointed to the board of the VHI.

At the moment of Magee's appointment, the HSE was facing a
€100 million deficit for 2010, which meant that patients would have
to put up with further cutbacks and reductions in services. An internal
financial report – leaked to the media after being presented to the
board – revealed that many of the local hospitals, especially in the
west of Ireland, were spending vastly over budget. It also emerged
that the Department of Health had cocked up its potential savings from staff cuts. It had been thought that €650 million of the

€1.2 billion reduction in the HSE's 2010 budget could be brought about through payroll savings. Forecasts for services, new equipment and other spending were based on these estimates. But they were wrong: predictions of the number of early retirements and people leaving the service were far too optimistic, leaving a major dent in the coffers. Other savings forecast by the HSE for 2010 did not materialize. The organization estimated that its drugs bill could be reduced by €140 million in 2010, but midway through the year the figure was revised down to just €96 million.

As ever, the HSE's financial projections were almost comically out of whack with reality. As a new chief executive prepared to take over, nothing of consequence seemed to have changed at Ireland's biggest and, arguably, most dysfunctional state agency.

5. The Minister for Limousines (and Other Tales of Parliamentary Waste)

Australian pop princess Kylie Minogue shares a birthday with former Minister for Arts, Sport and Tourism John O'Donoghue. Her 1988 number-one single 'I Should Be So Lucky' could have been penned for the Kerryman, who spent the best part of six years travelling the world, staying in some of the finest five-star hotels, eating in top restaurants and having the best seats at some of the most sought-after sporting and cultural events, all at our expense.

It began much more humbly. O'Donoghue was born into a well-known Fianna Fáil family in Cahirciveen, County Kerry, in 1956. His father – a county councillor – died when he was young, and his mother, also a councillor, reared the family while also running a pub and an auctioneering business. O'Donoghue was educated by the local Christian Brothers and at University College Cork, where he trained to become a solicitor. He married Kate Ann Murphy, whose father Michael Pat was a Labour TD for Cork South West for thirty years.

Following the family tradition, O'Donoghue became involved in local politics. He stood for Fianna Fáil in the 1981 general election, aged twenty-five, and polled well but not nearly well enough. He ran in both elections in 1982, again failing to win a seat. Faced with this reverse, O'Donoghue went into the trenches of local politics to build up his profile and was subsequently elected to Kerry County Council in 1985, becoming chairman of the council five years later. He was eventually elected to the Dáil on his fourth attempt, in February 1987, just a few months shy of his thirty-first birthday. O'Donoghue kept his nose clean on the back benches and crucially showed his loyalty to the then party leader Charles Haughey during Albert Reynolds's failed leadership bid in 1991. It was the first of many gambles in his career and initially it seemed to pay off. Haughey promoted him to Minister of State at the Department of Finance, with responsibility for the Office of Public Works. But Haughey's days were numbered. Within a few months he had stepped down as leader of Fianna Fáil, to be replaced by Reynolds. The Longford man booted O'Donoghue out as he installed his own people in key positions.

When the Reynolds government fell in late 1994, Bertie Ahern took control of Fianna Fáil. O'Donoghue was promoted to the justice brief and performed with gusto. He became the hard man of south Kerry, nicknamed 'The Bull' after a character played by Richard Harris in the film version of John B. Keane's play *The Field*. O'Donoghue harried Fine Gael's justice minister, Nora Owen, at every turn. Zero tolerance became his buzzword as he pushed for harsher sentencing of criminals. It was a popular stance.

When Ahern formed a coalition government with the PDs in 1997, O'Donoghue became minister of the enlarged and increasingly clunky Department of Justice, Equality and Law Reform. He was a key player on the negotiating team in the run-up to the historic Good Friday Agreement. And then, quite suddenly, O'Donoghue's star stopped rising. By 2000 the Bull was widely touted in newspapers as a prime candidate for relegation in an upcoming cabinet reshuffle. He fought his corner well and kept the brief, but his lack of dynamism had seen him surpassed by other Fianna Fáil young Turks. After the 2002 general election he was demoted to Minister for Arts, Sport and Tourism. O'Donoghue didn't tear up trees in the department, and was again widely tipped for demotion in the 2004 reshuffle, but he held on to his job. And, though it did not carry the power or profile of the justice brief, it was a pretty nice job: no other cabinet ministry comes with such excellent perks. O'Donoghue hoovered them up: his five-year tenure in Arts, Sport and Tourism was an orgy of over-spending and self-gratification. During a 42-month period between 2002 and 2005, O'Donoghue travelled abroad forty-eight times, with his wife Kate Ann accompanying him on at least twenty-seven of those occasions. This spending needs to be put in perspective. In October 2009 it emerged that the principal of St John's Girls National School in Carrigaline, County Cork, had written to parents asking them to help the school save money by giving their children loo paper to bring in to school. At the time of writing, a sixteen-pack of Kittensoft jacks roll costs €9.49, or about 59 cent per roll. There are around 3,300 primary schools in Ireland. O'Donoghue's travel and expenses bill would have provided each one of these schools with 280 rolls of decent loo paper.

In his five-year stint as minister, O'Donoghue attended some of the most prestigious events in the world sporting calendar. These weren't just events in which Ireland or Irish teams were prominent; he also turned up at events in which there was no Irish involvement, travelling the world at taxpayers' expense – often with his wife at his side. He attended the FIFA World Cup in South Korea in 2002 and in Germany in 2006; the UEFA European Championship in Portugal in 2004; a Champions League final; Rugby World Cups in Australia and France; a Heineken Cup final; golf's Ryder Cup; compromise-rules matches in Australia; race meetings at Cheltenham, Aintree, Royal Ascot, Melbourne; and the Breeder's Cup in Texas. Any sports fan would almost have joined Fianna Fáil for a shot at the job.

In his first year O'Donoghue ventured abroad five times. Warming to his brief, he upped the ante in 2003, making more than one overseas trip per month; his wife travelled eight times courtesy of the taxpayer that year. O'Donoghue's trip to see Willie Mullins's horse Holy Orders trail in down the field in the Melbourne Cup in Australia cost over €22,000 and included an extraordinary €4,545 for a five-night stay in a suite at the Park Hyatt Hotel in Melbourne. The taxpayer was also hit with a €136 bill for the rental of a tuxedo.

O'Donoghue had a cracking year in 2004, with the Olympic Games in Athens and the UEFA European Championship in Portugal. Ireland hadn't qualified for the football tournament, but O'Donoghue evidently took the view that it was worth spending €5,500 of taxpayers' money so that he could see what we all missed. He also went to the Ryder Cup in Detroit as well as visiting Brussels, Cheltenham, Hungary, Denmark and New York, where we paid €221 for tickets to Broadway shows for him and the wife. The most expensive jolly that year was a €22,000 visit to China.

The following year the Kerryman travelled abroad eleven times, with the taxpayer coughing up for Mrs O'Donoghue to represent us on seven occasions. After a US junket he claimed €10,800 for a car-hire bill, and he spent a staggering €9,164 on limos during the three-day

Cheltenham Festival. O'Donoghue also flew to Australia to see the Melbourne Cup again, with the whole shebang costing more than €30,000. (Dermot Weld's horse Vinnie Roe finished eighth that year.) The trip also featured spending of €207 on room service and dry cleaning as well as €210 for the use of a VIP suite at Sydney Airport.

The Cannes Film Festival was a big deal for O'Donoghue. The taxpayer spent about €35,000 to send him there in 2005, with the government jet sucking up a lot of the cost; and the following year the festival featured in some of his most outrageous abuses of his position and our money. In one six-day period in 2006 the minister – and the wife – used the government jet to fly back to Kerry from Cannes, where he'd gone to see the première of *The Wind That Shakes the Barley*, Ken Loach's movie about the Irish War of Independence. He then jetted from Kerry to Cardiff for the Heineken Cup final, where he saw Munster finally win the northern hemisphere's top club-rugby trophy by beating Biarritz 23–19 courtesy of a cheeky Peter Stringer try. O'Donoghue and his retinue returned to Cannes after the final to see *The Wind That Shakes the Barley* pick up the Palme d'Or for best film at the festival that year. He then jetted off to a Ryder Cup event in London and back to Dublin. The cost of using the government Learjet for this six-day whirlwind was €32,450, based on eleven hours of flying at the Department of Defence estimate of €2,950 per hour. The hotel bill for the trip to Cannes was a further €4,980, and limo hire cost us another €9,616.

O'Donoghue's decision to use the government jet to fly back to Kerry from Cannes for a constituency event – the cutting of a ribbon to open a new Fexco money-transfer office in Killorglin – was almost unbelievable in its arrogance. It was the sign of a man who had lost the run of himself. It was estimated that the cost of using the jet to fly home and back was around €11,300. But O'Donoghue didn't top the poll in Kerry South without being cute at local politics. Finance minister Brian Cowen was coming down to the constituency to cut some ribbons and make a speech. It's Local Politics 101: get in the photo beside the main man. Top government ministers didn't come to south Kerry every day and O'Donoghue needed to show his electorate that he was in the tent.

But the extraordinary use of the government jet for personal gain backfired when details of his travel expenses emerged in August 2009. His handlers tried to dampen down the ire. 'The use of the government jet in this case was in accordance with standard government guidelines for ministerial usage,' waffled a department spokesman. 'The department's understanding is that there was no commercial flight option available which could facilitate the minister executing his responsibilities as Minister for Arts, Sport and Tourism at a series of official engagements during the specified timeframe.'

Other highlights of 2006 included a trip to Royal Ascot, where he was entertained in the royal box; the limo bill for that trip was €3,500. O'Donoghue's free ways with taxpayers' money extended to his staff: his private secretary, Therese O'Connor, billed the state for the rental of not one but three pieces of headgear for the race meeting. She hired a white straw hat, an orange hairpiece and a buttermilk-coloured hat from Hattitudes in Lucan, for a cost of €120. We paid the bill.

In 2007 O'Donoghue's feet barely touched the ground between the luxury hotels, limos, expensive jets, VIP lounges and Michelin-starred restaurants. But his time was running out. An election was called in April of that year. The country was showing the first signs of financial meltdown. The Irish stock market had already begun to fall sharply and questions were being asked about the state of the banks and the property market. But O'Donoghue still made it to Venice for the art Biennale in early June 2007. The four-night jolly saw O'Donoghue, the missus and Therese O'Connor rack up major hotel bills at the Albergo San Marco as well as another €1,130 in food bills at the splendid Hotel Cipriani and the five-star San Clemente Palace, a seventeenth-century monastery that sits on its own island. The Albergo San Marco got a mention in O'Donoghue's resignation speech. It cost €312.50 per night, not €900, he said. Be that as it may, credit-card receipts for the department, released under the Freedom of Information Act, clearly show that €4,561 was paid to the Albergo San Marco in June 2007. O'Donoghue also clocked up a €250 bill for two water-taxis during his visit to La Serenissima. One of the water-taxis was to the airport, a journey that would have cost the entire party less than €45 if they'd taken a public vaporetto.

O'Donoghue's wife did well out of her husband's ministerial gig. Not only did she get to travel the world, with her hotels, flights and limos covered by the taxpayer, but, as we can reveal here, she also claimed miscellaneous expenses from the state. Buried in the 700-odd pages of John O'Donoghue's expenses and claims – released under the Freedom of Information Act in July and August 2009 – is an expense claim for €302.16, submitted in January 2006 by Kate Ann O'Donoghue 'for accompanying the minister in India'. It's stamped 'paid' on Valentine's Day of that year. (This was the trip that saw the minister spend €472.21 on limousines to take him from Terminal 3 in Heathrow Airport to Terminal 1 – a journey that would have taken less than 200 seconds on the airport's free shuttle service.) Another Kate Ann claim is for €105.86 for accompanying the minister to Birmingham and London in March 2007. Another one, for €105.05, covers trips to the World Cup final in Berlin, to Paris and to see Ireland lose 1–0 to Germany in a European qualifier in Stuttgart. Kate Ann O'Donoghue also claimed €16.21 for the trip to Royal Ascot and €212.91 for the trip to Venice. She put in a claim for €116.09 for a November 2006 junket to New York, where the taxpayer also stumped up for four nights in the Waldorf Astoria plus tickets to see *Spamalot* and two other shows. And there was a €70.94 claim for a trip to Turin for the opening of the Winter Olympics.

The fact that ministerial spouses can claim expenses for luxurious travel and entertainment in far-off countries is not something that the government is keen to publicize. Rules permitting ministers to claim expenses on behalf of their spouses are detailed in a 1959 circular that we obtained from the Department of Finance. A minister's husband or wife may travel on a jolly only if there has been a specific invitation from the host country to the spouse, or if the minister believes that it is in 'the public interest' – which evidently amounts to a rather vague way of saying that a spouse can travel if the minister needs a cuddle before going to sleep. Any travel by husbands and wives must be cleared by the Taoiseach's private office; once this approval is granted (and this appears to be a rubber-stamping exercise), the taxpayer will then cover all travel and accommodation costs. A ministerial spouse may receive half the subsistence rate that a minister can claim when travelling abroad. If hotels and flights are

paid for, then a minister is entitled to claim the 'conference rate' subsistence payment, plus up to an extra 50 per cent if travelling in the
US or Canada. A minister travelling to Florida with all flights, transport and accommodation paid by the state could claim about €105 per
night in subsistence payments based on the new rates introduced by
the Department of Finance in January 2010. The minister's wife or
husband could claim almost €53 per night in Florida. (In New Zealand, by contrast, ministers wishing to travel abroad with their spouse
or partner must get full cabinet approval. In June 2009 the deteriorat-
ing economic situation there saw Prime Minister John Key issue a
directive telling his ministers to leave their partners at home or else
pay for their travel themselves.)

Following the 2007 general election, O'Donoghue took a bullet for
his mediocre performance in cabinet and lost his ministerial brief. It
must have been disappointing to be dropped – but to be replaced by
Martin Cullen must have really stung.

   The Bull swung the post of Ceann Comhairle as compensation –
a largely ceremonial role that pays the same as a cabinet post. The
Ceann Comhairle sits in a comfy seat – something the well-padded
O'Donoghue rear was well used to – and directs traffic in the Dáil. It
is seen by some as a reward for has-beens and duffers.

   During his two years as Ceann Comhairle, O'Donoghue cost the
taxpayer nearly a quarter of a million euro on junkets, perks and self-
promotion expenses. Despite the largely ceremonial role of his new
office, O'Donoghue ramped up the staffing levels. His predecessor as
Ceann Comhairle, Rory O'Hanlon – father of comedian and *Father
Ted* star Ardal – had just three staff: a private secretary, a secretarial
assistant and a clerical officer. Their combined salaries cost less than
€142,000 per year. Under the reign of the Bull, staff bills rose to
€470,000. O'Donoghue personally appointed Dan Collins, formerly
his ministerial press officer, as his personal political adviser, at a cost
of €90,000 per year. None of O'Donoghue's predecessors in the post
had had his own press and policy adviser. O'Donoghue also had four
secretarial staff and a personal assistant, all working on constituency
queries. Ordinary TDs have one secretary and a personal assistant.

O'Donoghue's political career may have veered down a cul de sac, but he wasn't about to let his constituents forget about him. He famously described his office as being 'above politics', and the Ceann Comhairle is automatically re-elected to the Dáil, yet he still spent €11,900 advertising political clinics in his constituency. An Post also got over €2,500 for a direct-mail campaign aimed at constituents on behalf of O'Donoghue.

His travel bills – which added up to €90,000 over two years – were even less justifiable, given that the remit of the Ceann Comhairle does not extend beyond Leinster House. While in the post O'Donoghue – often with his loyal wife at his side – jetted to the four corners of the globe, visiting Cape Town, South Carolina, Hong Kong, Australia, Amsterdam, Paris, Edinburgh, Berlin, Prague, Houston, New Orleans and Lisbon. The eight-day jolly to Cape Town in April 2008, for the 118th assembly of the Inter-Parliamentary Union, worked out at: €10,511 for flights; €3,092.03 for hotels; €1,598.84 for other transport; and €575.37 for 'official entertainment'. On his St Patrick's Day junket in 2008 – away from Cheltenham for a change – O'Donoghue blew into Houston, Washington and New Orleans, with his limo bill alone coming to €4,956. Flights for Mr and Mrs Bull cost €12,404, with the politician leaving a $565 tip – at our expense – for his driver in New Orleans.

It seemed that O'Donoghue still thought that he was minister for sport. In June 2008 the O'Donoghues travelled to Paris and Toulouse. According to the Bull's subsistence claims, he attended a conference on 1–2 June at Chantilly. The Prix de Jockey Club (a.k.a. 'French Derby') just happened to be taking place at Chantilly at the same time. The Irish had no luck, with Dermot Weld's Famous Name beaten by a head into second place by French-trained Vision d'État. The other Irish horse, Aidan O'Brien's Achill Island, finished second last.

On a three-day jolly to Paris in October 2008 to address parliamentarians, the O'Donoghues attended the race meeting at Longchamp on two of the three days of their visit. The world-famous Prix de l'Arc de Triomphe was on at the time, and Aidan O'Brien's Duke of Marmalade was hotly tipped, but finished down the field. In the Prix de l'Opéra, Jim Bolger's Lush Lashes got turned over by an outsider. While O'Donoghue watched the racing, a chauffeur-driven limo remained on stand-by outside at a cost of more than €800. In December 2008 O'Donoghue and his wife flew to London for the state opening of parliament; the visit coincided with the Winter Festival at Sandown, which the pair attended.

Although it sometimes seems that south Kerry is another world, Cahirciveen is just five hours from Dublin by car. The Office of Ceann Comhairle comes not only with the padded seat in the Dáil chamber, but also a Garda driver and a ministerial Mercedes. Despite the full-time driver, O'Donoghue took 186 internal flights while in the role. His wife joined him on forty-four of them.

There was little in the way of controls to stop O'Donoghue burning through taxpayers' money on his little perks and junkets. In fact, O'Donoghue himself had a key role in deciding Oireachtas members' travel arrangements. Oireachtas jollies and work-related overseas trips by TDs and senators are vetted by a committee chaired by the Clerk of the Dáil, but it emerged that O'Donoghue himself chaired meetings of an Inter-Parliamentary Association – made up of members of both the Dáil and Seanad – where the details of some of these trips were planned. In effect, O'Donoghue was playing a role in regulating Oireachtas members' travelling while he himself was gallivanting around the world at the taxpayer's expense. The Bull was also the chairman of the Oireachtas Committee on Procedure and Privileges, which among other things deals with issues regarding TDs' and senators' expenses. There was no system in place to audit the value of overseas travelling, nothing to gauge whether there was any benefit to Ireland whatsoever.

O'Donoghue's fall, when it came, was car-crash viewing. From the end of June 2009 newspapers – the *Sunday Tribune* and Ken Foxe in particular – had been nipping at his heels, with one excruciating over-spending revelation after another appearing each weekend. Initially the stories related to his time as Minister for Arts, Sport and Tourism, and it could be argued that O'Donoghue was acting broadly within his brief when he incurred the enormous expenses. But once it emerged he was milking the system and junketeering as Ceann Comhairle, smoke started to appear from the toaster. He began to look extremely vulnerable.

For such a shrewd parish-pump politician, O'Donoghue didn't seem to grasp the seriousness of the issue. He threatened legal action against the *Sunday Tribune*. He told reporters that it was a matter for his former department. He refused to comment on his spending, claiming that he had to stay out of political debate because of the nature of his office.

On Tuesday, 15 September 2009, RTÉ's southern correspondent, Paschal Sheehy, doorstepped him as he was making a bet at the Listowel races and pressed him over the spending revelations. 'I regret this, but I've also explained that these were costs paid to service providers on my behalf,' said the ruddy Kerryman. Then O'Donoghue was asked whether he should make an apology. 'In so far as one regrets something, I think that is an apology,' he said. John O'Donoghue's head appeared to have inserted itself up his posterior.

Belatedly realizing that his career was imploding, O'Donoghue wrote to every member of the Oireachtas and later released a statement to the media. 'I was not aware of the cost of these arrangements. When I read the detail in the past weeks, I was embarrassed that such costs were associated with some of the arrangements made on my behalf,' he said. 'I sincerely regret that, although on official duty, such considerable costs were incurred. I apologize for this.

'I can fully understand how many people were shocked to read some of the detail. I apologize to these people, in particular, for the disquiet this controversy has caused.'

It didn't stop the relentless flow of damaging information on his spending as Ceann Comhairle. In a final gamble, O'Donoghue decided to come clean with every last detail of his spending. But he couldn't resist trying to pull a stroke in the process. At 3.15 p.m., on the Friday of the Lisbon Treaty vote, he lodged details of his expenses claims in the Dáil Library.

Any hopes that the referendum would overshadow his revelations were misplaced. The weekend newspapers gutted him. He was finished. There was discussion as to the procedural niceties of removing a Ceann Comhairle. The following Tuesday in the Dáil, Labour leader Eamon Gilmore dramatically told him that his position was untenable: he would have to resign or be sacked. At 10.30 that night, just as the new Maeve Higgins comedy cookery series *Fancy Vittles* opened on RTÉ 2, O'Donoghue released a statement announcing that he would resign the following week after making a statement to the Oireachtas. On 13 October 2009 O'Donoghue stood up and delivered a pompous 35-minute speech. 'I am not guilty of any corruption,' he waffled irrelevantly. Nobody had ever suggested he was corrupt – just that he was milking the system for all it was worth.

'In the fullness of time, it will become apparent that many matters have been distorted and exaggerated beyond the bounds of fairness. Simple techniques were used to create an ugly, grasping, black caricature of the man I am,' he said. And with that he returned to Kerry. He left behind an office that had been extensively refurbished, with almost €30,000 spent on new carpets and €11,380 on curtains.

The O'Donoghue 'defence', whereby a minister could claim that he or she didn't know how much flights, hotels or limos cost, will be harder to make in future, as the Department of Foreign Affairs has brought in new guidelines for Irish embassies involved in arranging ministerial travel overseas. Irish embassies must now send costings to the relevant minister's private office before any trip is made. The minister must sign off on expenditure on trips before he or she leaves the country.

While the Labour Party celebrated Eamon Gilmore's scalping of John O'Donoghue, its members seemed to have forgotten that they too were once in government with Fianna Fáil, and had got into a spot of bother over the use of the government jet. In October 1994 Joan Burton – a Minister of State in the Department of Social Welfare in the uneasy Fianna Fáil–Labour coalition headed by Albert Reynolds – was returning from a long trip to Tanzania, where she had accompanied President Mary Robinson on a state visit. The president's schedule changed at the last minute, leaving Burton, her husband, Pat, and other travellers stranded in Zurich. Although a scheduled flight was available the next morning, Burton and her entourage flew home on the government Gulfstream. There was outrage, with claims that Burton had demanded a flight home and that the whole trip had cost somewhere close to £30,000. This was emphatically denied by Burton in a letter to the *Irish Times* on 4 November 1994, in which she insisted that she hadn't 'personally initiated any request' for the jet to pick her up. 'The Government jet came to Zurich on October 13th to collect the presidential delegation. The jet was provided to facilitate the delegation, of which I was part, as well as senior civil servants,' she wrote. Burton also disputed the newspaper's estimate of the cost of the flight, calculating that the bill for the journey home was just £2,400 based on Department of Defence figures.

In the Dáil, Taoiseach Albert Reynolds was pestered about this trip by Proinsias De Rossa of Democratic Left. Reynolds outlined the circumstances in which the government jet was flown to Zurich, saying that Burton and her husband had travelled, at the request of the government, with the President and Mr Robinson on the state visit to Tanzania. It was customary for spouses to accompany ministers on state visits, he added. The scheduled return date was 13 October. But the arrangements for the president had changed at a very late date and she went to Rwanda. The rest of the party of nine returned to Europe as arranged. The Ministerial Air Transport Service (MATS) was used to bring Ms Burton and the other members of the presidential party home from Zurich on the evening of 13 October, as previously arranged.

The opposition continued to badger Reynolds, leading him to announce – in a fit of pique – that he might go off and look up how the jet had been used in the past. Reynolds warned the opposition that 'people might get red faces' if he started to open the files, adding: 'Maybe you are as well to stay a little quiet.' Reynolds described a trip by former Taoiseach Garret FitzGerald to the US, during which he had attended the Bilderberg Group conference, and met up with Massachusetts governor Michael Dukakis and Cardinal O'Connor of New York. 'If that represents a good fortnight's work on behalf of this country, I wouldn't even compare it with the sort of work that I do when I go abroad,' he commented.

Labour leader Dick Spring, Tánaiste and Minister for Foreign Affairs in the same government, got into a pickle over a trip to Corfu with his wife, Kirsti. The government jet flew to Warsaw to pick them up before flying the Springs to the Greek island for a meeting.

It then returned to Ireland to shuttle Taoiseach Albert Reynolds, Bertie Ahern and a number of officials to Corfu. Spring's wife flew back from the island on the otherwise empty jet. This caused understandable outrage. Spring threatened libel actions against newspapers that claimed he had arranged for the jet to come and pick up his wife. Those claims were false, but there was no avoiding the fact that the jet was being used incredibly wastefully.

At the time newspapers estimated the cost of the trip to be close to £30,000, which Spring described as 'untrue'. He was probably right, given that the cost of flying the jet was closer to £670 per hour back then. The entire journey, with a flight time of more than twenty hours, probably cost closer to €17,500, with the single five-hour flight taking Kirsti Spring back to Ireland from Corfu making up about €4,250 of that cost.

But, while Labour were happy enough when in government to settle into the deep seats of the Gulfstream and to avoid consorting with the plebs, Fianna Fáil and the PDs – Mary Harney in particular – have made the private jet their own over the past two decades. From September 2005 to September 2009, the use of government jets by country-hopping ministers has cost the taxpayer €10.6 million, according to figures released by the Department of Defence in October 2009. The department operates the Ministerial Air Transport Service, which runs private flights for members of the government. Dermot Ahern, then foreign minister, holds the record for running up the single biggest bill on the jet. His February 2008 trip to East Timor and Australia cost €259,000.

It was often difficult to see evidence of any return for this vast expenditure. The notorious 'mercy flight' in December 2008, when Mary Coughlan and Willie O'Dea jetted off to Texas to implore Michael Dell not to shut his factory in Limerick, was doomed to failure – and cost €189,000. The writing had been on the wall for Dell for a number of years, as the soaring cost base made Ireland ridiculously expensive to run in comparison with Dell's other manufacturing operations. It was clear that the government would have been better off trying to address the country's lack of competitiveness rather than sending the hapless Mary Coughlan to plead with Michael Dell.

On 21 September 2007 the Irish rugby team faced a crunch match with France at the Rugby World Cup in Paris. Failure to beat Les Blues would see Ireland dumped out of the competition. Tickets were like gold dust. The match also coincided with an awful lot of important Irish government business in Paris. On the day of the match the Gulfstream IV flew to Paris with Bertie Ahern and Minister for Foreign Affairs Dermot Ahern aboard. There were also ten unnamed 'officials' from the Department of Foreign Affairs and the Department of the Taoiseach on the plane. A day earlier justice minister Brian Lenihan had also flown to Paris, using the state's Learjet 45. 'I am sure they all had important business in Paris,' former minister Willie O'Dea told the Oireachtas when questioned by Labour's Brian O'Shea two weeks later. 'We do not inquire about that. Once the criteria are met we make the jet available. That is the function of the Department of Defence.' O'Dea would later have his own trip in the jet, when in November 2008 he joined Taoiseach Brian Cowen, education minister Batt O'Keeffe and Ceann Comhairle John O'Donoghue in the government Learjet on a flight down to Limerick to see Munster take on the All Blacks in a match to open the new Thomond Park stadium. The flight to see the match cost the taxpayer close to €2,000, based on Department of Defence figures.

In early 2009 the Department of the Taoiseach arranged a trip to Peru for Brian Cowen. Hotel rooms were booked for the Taoiseach and his entourage at an overall cost of €4,184 for two nights. The shocking state of the economy and conflicting schedules caused the trip to be cancelled, but state documents show that the hotel charges were non-refundable: the money went down the plughole.

Former Progressive Democrats minister Michael McDowell emerged as the top spender in cabinet for foreign travel in 2003, according to documents released to the *Sunday Business Post*. Justice minister McDowell racked up a hefty €37,015 on foreign and home travel, subsistence and official entertainment in the first six months of that year. This included a €12,060 trip to China for St Patrick's Day with an entourage worthy of a Hollywood A-lister: his wife, Niamh Brennan (now tasked with cleaning up the Dublin Docklands Development Authority), his special adviser, private secretary and press officer. The six-day jolly featured business-class flights and some pretty classy accommodation, with the party staying in the five-star Shanghai Okura Garden and Beijing Palace hotels.

Mary Harney has carefully nurtured a reputation as a ruthlessly efficient minister who understands business. But Harney is also one of the biggest junketeers and perk-merchants in the cabinet. A break-down of her expenses published in the *Sunday Tribune* in October 2009 showed that between February 2006 and September 2008 around €529,000 was spent transporting the Minister for Health on the government jet, and another €65,000 on hotels and limo hire. Speak-ing to reporters in the days after the revelations, the former Tánaiste claimed the outlay was justified, as she was on 'totally legitimate' government business. Harney added: 'I keep my foreign travel to a minimum and declined at least half the invitations I have got in recent years as Health Minister.'

The *Sunday Tribune*'s Ken Foxe uploaded some 600 pages of expenses claims and receipts relating to Harney's travels to the inter-net (they can be found at www.scribd.com). The limousines, hotels, meals and flight costs are quite obscene. But perhaps some of the smaller details are the most telling. Among all the receipts and bills for Harney-fronted junkets can be found one dated March 2008 for €115.57 for a 'guide tour of Prague'; a $50.80 bill for two Bushmills and a glass of white wine in Vienna; and one for just $7.17 dating back to October 2006 for a Snickers and a packet of Yukon Gold crisps in the Four Seasons Hotel in Chicago (where the nightly room rate was $465).

Harney spent more than €10,000 on chauffeur-driven cars in just five overseas trips in 2006: Toronto, Brussels (twice), New York and Philadelphia. Even as the economy was going down the plughole, Harney's use of limos didn't let up, as she got chauffeured around in Prague, Milan, Copenhagen, Washington, DC, Phoenix, Houston and Helsinki. Then there were the VIP lounges at airports, including €181.31 at Prague Airport in March 2008 and €727 for 'VIP service' on two journeys through Stockholm Airport in March 2007.

Harney and her husband, the former FÁS chairman Brian Geoghe-gan, spent St Patrick's Day 2006 in sunny Bahrain. In March 2007

Harney and Geoghegan and three staffers went to Stockholm for five days, bypassing the mess at Dublin Airport by using the government jet. In February 2008 Harney and her husband embarked on a bizarre €190,000 'fact-finding' trip to investigate dental and cancer policy in the US, taking the government jet; while there, she stopped by the Super Bowl in Arizona. Details of her jolly emerged only after explanations were sought as to why she had missed an important debate on the health service.

Harney and her fellow travellers were put up in the Enchantment Resort and Mii Amo Spa in Arizona – the winner of the World's Best Destination Spa in the *Travel + Leisure* awards in 2009 – for three nights, racking up a bill of $4,932.07. Overall the hotel bills from the trip hit €11,000, with another €3,380 for food and booze and just over €11,000 for minibuses to chauffeur the eleven-strong party from venue to venue, according to figures released by the Department of Health under the Freedom of Information Act. The jet snaked across the US, dropping in at Washington, DC, Houston, and Phoenix and Prescott in Arizona. But at least Harney had her luggage with her. A trip to Washington in May 2006 with a group of HSE and Department of Health officials saw Harney's entourage clock up a $9,480 bill from the Admiral Limousine Service over a three-day period. This included $192 for use of a 'luggage van' to accompany the delegation.

Responding to criticism of the trip, Harney's spokesman said the fruits of the minister's inspections of the 'ground-breaking' dental facilities in Arizona would be visible when her new dental-services strategy was published. 'It was a trip that lasted six days and it was a very busy itinerary directly related to the work of the Department of Health,' Harney said. Her spokesman described the bringing of a spouse on an official trip as 'normal'.

For such a busy man – Geoghegan was IBEC's director of economic policy and the chairman of PR and lobbying firm MRPA Kinman – he found plenty of time to follow his wife to the four corners of the globe. Geoghegan accompanied her to North America three times in 2006 alone, visiting Toronto, Washington, DC, Philadelphia and Chicago.

Harney's penchant for exotic long-haul travel predates her tenure as health minister. In 1999, as enterprise minister, she used the government Gulfstream eight times, visiting far-flung locations such as San Francisco, Bangkok and Kuala Lumpur. Harney's trade mission to Japan and Australasia in 1999 was spectacular in its length. She stopped in Novosibirsk in Siberia on the way, to meet dignitaries, drink vodka toasts, and chow through a five-course banquet of caviar, gravadlax and a selection of meats. After visiting Japan, her travels took her to the Solomon Islands and then on to Wellington in New Zealand.

The next time Harney visited New Zealand was an altogether less peaceful affair. In March 2010 Harney led a fifteen-day expedition to see the Kiwis, costing €34,318, including €19,990 in flights, €5,165 in hotels, €2,390 on taxis and limos and €665 on a dinner hosted by her for the honorary consul and an Enterprise Ireland client. The trip became highly controversial when Harney refused to cut it short after it emerged that over 57,000 X-rays taken at Tallaght Hospital between 2005 and 2009 had been left unchecked by a consultant radiologist.

Harney's excuse for her New Zealand junket was to see how the country's healthcare system worked. One highlight of the tour was the St Patrick's Day piss-up in the five-star Langham Hotel. Guests paid $180 for 'Green Tie' tickets to the beano, feasting upon oysters and fillet steak, as well as the best of New Zealand wines. Champagne, Guinness, Bushmills, Baileys and Kilkenny beer were on offer until the small hours.

Closer to home, Harney's use of the Ministerial Air Transport Service was shabby at best. In April 2005 Harney and other members of the government delegation flew back to Dublin Airport after attending the funeral of Pope John Paul II in Rome. The government Learjet took off again with Harney on board and made the short flight to Cork, where the Progressive Democrats' conference was being held that evening. Harney was able to pay her respects to the Pope *and* attend her own political party's shindig, because the taxpayer was hit with the tab.

In August 2009 Fine Gael's Michael Ring got his hands on records of domestic ministerial flights between January 2007 and June 2009.

The records, released by the Department of Defence in response to a parliamentary question, showed that government ministers using state aircraft and helicopters had cost the taxpayer over €350,000 during the two-and-a-half-year period, criss-crossing Ireland on 144 internal flights. Harney was the biggest user of Air Corps transport: she'd clocked up twenty-four internal flights, including ten on the government jet. Former enterprise minister Mary Coughlan had taken seventeen internal flights, while foreign affairs minister Micheál Martin made twelve flights during the period.

Harney and her fellow jet-setting ministers were accused of using the Air Corps as 'a glorified taxi service' by Ring. It wasn't far off the mark. 'It's not on,' Ring said. 'All the Ministers have a State car and two drivers. That's why they are there. There's no need for them to take flights inside the country. It's unacceptable and it's outrageous. You have the ludicrous situation where the State car goes down the country or comes back from a place empty because the Minister is travelling by jet or by helicopter.'

A classic instance of this was the notorious episode in 2001, when it was revealed that Harney had ordered an Air Corps plane to fly her the 130 miles from Dublin to County Leitrim so that she could open an off-licence in Manorhamilton. The offie was owned by her barrister friend Bernard O'Hagan. The ministerial Merc followed the jet from Dublin all the way up to Sligo, where it picked up Harney and her husband when they landed at Sligo Airport, ferrying them to Manorhamilton for the shindig. Afterwards, Harney and her husband met some local business people, then flew back to Dublin. Her spokesman said, 'The Minister is very scrupulous on the use of state resources and would not use this plane for personal, party or constituency business.' A month later it emerged that the Air Corps Casa plane was part-funded by the EU for fishery surveillance and shouldn't have been used to ferry around a minister at all. The EU had picked up the tab for half of the cost of the aircraft on the condition that 90 per cent of its flying time was spent on fishery protection duties. The EU ordered a probe into the matter. Harney subsequently apologized, telling RTÉ, 'At least I know the honeymoon is over. I can understand how people are annoyed. I'm sorry that this situation has arisen. But you do have to use, on a frequent basis, air transport and I hope I always use it wisely.'

The Ministerial Air Transport Service squadron operates three state planes for the use of government members and dignitaries. The service is provided by the Air Corps, with the aircraft based at Casement Aerodrome at Baldonnel.

It's like pulling teeth getting detailed information about the cost of MATS from the Department of Defence. Although there are no figures, we've been able to sift the raw data and figure it all out. Despite the economic hardship faced by almost everyone in the country, the government has been using its main jets more than ever. In 2009 the MATS flew its fancy jets on 188 missions. This is more than in 2006, 2007 and 2008.

Government-spending estimates for 2010 show that while budgets were slashed in health and education, the MATS budget has continued to rise. In 2009 the allocation for 'support services' for MATS was €666,000; this leaped to €975,000 for 2010. The Air Corps had its overall budget shaved by 6 per cent in the same period, so there's more money to ferry ministers around and less money for its other roles, including providing rescue back-up for civil defence and keeping an eye on sneaky Spanish fishermen trying to swipe our mackerel.

As well as the aircraft run by MATS, the Air Corps also makes some of its other planes and helicopters available to the government for internal flights. The costs of these trips are absorbed by the Air Corps's own budget. The latest annual report for the defence forces shows that an Augusta Westland 135 helicopter was used on twenty-five occasions and a Eurocopter EC-135P was flown twenty-one times by ministers in 2008.

The most elderly of the MATS aircraft, a Beechcraft Super King, is the rubbish one, and is being phased out. The aircraft has a cruising speed of 333 miles per hour and room for thirteen passengers. The Australian Flying Doctors and the US Air Force still keep a few in service. Heads of state have had some bad luck in the Beechcraft Super King: Macedonian president Boris Trajkovski was killed when his crashed in February 2004, and Ecuador's president Jaime Roldós Aguilera was killed when his collided with a mountain in 1981.

We also own a Learjet 45. This is way cooler than a Beechcraft, although it carries only seven passengers. The Learjet 45 travels at a decent pelt, hitting 525 miles per hour, with a range of 2,440 miles. It's our newest plane, having been bought for about €8.4 million in 2003 on the eve of Ireland's presidency of Europe.

Our swankiest jet is the Gulfstream IV. Charlie Haughey, who bought it in 1991, dispatched two architects from the Office of Public Works to Grumman's headquarters in Savannah, Georgia, to oversee the interior design of the cockpit. Their brief from Haughey was to incorporate quality Irish materials, such as carpets and linens, into the décor. The jet has clocked up some serious mileage: in 2007 Bertie Ahern said, 'The aircraft is 16 years old and I'm told there's not an aircraft in the world, or third world, that has done that amount of hours.' The jet has broken down on a number of occasions, including leaving poor Micheál Martin stranded for a bit in Georgia in 2008. It also left Bertie Ahern and Celia Larkin trapped in sunny Mexico when it conked out on the runway back in 2003. But, despite the lengthy service and whispers about a 'curse', the Gulfstream is the real deal. It can carry fourteen passengers and has a range of 4,872 miles.

If Fianna Fáil had had its way, we would have had an even bigger jet. In early 2003 the government agreed to buy a swish new forty-seater Airbus Corporate Jetliner for €41.7 million. It would have given the government enormous prestige ahead of its presidency of the European Union – enormous prestige among airport workers and plane spotters. The government quietly reversed its decision to buy the new jet, with Bertie Ahern saying the volte-face had been made 'in the context of a review of expenditure and budgetary issues'. Labour's transport spokeswoman, Róisín Shortall, claimed the acquisition was pulled only because 'the Government found that it could simply not secure a new jet' in the sort of time available before the EU presidency began.

'I am not convinced that this is a case of the Government seeing sense at a late stage,' she said at the time. 'The plan to acquire a lavish new jet would have been an outrageous waste of taxpayers' money at a time when crucial public services are being cut back.' But it wasn't all bad news for those members of the government who like the comfort of their own plane: the government bought the smaller €10 million Learjet 45 instead.

Fianna Fáil has always had a bit of a taste for executive jets. State papers from 1972 reveal that Jack Lynch's government agreed plans to buy a private plane in December 1972. The papers include a letter from Dublin businessman Patrick O'Brien to Lynch, arguing that the jet would not help 'unfortunate people who have to struggle on small means and little heat, particularly at this time of year'. The Lynch government reversed its plan to buy a plane in March 1973.

For all the complaints ministers make about the government jets – they say they're small, and you can't stand up – it remains a far more pleasant method of travel than Ryanair or Aer Lingus. The Gulfstream IV jet is comfortable, with armchair-style seats, a fully equipped galley and a spacious loo. The grub on the government jet isn't bad either – or at least it isn't cheap: in March 2003 it emerged that the government had spent almost €105,000 on catering and bar bills on the jet for the previous year. This included €18,256 for drink. Over €5,200 was spent on hot towels, perfumes, deodorants, shower gels and other toiletries. Remarkably, the taxpayer also spent €1,264 for special presentation boxes of hand-made chocolates. In November 2003 John Gormley, then a mere Green TD in opposition, harangued Bertie Ahern in the Dáil over the catering costs for the jet; he wanted to know about 'indulgences such as chocolates and champagne' being consumed on board. Ahern retorted, 'I do not eat chocolates. I have never seen champagne on the government jet. I will suggest to the Air Corps that we have organic lettuce.'

Gormley's questioning had no evident effect: the following year some €123,000 was spent on booze, food and other goodies for the government jets. This included €1,500 for flowers and another €1,000 for chocolates. The government also spent €230,000 to hire 'air taxis', or private corporate jets, on seven occasions in 2004. In July of that year, after newspaper revelations about the spending on non-state-owned executive jets, Ahern announced that the government would cut down its use of privately hired planes.

The recession has seen cutbacks on some of the more flippant journeys. The cost of ministers zipping across the country on internal flights using Air Corps planes and copters dipped in 2009, from €1.77 million to €1.06 million, and in the first three months of the year there were no internal flights involving ministers using Air Corps planes or helicopters. Even so, the cost of flights on the government jets in the first three months of 2010 was still €611,140, based on the cost-per-hour figures used by the Department of Defence. Taoiseach Brian Cowen's St Patrick's Day trip to the US on the Gulfstream cost an estimated €186,730, with stops at Chicago, California and Washington, DC. Foreign minister Micheál Martin's visit to Cairo and Sinai in February 2010 cost an estimated €92,050 – far more expensive than a scheduled airline ticket, even a business-class one.

Not all countries have private jets for government ministers. The Finnish president and government ministers take scheduled airline flights or charter a plane if necessary. Austria also charters flights, and the Luxembourg government uses both normal airlines and private charters.

The argument for using a government jet is that it allows a minister to squeeze the most out of his time. It saves them sitting around in airports waiting for connecting flights and it can plonk them down in places that other airlines fail to reach. There's a certain logic to this, especially for the more strategically important ministers. But using state aircraft to travel to party constituency meetings, sporting or cultural occasions, or even to open your buddy's off-licence, is quite simply indefensible.

Where does the buck stop? There are guidelines for use of MATS flights, which fall under the aegis of the Department of Defence. The Taoiseach's private office has to sign off on all trips using the state planes. The Department of the Taoiseach has said that 'use of air transport is strictly controlled, and permission is granted only after certain criteria are met'. The department also claims that 'Ministers and the Taoiseach have extremely busy schedules and would not always be able to keep appointments if they travelled on commercial airlines.'

But, despite this, it seems clear that these supposedly strict controls were little more than a rubber-stamping exercise in boomtime, as the jets took ministers to rugby matches in Paris, or Cheltenham, or on long-haul trips with uncertain benefits for the country.

To be fair to the hard-working ministers, flying in private aircraft hasn't been all fun. Poor old Martin Cullen, the Waterford TD who provided the state with useless e-voting machines to the tune of €52 million, nearly came a cropper in one of our helicopters. In March 2009 Cullen, who had replaced John O'Donoghue as Minister for Fun, had a traumatic experience when the left-hand-side door of the Air Corps AW139 in which he was travelling simply fell off. The helicopter was 150 feet up in the air at the time, somewhere over Killarney National Park, and was forced to make an emergency landing at the nearby Killarney Golf and Fishing Club. That morning it had flown Cullen from his Waterford constituency to Kerry, where he attended the Irish Hotel Federation annual knees-up. Cullen and his assistant were driven to Kerry Airport, where another AW139 – having been diverted from a military exercise in Cork – was waiting to fly them back to Dublin.

'Most of you know that I was nearly killed in a helicopter crash,' Cullen said in March 2010 as he announced his retirement from public life. 'It wasn't the door that fell off; half the helicopter actually fell off. I didn't lean on the door, by the way. My point is that five people were nearly killed that day. It was a quite extraordinary outcome but in the portrayal of it, suddenly I became a villain from nearly being killed in a helicopter accident.

'I don't know why the story should emerge in those terms other than it continues to perpetuate the view of a buffoon, a person who abuses his position in public life, who spends all his time flying around the world, that I take the helicopter home every weekend. All untruths, but most people believe this. The irony is that I was the lowest user of helicopters in the State. In the last five years I was in a helicopter four times. I can't stand them.'

His near-fatal trip cost an estimated €8,000, based on Department of Defence figures.

Ministers exult in luxury above the clouds in private jets; they also enjoy opulence in the way of chauffeur-driven ministerial motors when on terra firma. The automobile fleet, which is available to government ministers, former Taoisigh and senior government officials, includes seven Mercedes, seven Audi A6s, three BMW 5-Series, four Lexuses, two Toyota Prius hybrids, two Fords and one Citroën C6. Many of these cars are new, with a Mercedes S320, a Volvo S80, a Citroën C6, a BMW 525 and four Audi A6s all bought in 2008 to replace slightly shabbier ministerial runabouts. Finance minister Brian Lenihan and social affairs minister Mary Hanafin were allocated E-Class Mercedes, as was Martin Cullen before he resigned from the cabinet in March 2010. Foreign affairs minister Micheál Martin, education minister Batt O'Keeffe and chief justice John Murray use BMW 5-Series cars. Tánaiste Mary Coughlan and health minister Mary Harney flit about in Audi A6 Saloons, as do transport minister Noel Dempsey and justice minister Dermot Ahern. John O'Donoghue was also an A6 man before resigning as Ceann Comhairle. The Green ministers have been given the Priuses, although both John Gormley and Eamon Ryan tend to cycle in the city centre.

In February 2009 Joe Duffy's *Liveline* was abuzz with reports that a ministerial Merc had been seen driving about with just a dog as a passenger. Rumours over the identity of the mutt whizzed around the internet for several months. In August 2009 it was reported that Attorney General Paul Gallagher's Westland Terrier had been transported from Dublin to his holiday home in Kerry at Christmas 2008: the car had been dispatched to bring important papers to Gallagher and the dog 'hitched a lift'. Government sources insisted 'there was no impropriety and no extra cost to taxpayers,' according to the *Daily Mail* report.

Department of Justice figures show that the ministerial fleet costs at least €6.5 million a year to maintain, with drivers' salaries, expenses and car maintenance making up the bulk of this. There is another way. Soon after taking power in May 2010, Prime Minister David Cameron announced a new code of practice that severely restricted the use of chauffeur-driven cars. Certain ministers can be driven about if they are working on 'classified' papers and are travelling within a reasonable distance from London. Security issues mean that the prime minister, defence secretary, home secretary and foreign secretary retain a police driver, but in other circumstances the new Conservative and Lib Dem ministers have been encouraged to use public transport. Cabinet members should when possible finish working on classified papers in the office, in order to avoid the need for escorts. Such measures could work in Ireland. Why on earth is the transport minister not seen on the train every morning? Does the Minister for Social Protection really need to arrive at some facility for the unemployed in a shiny black Merc?

The Irish government's main belt-tightening gesture with regard to the ministerial car fleet was revealed in January 2009, when it emerged that Brian Cowen had declined to be chauffeured around in the new €160,000 S-Class Mercedes allocated to the Taoiseach; instead, he continued to use the Merc he'd been allocated as Minister for Finance. Government 'sources' told the media that this was due to 'the changed financial and economic circumstances' and concerns that this would send out the 'wrong message' in the current economic climate. The top-of-the-range Mercedes S350 that had been bought for Cowen's use by the Department of Justice in June 2008, after he took over as Taoiseach from Bertie Ahern, remained in a depot at Garda headquarters in the Phoenix Park for six months; it had to be plugged in to a charger to prevent damage to its on-board computer. 'The Taoiseach requested that the possibility of returning it to the supplier should be explored. This did not prove possible. The question of deploying it for alternative use within the fleet has also been considered. Appropriate alternative use has not been identified. Accordingly, the car will be allocated for the Taoiseach's use in the near future,' the Department of Justice said.

On 4 April 2008, shortly before he resigned as Taoiseach, Bertie Ahern used an Air Corps helicopter to fly from Drumcondra to Powerscourt in Enniskerry, County Wicklow – a distance of about twelve miles – and then back again. At the time we were a bit inured to the excesses of our masters after years of economic growth. Bertie still inspired a warm fuzzy feeling. The public hadn't realized that his short-sighted populist policies would lead us into deep recession, with up to 500,000 people unemployed, rising taxes, a shattered banking system and runaway public debt. But Bertie Ahern's victory lap in his final few months of power before handing over the reins to Brian Cowen really took the mickey. His travels during his final six months in office to pick up a few gongs, make some self-aggrandizing speeches and press the flesh cost the taxpayer €213,000, according to documents released under the Freedom of Information Act. During this period, Bertie made thirty-one separate trips covering 81,000 kilometres on the government jet.

Some €67,000 was spent sending Bertie off to wave at people in South Africa in January 2008. First-class outgoing flights cost €2,961 for each of the eight members of his entourage. The flights home – from Tanzania – were a bit cheaper, coming to a total of €13,000. The sum of €8,000 was spent on hotels and €1,555 on boozy meals. Limos added nearly €10,000 on to the tab for the week. The taxpayer also spent €80.26 on prescription drugs for one of the travellers.

The taxpayer picked up a €4,500 limo bill on Bertie's junket to see Manchester United play Manchester City on the fiftieth anniversary of the Munich air disaster in February 2008. A limo was dispatched from London and drove 302 miles to Newcastle-upon-Tyne, in the northeast of England, where it picked up the Irish ambassador to Britain, David Cooney. It turned left and crossed the Pennines on its way to Manchester, where it picked up Bertie from the airport and ferried him to Old Trafford. Ahern met with Prime Minister Gordon Brown before kick-off. After spending just six hours in Manchester, Ahern returned by limo to the government jet, after which the limo drove back to London with the ambassador. An altogether less fancy people-carrier accompanied the limo on its trip. This was to ferry Ahern's entourage.

Both vehicles were rented from Cartel, a company run by Terry Gallagher, the son of the former Fianna Fáil Gaeltacht minister Denis Gallagher. Terry Gallagher has done well out of the Irish taxpayer. John O'Donoghue's limo jaunts with Gallagher's company – four trips to the UK between 2006 and 2007 – cost €21,761. Three of these four journeys coincided with race meetings at Cheltenham and Ascot. Minister for the Environment John Gormley spent €3,580 with Cartel during his St Patrick's Day visit to London in 2009, which included visits to the London Eye and a West End show.

'In this business, you use your contacts to get in wherever you can,' Gallagher has said. 'I did use a networking opportunity to get to talk to the Irish embassy, which I have done with other embassies here. For the record, if you look at our company accounts, we turned over close on £2 million last year and the Irish embassy contribution to that was less than 5 per cent.'

Gallagher has pointed out that Fianna Fáil ministers are not the only ones who use his service: 'The Fine Gael office in Dublin has an account with us and we also provided cars for the Fine Gael administration through the embassy in London.'

Gallagher's Cartel earned a quite extraordinary €580,000 between 2002 and 2008 ferrying dignitaries, ministers and officials on behalf of the Irish embassy. For thirty years it had been the practice of the embassy to dispatch a functionary to Heathrow to meet any Irish minister as soon as he'd touched down – even if he was only transferring to another flight. This extraordinary waste of resources was stopped following a review at the embassy in the wake of the revelations about John O'Donoghue and his limo use. The Irish embassy in London invested in a seven-seater people-carrier and drastically reduced its spending on limos. In 2009 Gallagher's Cartel company earned just €394 from the embassy, compared with €99,343 a year earlier.

The high point of the Bertie Ahern farewell tour – his jolly to address the US Congress in Washington in May 2008 – cost us more than €65,000. This included €4,500 for Bertie to spend two nights in the penthouse of the Mayflower Hotel in Washington – labelled Washington's 'second best address' by President Harry Truman. Ahern's limousine bill came to €16,650, including a tip of €2,500. Bertie also charged a 'pay-per-view' movie to the room. He didn't forget to file for his Oireachtas expenses, submitting a €410 claim for subsistence, which we picked up.

Ahern knows the presidential suite at the Mayflower well, having stayed there for his St Patrick's Day junket in 2008, which cost us a total of €17,200. The suite – which is larger than many of the small apartments that first-time buyers bought during the boom – cost €4,700 for two days that time around.

Ahern also cost us €3,500 for two nights at the Conrad Hotel in

Brussels in 2007 and 2008. The hotel's two presidential suites are on the second and third floors, with 'lovely views over Avenue Louise'. We also spent €2,400 so Bertie could get a good night's kip in the Dorchester Hotel on Park Lane in London.

All in all, we paid €15,100 for seven nights' worth of B&B for Bertie. That's the same as eighteen months' worth of Jobseeker's Allowance for someone on the dole, someone who lost their job because Ahern and his government wrecked the economy. Seven nights' sleep. Let's hope he slept well.

After our initial deadline for this book, but before it went to press, the expenses of the controversial North Dublin Fianna Fáil Senator Ivor Callely became one of the stories of the summer of 2010. It emerged that Callely had been claiming Oireachtas allowances and travel expenses from his holiday home in west Cork while maintaining his house in Dublin. Callely, the long-time Dublin North Central TD, claimed to have moved his primary residence to west Cork after losing his Dáil seat in 2007. Callely was suspended from the Seanad for twenty days and a series of investigations was launched into his behaviour. It subsequently emerged that he had submitted expense claims using mobile-phone receipts from a defunct company.

Despite the supposed recessionary clampdown on government spending and waste, the message still hadn't got through to some members of the cabinet by the summer of 2010. In August, Minister for Transport Noel Dempsey racked up a bill of nearly €13,000 travelling to the MacGill Summer School in Donegal. Dempsey's trip started when he was driven from his Navan home to Baldonnel, where he boarded the government Gulfstream jet for the short flight to Derry. His ministerial Audi A6 was driven from Dublin to Derry and then used to ferry the minister over to Glenties. Dempsey was then brought back to the airport and flown to London for a meeting. Speaking after the controversy, Dempsey told the Ógra Fianna Fáil Summer School at Queen's University that, with the 'wonderful benefit of hindsight', perhaps alternative arrangements should have been sought.

6. The Social-Partnership Industry

It was 16 June 2008 – Bloomsday and conferral day at University College Dublin. There they were, the king and the queen of Ireland's quangos, wallowing in the sunshine and the approval of the academic establishment: Des Geraghty and Olive Braiden were being awarded honorary doctorates.

Out in the midsummer sun the two quangsters were in good company in their academic gowns, flanked by *Irish Times* editor Geraldine Kennedy, UCD president Hugh Brady and five professors. According to UCD *News*'s grammatically challenged account of the ceremony, entitled 'UCD honours "catalysts of change"', Des Geraghty had 'led Ireland's largest trade union (SIPTU) during the period of greatest prosperity in the country's history and his role as a negotiator within the social partnership helped change Ireland from a relatively poor, peripheral country who exported its young to the Celtic Tiger whose economic growth outstripped all of its EU partners for a decade'.

So there we had it. Des Geraghty was responsible for Ireland's prosperity. An honorary doctorate was the least he deserved.

The citation went on to laud Geraghty's other achievements. From 1992 to 1994 he had been a member of the European Parliament, where he sat on the Committee on Economic and Monetary Affairs and Industrial Policy. The text was a bit light on his academic achievements but credited him as the author of a book on the singer Luke Kelly of the Dubliners. It continued: 'He has written extensively on industrial relations and economic topics . . . he is currently chairperson of the Institute for the Development of Employee Assistance Services (IDEAS).' Finally, the citation listed the public-service achievements of Dr Des. He had been appointed a member of the RTÉ Authority. He was a director of Poetry Ireland. He was an elected shareholder of the Abbey Theatre. He served a term on the National Competitiveness Council. And he had been on the board of FÁS, the national training and employment agency, for nearly ten years.

For nearly twenty years, eight seats on the board of FÁS were reserved for the favourite sons of the big employers and the unions. The chairmanship of the board – with its €24,000 salary – rotated between a top boss at the big employers' oufit, IBEC, and a union chief. Geraghty was one of the insiders who drew €14,000 a year for the privilege of sitting comfortably beside so many other 'social partners'.

Four months after the UCD conferral, FÁS would be exposed as a hotbed of waste, junketry and mismanagement. A year later, at the end of 2009, the entire seventeen-member board of FÁS, including Geraghty, was forced to exit, some exposed as junketeers, others (like Geraghty) simply ineffective.

Social partnership did not propel Geraghty merely to the dizzy heights of an honorary degree and board membership of FÁS. In 2005 a little quango called the Affordable Homes Partnership (AHP) was created under the terms of the most recent social-partnership agreement. The Minister for the Environment, Dick Roche, offered the chair to Geraghty, who accepted. The chairman's fee was settled at €13,000. Geraghty received only €8,000 in 2005 because it was a short year, but the quango paid him €30,000 in 2006, another €30,000 in 2007 and €25,000 in 2008. Geraghty could have funded his own home from the fees he took from the social partners' little creation. A spokesman for the AHP maintained that Geraghty was paid a multiple of the originally agreed fee because he took on 'extra work above and beyond the usual responsibilities of the chair'. Add that to his fee at FÁS, his pension as general secretary of SIPTU and other perks, such as a stipend from his post as chairman of the Irish Print and Packaging Forum, and an observer might conclude that Geraghty has been in the right place at the right time. Social partnership has been good to Geraghty.

In his youth Geraghty was a member of the Labour Party. In 1969 he joined Sinn Féin, and after the party split was a member of its 'Official' wing and of the various successor parties that grew out of it: Sinn Féin The Workers' Party, the Workers' Party, New Agenda, then Democratic Left and finally back to the Labour Party after DL was absorbed into it. He stood unsuccessfully for the European

Parliament as a Workers' Party candidate in the Dublin constituency
in 1984; in 1992 he was co-opted to the parliament after Proinsias De
Rossa resigned his seat, but he did not stand for re-election in 1994.
He stood for the Senate as a Labour Party candidate in 2002 but failed
to inspire the party faithful to back him.

It was as a union leader – president of SIPTU 1999–2004, deliv-
erer of partnership deals time after time – that Geraghty, the old
radical, was richly rewarded. His fees from FÁS for ten years, his
income from the Affordable Homes Partnership over five years and
his stipend from RTÉ over five years must have amounted to little
short of €250,000.

The new Doctor of Laws, Des Geraghty, might have found himself shaded by his fellow UCD honorary doctor on that Bloomsday,
Olive Braiden, had he compared his income from the quangos with
hers. Like Des, Olive was an unsuccessful wannabe politician, but she
too need never have fretted.

Braiden's early career was as a progressive feminist. She joined the
Rape Crisis Centre as a volunteer in 1983 and worked her way up to
director by 1990. Her politics were regarded as liberal left, so it caused
a stir when she was persuaded to let her name be added to the Fianna
Fáil ticket in the European elections of 1994. This was a coup for
Fianna Fáil, but she failed abysmally at the polls, losing her deposit in
the Dublin constituency.

That was the end of Braiden's career in electoral politics, but her
decision to fly the flag for the Soldiers of Destiny changed her career
path. Her feminist credentials were a godsend to a party with little
profile on the liberal agenda. Fianna Fáil exploited her record craft-
ily, placing her up front on task forces by the bucketful. In the years
after her defeat she was a constant appointee to sensitive committees
investigating violence against women and child abuse. She was articu-
late, gregarious and popular.

Braiden's willingness to act as Fianna Fáil's eyes and ears in such
areas may have initially been tedious for her, but the party repaid her
in spades. During the years when she was playing the role of their
representative on such unrewarding bodies, she was also picking up a
number of more powerful posts.

In 1998 Braiden became a member of the Broadcasting Commission of Ireland at an annual fee of around €7,000. This was followed by a stretch on the board of the Courts Service (€10,157) and an appointment to the Human Rights Commission (€12,693). In 2003 Fianna Fáil's arts minister, John O'Donoghue, gave her the plum post of chairperson of the Arts Council, at a fee of €7,618. Prior to that Braiden had not been noted for her interest in the arts; the impressive CV summarized in the Department of Arts, Sport and Tourism's own press release announcing the appointment did not include a single arts-related position or interest.

At the turn of the millennium Braiden was picking up appointments from her Fianna Fáil patrons at a rate of knots, but she hadn't yet broken into the expanding social-partnership industry. In 2002, as we shall see below, Braiden was given her big break as part of the 'benchmarking' process that had been introduced into national pay agreements.

Funnily enough, the citation to Dr Braiden on Bloomsday 2008 never mentioned her flirtation with the politics of Fianna Fáil back in 1994. Nor were the scripted paeans of praise to Des and Olive tactless enough to hint that the social partnership of 2008 was a million miles away from the spirit of the first national pay pact hammered out back in 1987.

It is often conveniently forgotten by devotees of social partnership that it was the creation of Charlie Haughey.

The grim eighties were marked by a series of major disputes between employers and unions. Haughey, counting the economic and political cost of industrial unrest, saw the potential of a tripartite arrangement in which the state would join employers and unions at the negotiating table. His conversion to social partnership is often put down to a conversation he had with the German chancellor Helmut Schmidt at a European summit. Schmidt told the Fianna Fáil leader that he was going to consult German trade unions about how to sort out his country's economic ills. Charlie was initially puzzled, but quickly took up the idea and floated it to his trade-union contacts at home.

During his period as leader of the opposition in the mid eighties, Haughey was hopelessly bored at home, condemned to mixing with less lofty people than chancellors and presidents. He often sent out his press officer, P. J. Mara, to beat the bushes in search of people to amuse him at lunchtime. He would end up dining with the impresario Noel Pearson, or the twins Jim Hand (a showband manager) and Michael Hand (the legendary *Sunday Independent* editor).Shane Ross recalls lunching with Mara and Haughey around this time.

Another of Haughey's dining partners during this period was John Carroll, former president of the Irish Transport and General Workers Union (ITGWU) and boss of the Irish Congress of Trade Unions. Sometimes the two met in the Howth Lodge Hotel, close to Carroll's Sutton home and not far from Haughey's Kinsealy mansion, to discuss the financial crisis.

Carroll, although a lifelong member of the Labour Party, satisfied Haughey's need for stimulation and found a willing listener in the leader of the opposition. He was a fierce critic of the Fine Gael–Labour coalition that governed from 1983 to 1987, even though he had been nominated to the Seanad by Labour leader Michael O'Leary in 1981. He saw Fine Gael as basically hostile to the trade unions, convinced that Garret FitzGerald's government was stuffed with stuck-up amateurs. Charlie charmed him into believing that Fianna Fáil was more pragmatic.

Later Carroll was to speak admiringly of Haughey: 'The focus of the government was on low wage levels and reducing unemployment. They wouldn't gamble as Charlie did [later], on low inflation and tax cuts to offset moderate pay increases.'

According to an article by Pádraig Yeates in *Business & Finance*, Peter Cassells, assistant general secretary of ICTU, had written a document in 1985 called 'Confronting the Jobs Crisis'. It flew a heretical kite. Cassells, according to Yeates, was sending out a signal that 'after five years in which take-home pay had fallen by 11 per cent for some workers, the unions were now willing to trade pay restraint for tax cuts, anti-inflationary measures and job-creation initiatives.' Tax cuts accompanied by voluntary pay restraint were being considered as a real alternative to the old spiral of wage increases being rendered meaningless by penal taxation and runaway inflation.

Despite ICTU's traditional ties with Labour – the smaller partner in coalition – the Cassells proposal fell on deaf ears. Neither Fitz-Gerald, nor Spring, nor any of the other supposed social democrats in that government picked up the ball and ran with it. Yeates quotes Cassells as saying that '"Confronting the Jobs Crisis" was aimed at the government, but Haughey took up the challenge.'

Although he befriended dodgy businessmen and aped the aristoc-racy, Haughey never failed to emphasize his own working-class roots if it suited his needs. In the period following the Arms Crisis, when he was banished from the cabinet, he maintained friendships with key union leaders, including Micky Mullen, general secretary of the old Irish Transport and General Workers Union. He spoke their lan-guage and shared their background in a way that the more refined FitzGerald and Spring never could.

A few months before the Fine Gael–Labour government fell apart in a hopeless ideological split over the economy, Haughey was mak-ing passes at the union leaders. On 16 December 1986, as the coalition was entering its death throes, Billy Attley, general secretary of the Federated Workers Union of Ireland, signalled a desire for what he called 'co-ordinated economic and social planning'. He spelled it out: 'To achieve this, the trade-union movement is willing to negotiate with government and employers, a National Plan for Economic Recovery.'

Less than twenty-four hours later, Haughey responded: 'I wel-come the statement made yesterday by Mr Billy Attley . . . offering wage moderation in return for consultation on economic and social planning. Fianna Fáil governments have always sought close co-operation and consultation with the social partners and in particular with the trade-union movement.'

The mating dance had begun. Haughey was poised to cuckold not only Fine Gael but also the trade-union movement's traditional part-ner, the Labour Party.

Haughey's engagement with the unions was a political master-stroke, setting the stage for decades of divided party-political loyalties within the trade-union movement and driving a wedge between union bosses and the Labour Party. Labour was hampered by its political reliance on Fine Gael – it was perennially the third most popular party – and over the following quarter-century it would spend less than five years in government. The pragmatic union bosses saw little point in holding huge influence within the higher echelons of a party that was rarely in power. In the words of bricklayers' union leader Kevin Duffy in 1987, they could become 'Whingeing Willies on the fringes of society' or insiders with real clout.

They opted to sup with the devil. Within months of the formation of Haughey's third administration, the government, the employers and the unions negotiated a pact that was much more than a pay deal.

Revealingly, Haughey was close to contemptuous about the attitude of the other main party to the deal – the employers. After absorbing a wave of flak from the employers at the prospect of such a centralized deal, he witheringly downgraded the business lobbyists: 'When the government and the unions have agreed a common approach to solving a national crisis, it is not really possible for the employers to say no.'

He was right. It never was. In the next twenty years the tripartite deal generally turned out to be a pact between the government and the union bosses.

Back in the eighties the state of the economy was woeful. There were constant rumours of intervention by the International Monetary Fund – and occasional pleas for such intervention. Political instability had crippled governments. Haughey had originally come to power in 1979 but postponed tough measures because he faced a general election. Two unstable governments in the 1981–2 period were unable to break out of the economic death-spiral threatening the nation's solvency. The FitzGerald–Spring 1983–7 coalition was cursed by policy splits that paralysed its ability to balance the books. The Irish economy was in a state of chronic sickness for eight years. At the time the disease looked terminal.

PAYE workers had taken to the streets demanding lower tax; the national debt had doubled; unemployment had risen to 18.5 per cent of the workforce; interest rates were sky high; servicing the national debt devoured one third of tax revenue; gross domestic product per head was only 64 per cent of the European Union average; and agriculture was in decline. Emigration was running at close to 30,000. Perhaps worst of all, strikes were an everyday event.

When Haughey was elected Taoiseach in 1987, the country was not far from bankruptcy. He was convinced that Ireland needed industrial peace if there was ever to be a recovery; the unions alone had the power to deliver it. Workers wanted reductions in the punitive income-tax levels of the eighties; the government had the power to deliver them.

Struck in October 1987, the 'Programme for National Recovery' was the first social-partnership deal; it would be followed by six other national agreements between employers, unions and the state.

The government committed itself to reductions in tax through increases in PAYE allowances over a three-year period. In return, the unions accepted voluntary pay restraint. Wages would rise by no more than 2.5 per cent annually over the following three years.

Elsewhere the programme read like a mini-election manifesto. There were sections on education, health, fisheries, agriculture, horticulture and tourism. There were scores of projects and heady aspirations for existing semi-state bodies. Ominous seeds of future quango policy were sown in the arrival of two new state bodies: one for forestry (Coillte) and one for horticulture (An Bord Glas). Legislation on housing, unfair dismissal and employment equality was promised. The trade unions were now players in the game of government.

At the time of the first deal, Bertie Ahern was Haughey's Minister for Labour. Bertie was instructed by the Taoiseach to open talks with the social partners about changes in industrial relations. Suddenly the union brethren had a true friend at court. The young minister had long hair, a battered anorak, a thick working-class Dublin accent and a sympathy with their cause unmatched by anything they would encounter within their Labour Party comfort zone. A lasting alliance was formed.

The first partnership deal ran to thirty-two pages. The second deal, agreed in 1990, stretched to ninety-six. By 2000 the fifth national agreement of the social-partnership era broke new records with a page-count of 132. There was usually an element of drama – eleventh-hour crises and walkouts – to preserve the myth that the negotiators were fighting tooth and nail against entrenched opposition, but in truth the first six partnership deals were agreed with almost embarrassing ease.

The fifth programme revealed a well-plotted expansion strategy. The words 'institutional support' had crept into the partnership lexicon. They were ominous. Specifically, the programme spelled out the need for 'supportive institutional bodies'. One such was the National Centre for Partnership and Performance (NCPP). There was plenty of waffle about the great work it was about to do.

The Centre, which will be located within the Office for National Economic and Social Development alongside NESC [National Economic and Social Council] and NESF [National Economic and Social Forum], will work with IBEC and ICTU in supporting the deepening of partnership including through:
- deliberation, consensus building and dissemination;
- monitoring;
- research and analysis;
- training and facilitation.

As if that was not bad enough, the agreement of 2000 went on to assert that 'the roles of other organizations in both the public and private sectors which contribute to partnership development will also be considered in this context as will funding issues arising.'

'Funding issues'? Giveaway words were slipping into the mix. The state was willing to pump money into the emerging bodies.

Partnership was on the march. It was no longer pretending to be a quick fix for pay deals. The fifth programme wandered far from pay negotiations when it loftily mentioned the social partners' commitment to the Good Friday Agreement, their fidelity to European Union objectives, even their united belief in Third World debt forgiveness. All perfectly acceptable as government policies, but miles away from pay negotiations. Social partnership had become an industry unto itself. Quangsters were stumbling into a new paradise.

The NCPP was formed in July 2001. Happily for Peter Cassells, its foundation coincided with his departure as general secretary of ICTU, and he was installed as its head. According to one of Cassells's own pieces of self-promotion, the NCPP 'was established to promote workplace change and innovation through a partnership approach. He [Peter] is a member of the Board of NESDO (the National Economic Social Development Office), which oversees the work of the National Economic and Social Council, the National Economic and Social Forum and the NCPP.' Such is the navel-gazing nature of social partnership that there is nothing remarkable when the person who heads the overseeing acronym is the same person as the head of the overseen acronym. It is unlikely that, back in 1986, when Haughey picked up Cassells's ideas on sorting out the industrial-relations mess, he could have foreseen a time when Cassells would be the head of two state agencies and the beneficiary of so much semi-state largesse (board of Forfás, board of the Digital Hub Development Agency, consultancy work for An Post, the ESB and St Patrick's Hospital). But that was the way partnership developed. Former opponents were supping happily from the same trough. The top brass in Fianna Fáil, ICTU and IBEC found common cause. The role of the government in the pay deals was deeply conflicted. As the biggest employer they instinctively wanted to keep pay low; but they also wanted to get re-elected and, as a result, they often bowed to the desires of the trade unions.

The other two big blocs of employers were IBEC, negotiating on behalf of traditional unionized industries, and the Construction Industry Federation (CIF). During the years when pay restraint gave way to generous pay increases in national agreements, the construction industry was coining it; its main concerns were a steady supply of labour and avoiding unrest, and it would probably have paid far more if necessary to achieve those things. The CIF was almost invisible in the pay talks for nearly twenty years.

IBEC's membership was far more diverse and, like the government, often hopelessly conflicted. Far from being the voice of buccaneering business, IBEC's membership was stuffed with banks and semi-state bodies that were joined at the hip to the state's agenda.

Monopolies such as An Post, the ESB, the Dublin Airport Authority and CIÉ kept IBEC afloat, handing over lorryloads of taxpayers' money in bloated membership fees. Consequently IBEC was often a proxy for the government because of its heavy semi-state membership profile. It made macho noises but regularly danced to the government's political agenda. Even FÁS was, inexplicably, a member of IBEC, paying more than €50,000 a year into its coffers. IBEC was an employers' trade union first, a state sycophant second and a crusader for business interests a very poor third.

Danny McCoy became IBEC director-general in July 2009. His experience in business had been minimal. He arrived in IBEC from the state-funded Economic and Social Research Institute. Prior to that he was an economist at the Central Bank and a lecturer at Oxford, Trinity and Dublin City University. He had also served on the board of FÁS.

His predecessor as director-general, Turlough O'Sullivan, was a career IBEC man, having spent thirty-four years there and at its predecessor, the Federated Union of Employers. His CV mentions private-sector experience but is thin on detail.

Brian Geoghegan, director of Economic Affairs at IBEC until 2005, offered its members even less of a business-enterprise profile. He came to IBEC fresh from thirty years in the service of the state, from no less a backwater than the Central Statistics Office.

During the partnership era, IBEC, ICTU, the CIF and the government became far too cosy. The unions and the employers loved their access to the top tables. They had achieved far more recognition and political leverage than ordinary TDs or even many ministers. Hardly a speech passed through Brian Cowen's lips in the Dáil and the Seanad when he was finance minister that didn't include a mention of the need to consult with the 'social partners'. They wallowed in the attention. They became the guys who were seen to divide the spoils, who carved up the national cake. They had achieved a status that would never have been dreamed of by Haughey in 1986.

The social partners became the stuff of myth. The mantra that social partnership was the mainstay of the economic boom gained general acceptance. Industrial peace, credited to the partnership

process, was greeted as the ingredient that sustained the long boom –
an argument that can never be proved, or disproved. But it became
the accepted wisdom – until the gravy train hit the buffers. When it
did, the huge awards given to the public service under social partnership began to be clawed back. Parallel public-expenditure projects
were scrapped.

Social partnership meant a quieter life, a new sense of importance
and lots of openings into well-funded 'supportive institutional
bodies'.

Billy Attley was one of the first social-partnership quangsters. He
retired as general secretary of SIPTU at the age of sixty in 1998, having helped to deliver four partnership deals to Fianna Fáil governments.
He was picked by Bertie Ahern as one of the original trade-union
directors of FÁS, and served for years alongside his pal, chairman
John Lynch, and another trade unionist, Christy Kirwan. There is no
known record of a moment's discord on this chummiest of boards.

Billy Attley had torn himself away from the joys of FÁS long
before the board was forced to leave office; but he made up for the
loss elsewhere. Despite his friendship with Bertie, he maintained his
Labour Party membership, a link that did him no harm when he was
appointed to the RTÉ Authority by Labour minister Michael D.
Higgins in 1995.

Attley's good working relationship with Bertie probably landed
him his seat on the board of Eircom in 1999. This was a real jackpot:
the part-time job carried an annual fee of €48,000. Attley stuck it out
there, surviving the worst attacks on a board that allowed its executives high salaries and an orgy of share options. He looked horribly
uncomfortable sitting on the podium at AGMs alongside fat cats such
as Bank of Ireland boss Pat Molloy and DCC's Jim Flavin; but he did
not make the same mistake as Labour Party leader Dick Spring, who
antagonized the shareholders by pleading poverty as an excuse for
not buying any shares himself.

In 2000 Attley became a member of the first body to have respon-
sibility for benchmarking public-service pay. He was joined by Phil
Flynn, a similarly loyal social partner and an equally firm friend of
Bertie. Phil was a former president of ICTU and ex-general secretary

of IMPACT. A few years earlier Flynn had been appointed chairman of the state-owned ICC Bank and was constantly in the market for government consultancy work.

On the employers' side sat John Dunne, former director-general of IBEC. Prior to that he had headed up its predecessor, the Federation of Irish Employers. After his exit from IBEC, Dunne had been appointed by the state to the chair of the IDA at a fee that had risen to €24,000 by the time he left in 2009. He also made it to another state board, that of the Financial Regulator. Others on the seven-person benchmarking body included Maureen Lynott, formerly a director of the state-owned VHI – who, as we have seen, was later to receive a lucrative contract to serve in Brendan Drumm's kitchen cabinet at the HSE – and Paddy Mullarkey, former secretary general of the Department of Finance. Chairing the body was Mr Justice Quirke of the High Court. All but one of the members were either public servants or recipients of bulky amounts of state funds at some point in their careers. (The one exception was Jim O'Leary, chief economist at Davy stockbrokers.)

Sceptics suggested that the social-partner-dominated body was predestined to deliver a report richly rewarding public servants. John McManus, the business editor of the *Irish Times*, was highly critical of the exercise in a typically perceptive article in March 2003. Naming Attley, Dunne, Flynn and Mullarkey, he wrote: 'These are the grandfathers of partnership, steeped in its culture and hubris. They are high priests of the culture of the national pay deal, which holds the partnership agreements to be the godhead of our economic revival. It now looks like they believe partnership is so important that, in order to ensure the continued participation of the public sector unions, they will recommend pay rises that are not deserved which the taxpayer cannot afford.'

Prescient words, but at the time it was considered deeply suspect to criticize social partnership and its 'high priests'. Initially a pay deal, then a programme for the nation, social partnership had transformed into a religion.

The members of the benchmarking body were very well paid. The chairman, Justice Quirke, accepted nothing, but the other six members shared €329,000 over the two years in which the group did its work.

The proceedings remained shrouded in mystery until April 2002, when, two months before the body was due to report, Jim O'Leary resigned. The resignation was a bombshell. O'Leary, the only member of the group with serious private-sector experience, was seen as carrying the flag for the financial sector and for entrepreneurs. This, along with his past associations with Fine Gael, meant that his imprimatur was considered important to the report's credibility.

At first O'Leary tactfully cited time constraints as the reason for his sudden exit. But, speaking to the Dublin Economic Workshop in Kenmare later in the year, the economist revealed that he had resigned because his skills were irrelevant in drawing up the body's final recommendations. He insisted that the benchmarkers had offered 'precious little' justification for the pay awards they recommended. He asserted that the body 'had been a hostage to the sensibilities of the public-sector unions and employers'.

The benchmarking body's proposal for an overall 9 per cent increase in public-service pay stunned even the optimists in the public-service union leadership. The award was ordered in staged payments, with the final instalment – linked to productivity – to be paid not earlier than October 2002. It would cost the state over a billion a year. The icing on the cake for public servants was the decision by the government that a full quarter of the increase would be backdated by six months to 1 December 2001.

The benchmarking awards confirmed the dominance of the public-service unions over the other social partners. A one-off award of this dimension was unprecedented, and marked their unstoppable march. In other pay deals negotiated between the social partners, the public service had been awarded phased increases of dramatically less value than the benchmarking giveaway – and phased over far longer periods. The Programme for Prosperity and Fairness, which ran from 2000 to 2003, gave public servants 5.5 per cent a year in each of the first two years and 4 per cent in a final nine-month period. It was followed by the Sustaining Progress deal, which started with a six-month pay pause that was followed by three half-yearly increases – the first being 3 per cent, and the last two, 2 per cent.

The 9 per cent benchmarking award was an inflation beater. After peaking at 5.6 per cent in 2000, Ireland's rate of inflation retreated to 4.9 per cent (2001), 4.7 per cent (2002) 3.5 per cent (2003) and 2.2 per cent (2004). Benchmarking was, in the words of former trade-union leader Senator Joe O'Toole, 'equivalent to walking up to an ATM machine'.

The government embraced the pay proposals. Opponents complained that none of the data on which the report had based its conclusions was ever published, and it was suggested that the evidence was destroyed because it did not support the findings. We will probably never know the truth because the body's deliberations were specifically and conveniently excluded from the Freedom of Information Act.

The seeds of future insane pay expectations were sown on that day in July 2002. When the crisis hit the Exchequer's finances in 2008, its origins could be partly traced back to the benchmarking deal of 2002. Although at the time of the benchmarking the nation's economy was taking a brief post-election breather in the middle of the boom, during the two previous years public spending had been allowed to run completely out of hand as the government faced the 2002 polls. In 2000 spending shot up by 14.4 per cent and in 2001 by a sensational 20.7 per cent. The public-service unions and their allies on the benchmarking body spied this riot of expenditure and resolved to strike while the iron was hot.

The Fianna Fáil giveaway philosophy won the general election of 2002, but benchmarking saddled us with an albatross we could not carry when tax revenues dried up, as they inevitably did once the property market turned, the banks went bust and the economy crashed.

Compared with the catastrophic cost of the multibillion-euro bank bailout, the long-term cumulative cost of benchmarking was a flea bite; but the consequences of binge–purge economics would have come home to roost even without the banking implosion. The 9 per cent benchmarking award was not, in theory, meant to be paid without strings attached. Under the deal, employees were obliged to justify their increases by improved performance and modernization in their workplaces, though the benchmarking report was hopelessly vague on the subject:

The Body strongly recommends that implementation of the pay awards should be made conditional (apart from the one quarter of any award to be implemented with effect from 1 December of 2001 as agreed between the parties) upon agreement on relevant modernisation and change issues at the appropriate local bargaining levels. It will be a matter, in each case, for managements and unions/associations to determine the agenda for this local bargaining, but it is the firm expectation of the Body that real outputs will be delivered. The establishment of appropriate validation processes is recommended to ensure that agreements on issues such as adaptability, change, flexibility and modernisation are implemented.

Five Performance Verification Groups (PVGs) were born, covering justice, education, the civil service, local government and health. The composition of the five groups selected to sit in judgement – and to give the green light to the pay hikes – was left up to the government. They chose their candidates carefully. Very carefully. They were a mixture of trade unionists, public-service managers, social-partnership junkies and independent government nominees.

The trade-union members appointed to each PVG were instantly onside, as some of their top leadership had signed the benchmarking body's report. Similarly, the representatives of the departments were unlikely to delay their own pay increases. With such a loaded line-up, an independent chairman might find himself or herself isolated. It never happened. The chairs of each group were chosen even more carefully than the ordinary members. We have no way of knowing whether any individual decision made by a PVG was incorrect. The problem is that the composition of the groups left too much room for public cynicism about the exercise. It looked like the fix was in.

The name of the chairperson of the Health PVG was strangely familiar. It was none other than Maureen Lynott – a member of the benchmarking body itself. The appointment – for which Lynott was paid €1,080 per day exclusive of VAT – hardly raised a ripple.

In reality the train had already left the station. The report was out in the open. Public servants nationwide were rejoicing in the expectation of their 9 per cent awards. It was unthinkable at this stage that the payments would be withheld: there would have been blue murder from the public-service unions. The government, the civil-service management and the social-partnership industry would have been in turmoil.

The Health PVG gave the all-clear to the 'performance' of the health workers. Its decision cannot have been hindered by the presence on the group of social partner Liam Doran, the boss of the nurses' union.

The Justice PVG did the same, although there was a minor delay because of a dispute among prison officers. Its chairperson was none other than Olive Braiden, the woman with the honorary degree from UCD, the Fianna Fáil nomination for Europe in 1994, the chair of the Arts Council in 2003 and the undisputed queen of Ireland's quangos. She was paid €15,700 for the gig – her first in the social-partnership industry – over three years.

Beside Braiden on the Justice PVG bench sat John Clinton of the Prison Officers' Association and Rosaleen Glackin of the Civil and Public Services Union (CPSU). John Clinton was hardly likely to return to his prison officer flock and tell them that he had decided to oppose their pay increase because they were not performing properly. Rosaleen Glackin was more interesting. After a long stint as deputy general secretary of the CPSU, she graduated to the lucrative state-funded post of rights commissioner, attached to the Labour Relations Commission. A few years later Fianna Fáil also made her a member of the Dormant Accounts Board, which distributes funds to good causes.

Glackin was unlikely to make a name for herself by finding that civil servants hadn't performed adequately. She didn't.

Nor did Arthur Coldrick, the independent chairman of the Local Authority PVG. Coldrick was managing director of an unknown company called AC Network. A little digging unearths that AC Network networks principally in the social-partnership industry. It has open links with Peter Cassells's National Centre for Partnership and

Performance. AC Network's own blurb boasts of its 'excellent working relationship with social partner groupings, eg IBEC/ICTU'. It goes on to list its closeness to FÁS and similar quangos such as the moribund Irish Productivity Centre, itself an IBEC/ICTU operation. A few years later he found himself on the government-appointed 'Advisory Board on Partnership and Change in the Workplace'.

The Civil Service PVG was chaired by Donal de Buitléir, a man with decades of public service behind him, including stints as a council member of the ESRI, secretary to the Commission on Taxation and chair of the National Social Service Board. The final PVG, covering teachers and education, was guided to its unsurprising conclusion by Dr Seamus McGuinness of Trinity College Dublin.

(One month after the five PVGs had waved public servants through the 'adaptability, change, flexibility and modernisation' hurdles, Shane Ross received his monthly pay cheque as a Senator. Puzzled by a sudden unexplained increase, he rang the Department of Finance to inquire about it.

'The increase is your performance bonus,' replied the frosty mandarin.

'But my performance in the Senate has deteriorated in recent months,' replied Ross mischievously.

'That is of no consequence,' replied the mandarin. 'You have to accept it.')

After the dust settled, benchmarking was promised to the public-sector unions as a permanent feature of social partnership, and in 2006 Brian Cowen, as Minister for Finance, announced the appointment of a second benchmarking group. This one was as reliable as its predecessor. Its composition was different, but it contained familiar names and several safe pairs of hands.

The first name out of the hat was none other than that of the old warhorse Billy Attley − the only man in Ireland to do the benchmarking body on the double. The other trade unionist on the panel was Tom McKevitt, former deputy general secretary of the Public Service Executive Union. Olive Braiden, the chairperson of the first Justice PVG, was another familiar name on the body. Chairing the new benchmarking group was Dan O'Keeffe, a Senior Counsel who had been chairman of the stock exchange takeover panel. (After he completed the 2007 benchmarking report, O'Keeffe would be elevated by the government to the High Court.) The employers were represented by Willie Slattery of State Street, a US-based financial services holding company, and John Malone, former general secretary of the Department of Agriculture.

On this occasion the mandatory economist was Brendan Walsh, emeritus professor of economics at UCD. He did not follow Jim O'Leary's lead and jump ship, but the second body was operating in different times: by 2007 restraint, not generosity, was the government's motto. Besides, Bertie and Brian Cowen had just won an election, and they wanted cover for a skinflint settlement. They needed a report that preached the virtues of the hairshirt as the economic storm clouds gathered.

Despite the different climate, the fees paid to the benchmarkers were staggering. Chairman Dan O'Keeffe charged the taxpayer €2,000 a day plus €35,000 as a 'reading fee', according to a well-documented piece by Maeve Sheehan in the *Sunday Independent*. He eventually took €379,000 in fees for chairing the body. Attley, Braiden, McKevitt and the rest were paid €30,000 a year for a gig that lasted a month short of two years. Partnership was again lining the pockets of a few politically favoured old reliables.

Meanwhile, nearly all the top union leaders were landing handy part-time state positions. Peter McLoone, boss of the public-service union IMPACT, not only held the chair at FÁS for €24,000 a year but was appointed a director of the Labour Relations Commission at €14,000 a year. Senator Joe O'Toole finished up his term as president of ICTU, only to find himself on the board of the Irish Auditing and Accounting Supervisory Authority at around €9,000 a year and as the ICTU nominee on the Personal Injuries Assessment Board at a fee rising to €14,000 in 2008. Christy Kirwan, formerly head of the Irish Transport and General Workers Union, had earlier totted up several other semi-state board posts including Aer Rianta and the chair of FÁS; he even landed a Taoiseach's nomination to the Senate courtesy of Labour leader Dick Spring as far back as 1983. SIPTU's

Patricia King, another loyal survivor of the 2002 PVGs, notched up lucrative terms on the RTÉ Authority and the National Roads Authority. Hardly a union leader with a partnership pedigree was forgotten.

One particularly useful vehicle for rewarding social-partnership veterans in the twilight of their careers was the office of rights commissioner. Rights commissioners were creatures of the Labour Relations Commission, established under partnership deals to 'promote the improvement of industrial relations'. The LRC's first chief was Kieran Mulvey – a former general secretary of the powerful teachers union ASTI – who in 1989 had sought a nomination for Fianna Fáil in the Dun Laoghaire–Rathdown constituency; its board included not only Peter McLoone and Peter Bunting of ICTU but also Brendan McGinty of IBEC. Rights commissioners were appointed to investigate workers' grievances under various acts of the Oireachtas. By 2008 their number had expanded to fifteen after a promise made to ICTU in the most recent partnership agreement, 'Towards 2016'. In April 2010 the Rights Commissioner Service admitted to us that in 2009 each commissioner was paid a per diem fee of €470. The spokesman also noted, incomprehensibly, that most commissioners 'work a five-day-week basis, others choose to operate a lesser regime in terms of availability'. Those who work the five days receive €2,350 a week for their trouble, comfortably exceeding €100,000 a year.

An examination of the names of those appointed rights commissioners throws up some usual suspects from the second division of the trade unions.

Joan Carmichael is one of the chosen ones. She has been assistant general secretary of ICTU and a member of the Equality Authority, the NESC and the National Competitiveness Council. Carmichael's fellow commissioners include Gaye Cunningham, who retired from the ESB after thirty-four years' service in 2007. She was secretary of the Women's Committee of ICTU. In 1989 Cunningham was appointed to the Employment Appeals Tribunal by Bertie Ahern. According to a farewell tribute made to Cunningham at the ESB, she was 'a true advocate of partnership and developed a very constructive partnership group in Poolbeg'.

The Rights Commission begins to sound like a gentle retirement home for those who have passed the social-partnership loyalty test.

Carmichael, Cunningham and their fellow champions of the underdog drew more than three times the average wage for their devotions, even though few boasted legal qualifications.

Joan Carmichael's attachment to social partnership extended to Europe. From 1998 to 2006 she served two terms as a member of the European Economic and Social Committee (EESC). This mysterious committee is a fascinating feature of social partnership. Its outgoing Irish membership in 2010 featured a list of battle-hardened social partners who had been put out to grass.

First on the list was none other than Billy Attley. Attley, who was last nominated to the EESC in 2005 by none other than his old buddy Bertie Ahern, somehow manages to find time, despite all his other activities on behalf of the state, to travel to the capitals of Europe representing Ireland at this energy-sapping committee.

For the past four years he has been accompanied on his tireless voyages by Sally Anne Kinahan, assistant general secretary of ICTU. He probably knows Kinahan pretty well as they were both members of the board of FÁS. She was a happy camper at the Equality Authority and served her time at NESC as well.

Among the other former partnership hotshots who have done time on the EESC are Frank Allen, former president of the Irish Creamery Milk Suppliers Association; Brian Callanan, former director of IBEC; John Dillon, former president of the IFA; and Jim McCusker, former general secretary of the Northern Ireland Public Service Alliance. Making up the numbers are Heidi Lougheed, head of IBEC (Europe); Thomas McDonogh, a big builder's supplier from Galway; Jillian van Turnhout of the Children's Rights Alliance; Fianna Fáil fundraiser Roy Donovan; John Carroll, former president of the ITGWU; and John Freeman, former president of ICTU.

The committee meets nine times a year in plenary session. Travel expenses are covered. The daily allowance for days on which they

Seán Lemass (*left*, as Minister for Industry and Commerce, with the secretary of the department, John Leydon, and his private secretary, Tadhg O'Carroll, on a transatlantic trade mission) spearheaded the creation of state industries with a mixture of idealism and pragmatism; today, the sector is bedevilled by cronyism and waste

Bernie Cahill, the Fine Gael-appointed Irish Sugar chairman who became pals with Charles Haughey and survived as chairman of Greencore, despite the company's botched privatization

Noel Hanlon, who exercised power on a number of state boards, most notably at the deeply politicized airport authority Aer Rianta

Bertie Ahern with Celia Larkin, his one-time life partner,
whose appointment to the board of the National Consumer
Agency torpedoed the credibility of the fledgling quango

Des Richardson, a
key figure in Bertie
Ahern's Drumcondra
Mafia and Bertie's
eyes and ears on the
Aer Lingus board

FÁS Director-General Rody Molloy at a jobs fair with Bertie Ahern in 2008 – not long before Molloy's career imploded over junketeering at the agency and Ahern resigned under pressure arising from his financial arrangements

The authors, who broke the story of the culture of junketeering at FÁS, outside the agency's headquarters in Dublin

Mary Harney and Brian Geoghegan at the wedding of Ryanair boss Michael O'Leary to Anita Farrell in County Westmeath in 2003

Health Service Executive chief executive Professor Brendan Drumm (*centre*), accompanied by press officer Alex Connolly (*left*) and adviser Karl Anderson (*right*). Press officers and advisers were thick on the ground in the HSE during Drumm's tenure

Bertie Ahern flying in style on a government jet. Despite being under pressure in relation to his hard-to-explain financial arrangements, Ahern pursued an extraordinary programme of junkets in the dying weeks of his tenure as Taoiseach

John O'Donoghue's travels as 'Minister for Fun' took him to sporting and cultural events in some of the most salubrious corners of the globe – but let it not be said that he did not also heroically turn out to race meetings on blustery days at the Curragh, as he did here in 2005

Minister for Transport Noel Dempsey (*left*) with John Lynch, executive chairman of CIÉ, which has been exposed as a hotbed of waste and dubious practices

Des Geraghty (*second from right*), the SIPTU head and quango king, at a riveting trade union event

George Redmond alighting from a prison van at the Mahon Tribunal at Dublin Castle in 2004. As assistant city and county manager for Dublin, Redmond signed the agreement for the controversial West Link toll bridge

Pádraig Flynn (*right*) with Albert Reynolds at Croke Park. Flynn signed the West Link agreement on behalf of the government

Bertie Ahern embraces Lar Bradshaw, chairman of the Dublin Docklands Development Authority (and future Anglo Irish Bank director), at the launch of the Grand Canal Harbour project in 2000

U2 frontman Bono with Peter Coyne, then head of the Dublin Docklands Development Authority, at the launch of a design competition for the U2 Tower in 2002. The entries to the competition were at one stage lost by the DDDA, and the project has been shelved

Light at the end of the tunnel for NAMA chairman Frank Daly and Taoiseach Brian Cowen? Not a chance. This photo was taken in March 2008, when Daly was still chairman of the Revenue Commissioners and Cowen was still Tánaiste and Minister for Finance, at the opening of the Revenue Museum at The Crypt in Dublin Castle. Two years later, NAMA started looking at the toxic assets it had bought with taxpayers' money from the banks – and realized they were even more toxic than they'd imagined

Minister for Finance Brian Lenihan with NAMA chief executive Brendan McDonagh

meet is €233, while an extra €145 is given per diem for what are known as 'travel days'. The committee has numerous subcommittees that meet all over Europe at various times of the year. It even has an old boys and girls association for former members.

The 'Association of Former Members of the EESC' is blessed with secretarial support and holds a 'fact-finding' trip every year. Last year they headed to Riga and Vilnius for a four-day visit. The theme of the trip was 'Financial crisis, employment, wages, economic developments, financing of business'.

UCD and Maynooth have seen fit to bestow honorary doctorates upon the most distinguished of the social-partnership junkies; but the quangsters also have their very own seat of learning.

The National College of Ireland (NCI) began its existence in Ranelagh in 1951. Originally the Jesuit-run Catholic Workers College, in 1966 it was renamed the National College of Industrial Relations and, according to its website, 'assumed an educational leadership role in workforce development, industrial relations and social justice issues'. In 1998 it changed its name again, to the National College of Ireland, and soon relocated to the International Financial Services Centre (IFSC).

From Catholic workers to industrial relations to international financial services may sound like a long and winding journey, but the NCI's progress merely symbolized the arrival of the social-partnership industry and its apostles at the highest level of the Irish establishment. This is reflected in conferral ceremonies every year. Among the trade unionists who have dressed themselves up to look like hen pheasants to receive honorary fellowships are our old friends Billy Attley and Christy Kirwan. Attley even made it on to the NCI's governing body along with another FÁS old boy, IMPACT's Peter McLoone. On the employers' side, the NCI has awarded fellowships to IBEC heads such as Gary McGann, Tony Barry, Maurice Healy and Patrick Wright.

On the day in December 2005 that Attley received his award, the citation was presented by former Taoiseach Albert Reynolds. Also picking up a scroll at the same ceremony was Paddy Kelly, the developer who had built the NCI's IFSC campus, and who later went bust owing hundreds of millions of euros to the state-owned Anglo Irish Bank and other financial institutions.

The only politician ever to have been anointed with an honorary fellowship from the NCI was none other than Ireland's champion of partnership and cronyism: Bertie Ahern.

7. Off the Rails

It was close to midnight when the phone rang at Shane Ross's home one evening in early September 2009. It was not unusual for nutcases to ring journalists after hours with tales of skullduggery – ever since the FÁS scandal had broken headbangers with all kinds of grudges had been ringing us with stories – but midnight was a bit late for anyone to call. Still, curiosity got the better of Shane. He picked up the phone.

The female voice on the other end of the line was stressed and urgent. 'I have a massive story for you,' volunteered the midnight caller.

'Who is calling?'

'Just call me Maggie,' insisted the voice. 'Listen to me for a minute. If you think FÁS was bad, this is worse. There is corruption, graft and theft in CIÉ.'

The tone was not altogether unfamiliar. The FÁS orgy of waste and extravagance nearly a year earlier had triggered a wave of semi-state malcontents eager to air the injustices inflicted upon them by their employers.

Shane asked for evidence.

'No problem,' the caller responded. 'I have it in front of me. You will not believe your eyes.'

'Go on.'

The caller told Shane that she had a report, compiled by the accountancy firm Baker Tilly Ryan Glennon, that CIÉ had tried to bury.

The story began to sound more promising. Shane had never heard of the Baker Tilly report – the news of its very existence was a show-stopper.

'What is in this report?' asked Shane.

'Dynamite. And it is top secret.'

As it turned out, the whistleblower was telling the truth on both counts.

The report was so 'top secret' that neither the board of CIÉ nor the Minister for Transport, Noel Dempsey, had ever caught sight of it. The minister did not even know of its existence.

Nick, Shane and Maggie arranged to meet the next day at a discreet location in the vicinity of Leinster House. Maggie telephoned from an unidentifiable mobile before arriving, giving a brief description of her appearance and clothing.

She was understandably nervous. Nearing retirement, she was well known to staff at Iarnród Éireann, the CIÉ rail subsidiary that was the source of the corruption documented in the report. To protect her identity we can say no more about her, except that she is not a dismissed or unhappy employee with a personal axe to grind. She was simply disgusted with the corruption at her place of work and the failure to stamp it out.

The report she handed us that day was a heavy tome, initially indigestible, but on a second reading the message became clear.

The report's initial priority was to spell out the importance of its own secrecy. The first page was pure cloak and dagger. Headed 'CONFIDENTIALITY', it insisted that the report was only for the benefit of the three-man Iarnród Éireann steering committee.

As we waded through the pages it became clear that they were never meant to see the light of day. And more than one year after it was completed, it had been seen by only a handful of trusted confidants of the top brass in Iarnród Éireann.

Baker Tilly had been asked by the Iarnród Éireann steering committee to ascertain the extent of the abuses. According to Iarnród Éireann chief executive Dick Fearn, the steering committee originally consisted of himself as chairman, human resources boss John Keenan and chief financial officer Richard O'Farrell, later to be replaced by Aidan Cronin.

The findings were damning. Baker Tilly reported corruption, theft, kickbacks, bogus orders, manipulation of contracts and a host of abuses at Iarnród Éireann. The word 'fraud' appeared with alarming frequency. Procurement policy was a shambles because collusion with vendors was rife. It was mind-boggling stuff. This was a state company receiving over €300 million a year as a subsidy, some of which had been finding its way into the pockets of criminals.

Specifically, Baker Tilly found that some employees were 'manipulating transactions so that they remain within their procurement authority thus enabling them to appoint their chosen contractor. There is a high likelihood of collusion between one of the [key maintenance staff] and one of the vendors.' The report told of a 'serious breach' of procurement policy, as large-volume transactions were manipulated in such a way as to bypass controls. It noted that its investigation had been hindered by missing and faulty documentation.

In one case, an unsuccessful tenderer for the removal of soil from a development site owned by CIÉ in the Dublin docklands sent in invoices that were paid, although the company never did a minute's work on the project. The 'mistake' cost Iarnród Éireann several hundred thousand euro and exposed it to the loss of €257,000 in European Union grants because its behaviour was in breach of European rules on procurement.

Under the heading 'Collusion with Contractors' Baker Tilly highlighted an instance where an inspector had been signing fraudulent timesheets and requesting labour and plant hire when not required.

We were flabbergasted by the report's findings. We had heard rumours over the years of a handy little racket involving the theft of sleepers, but never suspected an endemic procurement problem. Yet this was the message of the report.

We initially resolved that we would publish the contents of the leaked report, and that Shane, as a Senator, would seek an early meeting of the Joint Oireachtas Committee on Transport to question the CIÉ and Iarnród Éireann boards about Baker Tilly's findings.

In the 11 October edition of the *Sunday Independent* we published the bones of what Maggie had given to us, under the headline 'Kickbacks, Waste and Bogus Orders Costing CIÉ Millions'.

CIÉ did not deny the story. Instead it sent out the spinners to pooh-pooh it, suggesting that the semi-state was well on top of implementing Baker Tilly's 156 recommendations, that there was nothing new in the report and that the *Sunday Independent* story had been a massive exaggeration.

A witch hunt then started in CIÉ to determine the source of the leak. To this day they have not come within an ass's roar of identifying Maggie.

Minister Noel Dempsey called CIÉ boss John Lynch and ordered him to publish Baker Tilly's report in full. The guts of a week was spent deleting what the state body claimed were commercially sensitive passages. Copies of the report, which ran to 220 pages, were available for TDs and Senators in the Oireachtas Library on 27 October, just a few hours before the transport committee was due to interview Lynch, Dick Fearn and CIÉ's PR man Barry Kenny about its contents.

When the report was finally lodged in the Dáil Library it was riddled with deletions. Whole pages of relevant facts and figures were blacked out. Happily, we held in our hands the original, unredacted report. We knew exactly what was typed under all those blacked-out bits. Even more happily, we had in our possession an earlier draft, from May 2008. Baker Tilly had estimated much higher figures for losses from corrupt practices in the earlier draft than had appeared in the final version: €8.7 million versus €2.6 million.

Why was the June figure for corruption-related losses so much lower than the May one?

Billed to appear before the Oireachtas committee was John Lynch, executive chairman of CIÉ and also chairman of its two big subsidiaries, Iarnród Éireann and Dublin Bus. Lynch brought along a far lesser mortal in the shape of Iarnród Éireann chief executive Dick Fearn, and an even lesser mortal again in Barry Kenny, spinner for all three companies.

John Lynch is a colossus of the semi-states, a clever operator without parallel in the sector. One ex-director who served on the board of CIÉ with Lynch described him to us as being 'completely in charge'. Another said that the only law in CIÉ was 'Lynch Law'. Equally significantly, the same director muttered that Lynch meticulously maintained excellent contacts with politicians.

John Lynch, bachelor and football fan, was a Christian Brothers boy who graduated from UCD before picking up a Ph.D. in manufacturing strategy from Trinity. After a seven-year spell as director of business policy at the Confederation of Irish Industry, he hit the quango gravy train. First he landed a job as boss of the Irish Productivity Centre, then one as chief executive of An Bord Gáis, before making an unusual, and possibly unique, switch from the chair to the director-general's job at FÁS in 1990. According to the *Irish Times* of 29 December, 'the appointment of the chairman of FÁS, John Lynch, to be its chief executive was not without some angst. The post was advertised last summer when the incumbent, Brendan Leahy, announced that he was leaving for a job in the tourism industry. Naturally enough, chairman Lynch sat on the interview board for the short-listed candidates. Not so usual was the fact that the interview board could not agree to make an appointment from among the candidates. Then Lynch's name was suggested and since he could hardly interview himself, the board was reconstituted and the Minister for Labour, Bertie Ahern, duly ratified Lynch as chief executive.'

Little analysis has yet been done on Lynch's tenure at FÁS because the organization only became subject to Freedom of Information requests in 2001, a year after Lynch had left.

On 28 March 2010 Lynch, aged sixty-eight and mired in controversy, was given a one-year extension to his term as executive chairman of CIÉ by Noel Dempsey. Five days later, Dempsey posted a press release on his website saying that Iarnród Éireann trains were on their way to Navan via an extension of the commuter line to Dunboyne, and claiming the credit. Both Lynch and Dempsey enjoyed a good week.

Lynch's closeness to politicians was never more evident than when he jumped from the FÁS frying pan into the CIÉ cauldron. He negotiated a unique deal that put his successor Rody Molloy's later payoff in the shade.

As Lynch departed from FÁS in 2000 he was handed a sudden salary boost, from €98,000 a year to €117,200 – a hike that gave him the salary he'd have been on had he served at that level for forty years, rather than the seventeen he'd actually served; this, therefore, gave a substantial boost to his pension, which was based on his final salary. The deal was topped up with a lump sum of €138,430, again, based on forty, rather than seventeen, years' service. While he was working for CIÉ he was receiving the increased pension of €105,000 a year achieved as a result of his late pay hike at FÁS. He secured a special arrangement solely for himself through a one-off statutory instrument signed by Minister for Finance Charlie McCreevy and Minister for Enterprise, Trade and Employment Mary Harney. Lynch had a knack for winning favours from politicians.

Even more fascinating was the identity of the civil servant responsible for the generous FÁS pension package given to Lynch: none other than his successor at FÁS, the man later to be deposed as chief executive for his extravagance, Rody Molloy.

Lynch also cultivated journalists. He understood exactly what made both management and ordinary hacks tick, and he was not above making protests to newspaper bosses when the journalists' copy was critical of himself or his organization.

He made one less than glorious appearance at the Mahon Tribunal investigation into planning controversies, strongly denying that he had arranged a junket to London for a councillor (also a FÁS employee), thus enabling the man to miss a vote on the controversial Quarryvale development in Dublin. Lynch was a friend of Cork developer Owen O'Callaghan, who was behind the Quarryvale project, later to become the Liffey Valley shopping centre. The two had been directors of Bord Gáis together. Lynch was also quizzed about alleged calls that he had made to Frank Dunlop, the lobbyist who was working as a consultant to O'Callaghan at the time. Lynch insisted that the calls had nothing to do with sending the councillor on a junket, but might have concerned O'Callaghan's idea of putting a FÁS centre in the Quarryvale development.

It was a battle-hardened Lynch, a veteran of quango wars, who came to the Oireachtas transport committee on 27 October prepared to explain the mysteries surrounding the Baker Tilly report. He read an opening statement that was robust in its attack on our *Sunday Independent* story. CIÉ investigations had already found that only three out of 11,300 employees had been involved in the corruption. The picture of backhanders and graft portrayed in the media was 'inaccurate, grossly insulting and a serious misrepresentation'. And, in a rousing scripted finale, he declared, 'Iarnród Éireann, not Baker Tilly Ryan Glennon, identified these issues and took the necessary steps to address them. We commissioned Baker Tilly to ascertain whether our systems were sufficiently robust. We did this to ensure that we deliver value for money, to protect our reputation and to defend the good name of our workforce. The actions of a tiny minority should not take from the good name of the rest of the workforce.'

Senator Ross quizzed Lynch about the board's level of awareness of the Baker Tilly investigation and its eventual findings.

SENATOR SHANE ROSS: Therefore the board was aware of what was going on in Baker Tilly at all times?

DR JOHN LYNCH: The board was aware through the finance and audit committee.

SENATOR SHANE ROSS: Therefore, both boards [i.e. the boards of both CIÉ and Iarnród Éireann] were in touch at all times with that. When did they get the Baker Tilly report?

DR JOHN LYNCH: When it came out.

SENATOR SHANE ROSS: Both boards got the Baker Tilly Report in June 2008, is that correct? If we have board members in before the committee, is that what they will tell us?

DR JOHN LYNCH: The finance and audit committee of the CIÉ board would have got it a little later because the Iarnród Éireann one was digesting it at the particular time.

SENATOR SHANE ROSS: When did the full board of both companies get it?

DR JOHN LYNCH: Probably four, five or six months afterwards.

SENATOR SHANE ROSS: Why did it take so long?

DR JOHN LYNCH: They were digesting the report in –

SENATOR SHANE ROSS: Is it correct that the full board got it in the end?

DR JOHN LYNCH: Yes.

Bingo. An unambiguous statement from the executive chairman. A few weeks later, however, we would be told something very different.

Senator Ross also asked Lynch why the Baker Tilly report had not been sent to the Minister for Transport.

DR JOHN LYNCH: Ministers decide policy. If I was to go to the minister with every single conceivable problem I have, I would never leave his office.

SENATOR SHANE ROSS: This is not a minor matter. It is serious . . . How much did the report cost, in total, by the way?

DICK FEARN: I do not have that figure in front of me. Three or four companies were approached and Baker Tilly won it by competitive tender.

DR JOHN LYNCH: The figure was roughly €50,000.

At this point Dr Lynch went into a huddle with Barry Kenny, his PR man.

DR JOHN LYNCH: Excuse me, I am told the figure is €450,000.

In fact the total figure, including VAT, was €499,632.

SENATOR SHANE ROSS: If Dr Lynch is prepared to spend €500,000 on an investigation, he must think there is something serious going on.

DR JOHN LYNCH: I would like to come back to the senator with regard to that figure.

SENATOR SHANE ROSS: Is it right or wrong?

DR JOHN LYNCH: I do not know.

SENATOR SHANE ROSS: To begin with, Dr Lynch said it was €50,000. When he was prompted he said it was €500,000.

DR JOHN LYNCH: The answer is that I do not know.

SENATOR SHANE ROSS: Mr Fearn said he did not know.

DR JOHN LYNCH: I was prompted. I do not know. We will check it out before we leave.

SENATOR SHANE ROSS: It is astonishing. I have never heard of a report costing that much.

The May 2008 draft report had been given to the Iarnród Éireann steering committee. Its findings were sensational. It calculated that the monetary loss to the organization from a litany of malpractices was €8,671,468.

What happened at the meeting of the three-man steering committee when they were given this unwelcome May draft report is crucial.

Dick Fearn agreed at the transport committee in October 2009 that he was given the €8.7 million figure by Baker Tilly in the earlier May 2008 draft report, but insisted that he had not sought a 'guesstimate' based on what the losses would have been if the issues had occurred elsewhere. Fearn is adamant that the steering committee had sought only a figure for actual loss. His favoured figure for this was €2.6 million. He says he gave the consultants 'clarification' of his wishes after he received the €8.7 million figure in the May draft, declaring that he did not want 'guesstimates'. Not even from forensic accountants. Baker Tilly obediently dropped the €8.7 million figure in accordance with the wishes of the men paying them the 450 grand.

But Baker Tilly insisted on giving a coded explanation of their views on Fearn's position. 'Following receipt of clarification on our Terms of Reference from the Chief Executive of the Steering Group [Fearn], we can confirm that we consider it impossible to assess the full extent of ACTUAL loss suffered by the Company in the period from 2004 to date, through breaches of procedures. This is due to the sheer volume of transactions which have taken place, the lack of information (reports) and underlying data . . . We have provided a monetary assessment of actual loss found (€2.6 million) and consider, based on our findings, that there is a higher likelihood that further loss occurred in the period under review.'

No one has disputed the accuracy of the €2.6 million figure, nor the authenticity of the €8.7 million figure: the two numbers reflected two different, but valid, calculations. The only point at issue is why the €8.7 million figure was dropped from the final report. It could have been helpful to the boards of both Iarnród Éireann and CIÉ, to the minister and to the wider public. But Fearn and Lynch did not want it to gain a wider audience.

The €8.7 million figure might never have seen the light of day had it not been for Maggie. At one point in the committee hearing, Fearn strenuously denied accusations that Iarnród Éireann had 'whitewashed' the report.

SENATOR SHANE ROSS: The draft was buried because its figures were inconvenient.

DEPUTY FERGUS O'DOWD: It was bloody well buried.

DICK FEARN: It is not a case of it being buried, it was not correct.

DR JOHN LYNCH: Through the chair, can we tone things down a bit? Someone wants to give an answer and we would be obliged if the answer could be provided.

Suddenly a Fianna Fáil voice rode to Lynch's rescue. Deputy Timmy Dooley – like Lynch, a favourite of Bertie Ahern's – entered the debate.

DEPUTY TIMMY DOOLEY: With respect they are playing to the cameras. They are trying to get on the *Six One News*. They are doing well in that regard.

DR JOHN LYNCH: Mr Fearn has been interrupted three times when he has endeavoured to answer.

The pressure came off as friendly Fianna Fáil faces began to ask various questions mostly unrelated to the Baker Tilly report. Deputy Michael Kennedy asked about computers, Senator John Ellis and Deputy Dooley lobbed the CIÉ duo softballs, and Deputy Thomas Byrne of Meath queried them on the price of tickets from Laytown in his Meath constituency to Dublin.

Lynch, Fearn and the rest of the CIÉ gang were bruised, but off the hook. They were due back for another round on 16 December.

Fergus O'Dowd and Shane Ross felt that human resources boss John Keenan alone could clarify what had happened behind closed doors between Lynch, Fearn, O'Farrell (before he moved jobs) and himself on the issue. Keenan was Iarnród Éireann's leading crusader against corruption. A bearded trade unionist, he had been a member of the Labour Party in chief whip Emmet Stagg's Kildare North constituency. At Iarnród Éireann he was constantly in hot pursuit of those suspected of being guilty of the theft of railway sleepers, breaches of procurement rules and other abuses. For obvious reasons he was far from universally popular with his colleagues or with some employees. If, as we suspected from our investigations, he was a dissenter from the decision to make the €8.7 million figure disappear, he would surely tell us as a witness at a future meeting.

At the same time we resolved to widen the investigation. We wanted to interview Baker Tilly partner George Maloney, the non-executive directors of both CIÉ and Iarnród Éireann, and finally the Minister for Transport, Noel Dempsey. But John Keenan, we felt, was the key.

We dug in for a series of transport committee meetings over the coming months with a long line of witnesses in mind.

George Maloney was the first person we wanted to question. He was due to appear on 16 December but contacted the committee to say he could not attend on that day because he was due in the Supreme Court in relation to another matter.

On the evening of 3 December, Shane Ross and Nick Webb both received urgent telephone calls from sources within CIÉ: a rumour was circulating that a member of staff had been suspended for leaking the Baker Tilly report.

Our hearts sank. Had our source been rumbled? In fact, the rumour we'd heard had been garbled. What had really happened was that John Keenan had been suspended by Dick Fearn. The reason given to Keenan was that he had taken ten days to report Iarnród Éireann's loss of an employment case at the Equality Tribunal to Fearn. The result of the case was a serious setback for Iarnród Éireann and Keenan. A female employee had been awarded €189,000 compensation for victimization and discrimination on grounds of gender. As director of human resources Keenan was in the front line. (A complaint against him for harassment was not upheld.)

Inside Iarnród Éireann the news was greeted with disbelief. Keenan had joined CIÉ when he left school. He had risen through the ranks to become the top man at human resources and head of the cost audit unit. In this role he had led the fight against fraud in the company.

In 2005 Keenan had spearheaded the discovery of a web of collusion between some contractors and employees suspected of defrauding the company. As a result of the activities of Keenan's unit, the Gardaí were called in and employees were dismissed. It was on Keenan's recommendation that Baker Tilly had been engaged to review procurement procedures and suspect financial transactions. In one report to the CIÉ audit committee in 2007, Keenan had estimated that potential losses from these malpractices could run to a 'seven- or eight-figure sum'.

Keenan immediately sought a High Court injunction to reinstate him in his former position, and later lodged affidavits to support his case that his suspension was due more to his ruthless pursuit of wrongdoing in the company without fear or favour than to any perceived delay in communicating the result of the verdict at the Equality Tribunal. The affidavits painted a picture of simmering warfare between Keenan and the top brass, tracing a pattern of hostility dating back to the Baker Tilly draft report of May 2008, and confirmed our suspicions that he had been against the decision to dump the €8.7 million figure. Lethally, in a letter to Fearn on 13 November, three weeks before his suspension, he had stated: 'I dissented from the decision to delete an assessment of loss, reducing the overall estimate from €8.7 million to €2.5 million. You recalled in our conversation that I strongly advised against this.'

The 13 November letter to Fearn had been prompted by Keenan's shock removal from his post as head of the cost audit unit, two weeks after the Oireachtas committee had questioned the two senior CIÉ men.

According to Keenan's affidavits, in the week after the initial exposé by the *Sunday Independent* he received an irate call from John Lynch accusing him of leaking the contents to the newspaper.

After further articles in the *Sunday Independent*, his affidavits declare, he took another angry call from Lynch telling him to 'button' his lip. In the same call the 'chairman threatened to remove me from my post unless I made the appointment of a Deputy Director of Human Resources'.

According to Keenan he felt undermined. Lynch denies the allegations.

So, in the months prior to the Equality Tribunal findings against Iarnród Éireann, he maintains that he had clashed with his colleagues on the treatment of the figures in the Baker Tilly report; that he had been accused of leaking the Baker Tilly report to the *Sunday Independent*; and that he had been threatened with the loss of his job long before the Equality Tribunal case. On the other hand, Fearn is adamant that the delay in telling him about the Equality Tribunal's verdict against Keenan was the sole reason.

When the transport committee was recalled on 16 December, Fergus O'Dowd again went straight to the crux of the matter. He wanted to know more about whether any member of the three-man steering committee had disagreed with the removal of the €8.7 million figure from the final report. There was no doubt that he had Keenan in mind. Although no affidavits had been opened in court by this date, O'Dowd appeared to be well informed. It was obvious from his line of questioning that he had been talking to insiders.

An additional drama at the 16 December transport committee meeting revolved around Lynch's U-turn on his claim, in response to Senator Ross's questioning at the October meeting, that the Baker Tilly report had been circulated to the CIÉ board.

DR JOHN LYNCH: I should like to rectify my statement at the last meeting that the Baker Tilly Ryan Glennon report was circulated to other CIÉ board members. It was not.

SENATOR SANE ROSS: Will Dr Lynch repeat that?

DR LYNCH: Yes, I want to clarify and rectify my statement at the last meeting that the Baker Tilly Ryan Glennon report was circulated to other CIÉ board members. It was not. What I meant to convey was that the board was advised of the report and the relevant issue on a continual basis. I have since clarified that the issues were brought to the board's attention at the first available opportunity.

So that was that. The board had never been allowed sight of the Baker Tilly report. All they had received was a summary of the issues from a key member of the board, Bertie Ahern's old pal Paul Kiely.

In response to a further request that he attend the transport committee at a later date, Maloney – who had had to miss the 16 December meeting because of a court date – pleaded that he could not give evidence on this subject for reasons related to commercial confidentiality. Yet we felt Keenan could still give us the information we needed. A formal decision to ask him to appear was debated in a private session on 10 March.

Up to now Fianna Fáil transport committee members had been merely unenthusiastic about, but not directly opposed to, pursuing the visitors from Iarnród Éireann. It was time to flush them out. Shane Ross and Fergus O'Dowd brought a motion requesting Keenan to come before the committee in public session to answer questions about the crucial meeting in May 2008 between Dick Fearn, George Maloney, Richard O'Farrell and Keenan. The committee's voting bells were rung and, on a division, the government Oireachtas members – consisting of five Fianna Fáil members and Ciarán Cuffe of the Greens – entered the bowels of Leinster House to defeat the invitation to Keenan by six votes to four.

The Fianna Fáil members had pleaded that it was wrong to bring Keenan before the committee because the issue was sub judice. By their action they helped, in the words of Keenan's own submission to the court, to keep him 'off the pitch'. The CIÉ top brass must have been glad that the government representatives had prevented the possibility of Keenan spilling the beans all over Leinster House.

On 22 January, Judge John McMenamin had delivered a High Court judgment in response to Keenan's first legal salvo. The judge confirmed that CIÉ employee Monica Murphy had been awarded €189,000 by the Equality Tribunal in compensation for discrimination and victimization by Iarnród Éireann, and that the decision was already under appeal.

The judge found that there was now such a lack of trust between the two sides that an immediate restoration of Keenan to his former position would be impractical. He refused the application for Keenan to be restored to his job, but he gave no judgment on the strength of his case. Many of his remarks were sympathetic to Keenan's pleadings.

Keenan upped the stakes. He had employed two high-profile lawyers, namely Labour Party Seanad leader Alex White and Labour Party Dáil candidate Oisín Quinn. He headed, all guns blazing, towards a full hearing, though it was assumed that settlement talks were going on in the background. The potential for mutual destruction was obvious.

At the 7 April 2010 meeting of the transport committee John Lynch was asked for a date when his non-executive directors could attend a hearing for questioning. He muttered about some of them living abroad. He was a little nonplussed when it was pointed out that they managed to fly in for board meetings once a month.

Such evidence of CIÉ's refusal to accept accountability is everywhere. After Nick Webb and Shane Ross put a series of specific questions to the company in November 2009, we received the following brush-off: 'We note your continuing biased and inaccurate reporting of the issues arising from our investigations into and actions taken on the area of Procurement and Internal controls. We will not be responding to these queries.'

Some of those questions related to board members. Some addressed the thorny topic of expenses or tackled businesses named in the draft Baker Tilly report, notably a client company of CIÉ known as KN Network Services.

CIÉ's frosty responses led us to believe that we were coming a little too close to the bone. We had heard stories of lavish hospitality being laid on for powerful CIÉ employees with lucrative contracts in their gift. CIÉ was not like FÁS, givers of largesse to their clients as a cover for enjoying the good life themselves. They were takers of it. When we probed this area, the shutters came down. The executives did not want this little genie escaping from the bottle.

So we went in search of CIÉ's directors – the noble guardians of the people's interests, the geniuses who had signed off on the accounts.

Who were they? How much did they know? And how much are they paid by the taxpayer for their task?

The board of CIÉ is a peach. It would make a classic case for a seminar on corporate-governance howlers.

Start with Lynch, the executive chairman. Back in December 2008 he told the Dáil's PAC that he had resigned from FÁS because 'I feel in any job, any less than five years or any more than ten years is more than sufficient.' Yet fifteen months later, in March 2010, he happily entered his eleventh year as executive chairman of CIÉ.

Lynch has eleven colleagues on the board, three of them worker directors. Who were the other eight, we wondered? And what expertise did they have in transport affairs?

Initially it was impossible to tell. The annual report, in what must be a uniquely contemptuous gesture, refuses to reveal anything about the board. The directors for 2008 are listed on page eighteen. No Christian names, just initials and surnames. No CVs. No photographs. They could all be escaped convicts from Mountjoy for all the information provided.

Finding out about them has proved fascinating. We have already met 'P. Kiely' – Paul Kiely of the Drumcondra Mafia and simultaneous holder of the chair of the CIÉ audit committee, finance committee and remuneration committee – in Chapter 2. First port of call to inquire about Kiely's qualifications for these responsible positions was CIÉ itself. Their public-relations department eventually provided us with brief CVs for the entire board. Paul's was a one-liner: 'Paul Kiely is chief executive of the Central Remedial Clinic, a position he has held since 1988.'

We decided to pursue Kiely's credentials with a little more vigour. At the transport committee meeting on 27 October, Shane Ross put a question to John Lynch about Kiely's qualifications. CIÉ's finances were opaque, to say the least, so it was important to ascertain that Kiely, the chairman of the audit committee, was not an amateur accountant.

SENATOR SHANE ROSS: What does Mr Paul Kiely do to merit being chairman of such a large audit committee?

DR JOHN LYNCH: He is an accountant and chief executive of the Central
   Remedial Clinic.
SENATOR SHANE ROSS: Is he an accountant like Bertie Ahern was
   an accountant or is he a real accountant? He is a friend of Deputy
   Ahern.
DR JOHN LYNCH: I do not know.
SENATOR SHANE ROSS: What qualifications does he have?
DR JOHN LYNCH: As far as I know he is ACCA.

Three months later Shane Ross rang Paul Kiely to ask what
accountancy qualifications he had to merit his position as chairman
of the CIÉ audit committee.

Kiely replied that he had none. He was an amateur, after all. Lynch
had been gilding the lily.

Kiely has served as chairman of the audit committee throughout
nearly the entire period of Lynch's term as executive chairman. It
would be reasonable to expect an executive chairman to ensure that
the key audit boss in such a vast company – with an annual budget of
around a billion euros – had the qualifications needed to read a balance sheet. Surely a qualified accountant or auditor could more easily
mix it with the forensic accountants at Baker Tilly than a friend of
Bertie Ahern who runs a rehab clinic?

Kiely has now been on the board since 1998, for even longer than
Lynch, although to be fair to him he has never – unlike Lynch – said
that ten years at any one job is enough.

At one stage in 2009 there were only two members on the notion-
ally four-person audit committee: Kiely in the chair, and beside him
a man the annual report refers to as 'Mr N. Ormond'.

And who is Mr N. Ormond?

A question from Shane Ross and Nick Webb to CIÉ about
Mr N. Ormond prompted the following response. 'Neil Ormond is
a retired former HR director of Jacobs Ireland. Previously he worked
extensively for the Bovril Group in the UK, including as head of
production.'

There was no indication that he could read a balance sheet, but we
had seen far less qualified people serving on state boards.

A little digging revealed that 'Mr N. Ormond' had other interesting qualifications. He was a dyed-in-the-wool Fianna Fáil supporter. He had sought a Fianna Fáil nomination for the Dáil in the late seventies and been a member of the party's national executive. His sister Ann is a long-time Fianna Fáil senator and constituency supporter of the late Séamus Brennan, the former transport minister. His brother Donie was a Fianna Fáil TD. Ormond and Kiely must have thought they were at a meeting of a Dublin Fianna Fáil cumann, not an audit committee, when they sat around shooting the breeze with the Baker Tilly report in their hands. It is hard to imagine that the mighty PricewaterhouseCoopers, external auditors to CIÉ, would have been shivering in their shoes as they approached the annual review of their stewardship of the CIÉ accounts with the two Soldiers of Destiny firing the questions.

These two Fianna Fáil loyalists were the only members of the CIÉ audit committee to last the full course during the Baker Tilly controversy. In early 2009 Mary Canniffe, an employee of the Financial Regulator, resigned for unexplained reasons, leaving the audit committee at half strength for six months. (The other vacancy was created by the retirement a year earlier of John Sorohan, the former chairman of RTÉ.)

Eventually Lynch filled one of the vacancies by installing a man called Dermot Killen. Killen ticked a few of the right boxes. The minimalist reply we received about his career from the CIÉ spinners revealed that he had been employed by the Smurfit Group in the past. His blurb spoofed endlessly about those experiences. It omitted to mention that back in the eighties he had been an old comrade of none other than John Lynch at the Irish Productivity Centre, a FÁS-like joint employer–union body set up in 1972 to promote greater productivity. It died a natural death in 2004.

The last man appointed to fill a gap on the audit committee was a guy called Graham Lightfoot. Although he had arrived on the board of CIÉ in April 2008, he was not appointed to the audit committee until long after the row over the Baker Tilly report had hit the public arena.

Our queries about Lightfoot left little space for manoeuvring by the spinners. Lightfoot was a Green Party nominee. Unlike nearly all his colleagues, he seems to sport one or two transport qualifications. His CV states that he has lectured widely on community transport, and that he is a board member of Sustainable Projects Ireland, which is building Ireland's first Eco Village in Cloughjordan, north Tipperary. He is a member of the Chartered Institute of Logistics and Transport Ireland and has a B.Sc. in Transport Management and Planning.

Lightfoot is likely to make all those hard-headed Fianna Fáil followers feel deeply uncomfortable as he shows off his knowledge of sustainable transport at board meetings. He appears to be one of the few directors who would recognize the difference between the back of a bus and a lorryload of stolen railway sleepers. Consequently Lightfoot must be hopelessly out of the loop on the CIÉ board.

CIÉ eventually provided us with superficially plausible, but painfully incomplete, career histories of the other directors. 'S. Sheerin' pricked a few memory cells. Surely, we thought, this could not be the same 'S. Sheerin' who had left AIB in a blaze of publicity five years earlier after a bitter dispute over foreign-exchange overcharging?

It was. Seamus Sheerin was the man who had claimed he was being 'scapegoated' by AIB. He took the bank to the steps of the High Court. The case was settled. Sheerin ended up on the board of CIÉ, appointed in 2008.

What was interesting about Seamus Sheerin was not his battle with AIB, in which he may well have been in the right. Rather, what was interesting was that he had given a €1,000 donation to the political war chest of Brian Cowen, then Minister for Finance, in 2006, and that his Capital Securities Corporation had its head office in Tullamore, in the heart of Cowen's constituency.

The Baker Tilly report's scope was severely limited. It examined procurement of plant hire between 2004 and 2007; it reported on the flourishing cottage industry of thieving rails and sleepers; it identified

breaches of procurement procedures, neglect of duty and misappro-
priation. It looked at what it called the 'relationship with contractors
of goods'. Its probe was restricted to a small part of CIÉ. It did not
investigate procurement practices beyond the Infrastructure Maintenance, Signals and New Works divisions. Baker Tilly noted that
the annual spend of the areas under review came in at €250 million, a
figure that would have amounted to less than 22 per cent of CIÉ's
total spend for the year.

While CIÉ was frantically attempting to peddle the message that
the cost was small, the company clean and the problem confined to a
tiny corner of the semi-state, Nick Webb and Shane Ross were being
regaled with tales of further embarrassing losses in other parts of the
massive semi-state.

In early January 2010 we were contacted by an insider from a company called Greyhound Waste. His story was disturbing. It was a
second front, way outside the scope of Baker Tilly.

Greyhound Waste is a big company whose blue-chip clients include
Dublin City Council. It had a contract with Iarnród Éireann to remove
the enormous volume of waste arising from its activities.

Our source told us that something had gone badly wrong with this
contract. The result had been the payment by Greyhound of a seven-
figure settlement to Iarnród Éireann.

The mind boggled. How had it happened?

John Keenan had been on the case. He had spotted alarming discrepancies in the amount of work done measured against the amount
of work billed for. He challenged the top brass at Greyhound, a large
settlement was agreed, and Greyhound paid up.

Without Keenan's cost audit unit it is doubtful whether Greyhound's overcharging would ever have been rumbled. He had
unravelled a complicated set of transactions involving subcontractors, Greyhound and CIÉ.

Iarnród Éireann had been overcharged a colossal figure – not less
than €1 million – by Greyhound Waste. After Greyhound had
received invoices from subcontractors for the collection of the semi-
state waste, it had added additional units of weight to its own invoices

and submitted the adjusted invoices to the state company. Iarnród Éireann had paid Greyhound's padded bills.

On 16 December 2008 Shane Ross asked Dick Fearn about the Greyhound case. Fearn started by outlining what we already knew about the overcharging and the settlement. He went on to explain that the contract had been re-tendered, and that Greyhound had been invited to tender and had done so, but that the contract had been won by a different company. Senator Ross pressed Fearn on the size of the settlement, which Fearn surprisingly said he could not recall. The chairman of the committee, Frank Fahey, then asked Fearn about the re-tender.

CHAIRMAN: The matter the Senator has raised is a cause of concern. A company found to have acted in the way Mr Fearn described was brought back in to tender again. That is most unusual.

DICK FEARN: No. I do not think that is correct. If we found something inappropriate and if there were some breach or if we had to report a matter to the Garda, then there would be no question of the company being asked to tender again. We found contractual matters which were wrong. Basically, the money charged did not tally with the actual work done.

SENATOR SHANE ROSS: That is quite serious.

DICK FEARN: It is serious but is it not good that we identified that and did something about it? If we had sat back as a management team, we would have blindly carried on paying and have done nothing about it. That was the opposite of what we did

SENATOR SHANE ROSS: Were Iarnród Éireann getting bogus invoices?

DICK FEARN: I cannot use the word 'bogus', but through good management we identified discrepancies between the amount invoiced and the actual work done –

SENATOR SHANE ROSS: Was it fraud?

DICK FEARN: No, it was not fraud. We had no evidence to believe that someone was deliberately doing it. Sometimes in business, one will find that if one has a good process for checking invoices against work done, one might well find errors. Sometimes they might be quite serious errors.

One cannot immediately, however, jump to the conclusion that someone is doing it in a fraudulent way.

DEPUTY THOMAS P. BROUGHAN: On a point of information, the company in question has tenders for household-waste collection with Fingal County Council and Dublin City Council and there is grave dissatisfaction with it. Is Mr Fearn saying collections were not made in some stations and areas or, as Senator Ross fears, there was some sort of fraud taking place?

DICK FEARN: No. What I am saying is that there were discrepancies relating to the amount of material picked up at locations, whether pick-ups were done routinely and so on. We believed that in some of the invoicing there were inaccuracies and errors. We believed, therefore, money needed to be refunded to Iarnród Éireann. We did that diligently. We sat down with the management of Greyhound Waste and, in due course, money was refunded to Iarnród Éireann. We did not have evidence of fraud and, therefore, did not go to the Garda. However, we did say to Greyhound Waste that as a result of our dissatisfaction, we had no alternative but to re-tender the contract. In such circumstances, it would be a breach of procurement law if one has no basis to bar a company. As the committee will be aware, in European procurement law one cannot bar companies from tendering just because there was some discrepancy with them in the past. We did re-tender but Greyhound Waste did not win it.

CHAIRMAN: With all due respect, Iarnród Éireann is a large organization. The point Senator Ross is getting at is the procurement and tendering process must be above aboard and watertight. If discrepancies of any type were found with a supplier's invoices, I would have expected Iarnród Éireann to debar the supplier from tendering again.

DICK FEARN: Our legal advisers informed us we could not do that.

Further evidence that Baker Tilly had uncovered only the tip of the iceberg emerged in late 2009, when documents we had requested under the Freedom of Information Act were released to us.

Every year a mandatory report on Compliance with the Code of Practice for the Governance of Semi-state Bodies went from Lynch to the minister. Every year it listed a series of breaches. While CIÉ is not subject to the FOI law, the Department of Transport's correspondence is covered by it. Letters between Dempsey and Lynch showed breaches of procurement policy at CIÉ in areas well beyond the reach of Baker Tilly.

Lynch's annual letters to the minister revealed a company working to its own rules. CIÉ Tours had for some reason 'sought and [been] granted, by the Board, a derogation from the Procurement Policy as it applies to the purchases of hotel/other accommodation services, visitor attractions and air travel and noted that all such services are purchased for resale to their customers'. CIÉ Consult, described on the company's website as the consultancy arm of CIÉ, was not in compliance in the hiring of consultants. And in yet another admission of a breach of procurement policy the Group Property Department had considered it 'inappropriate' to go to tender for certain unspecified items.

Dempsey's reply to Lynch was as near to a wigging as any semistate chief ever receives from a minister. First he raised the chairman's failure to provide a five-year plan, as required. He was even more concerned about procurement. 'I note', he said, 'the commitment of CIÉ and its subsidiary companies to the principle of competitive tendering. I expect a significant reduction or complete elimination of the number of procurement exception reports, particularly for high value contracts in the next annual report.'

And finally the most damning ministerial remark of the lot: 'I note that the submission of the accounts for 2008 did not adhere to the guidelines set out in the Code of Practice in relation to the deadline for the submission of accounts.'

God knows why CIÉ couldn't meet the deadline, given that the accounts revealed nothing about what was lurking beneath the surface of the transport company.

That was left to Maggie the whistleblower and John Keenan the overenthusiastic employee.

On Thursday, 24 June 2010, John Keenan headed for the High Court with an army of lawyers to take on his tormentors in CIÉ. The case was settled on the steps of the court on confidential terms. Keenan was restored to the Iarnród Éireann staff as a 'consultant'. John Lynch turned up at the court to sign off on the deal. It seemed that Keenan was yet another Irish whistleblower unable to blow his whistle. His legal costs were paid by the taxpayer. Once again CIÉ had wasted a fortune.

8. Bad Deals

In late 2004 a campaign was launched to tackle the tortuous daily tailbacks on West Dublin's M50 toll bridge. Motorists were sitting in queues for ninety minutes or more to pass through the West Link toll barriers. First they queued. Then they paid. Then they did the same thing again on the way home.

After Shane Ross was caught in the M50 trap one Friday evening in late 2004, we began to write articles about it in the *Sunday Independent*. Commentator and football pundit Eamon Dunphy rallied in support, speaking at a crowded public meeting in West Dublin's Red Cow Inn to mobilize public opinion. An action group was formed and a fighting fund was opened. Meetings with government ministers followed. Debates were held in the Senate seeking relief for the motorists. Ministers and TDs were overwhelmed by emails from commuters demanding that the toll booths be opened.

Initially Bertie Ahern's government pleaded helplessness. A watertight agreement had been signed back in 1987 giving a private company, National Toll Roads (NTR), the right to toll the M50 at a single point on a bridge over the Liffey. Government sources wrung their hands and mumbled that the wretched agreement was a lock-in and that they were prisoners of the private company, but that they would do their best to hasten the introduction of barrier-free tolling. They even promised to upgrade the approach to the West Link toll bridge and to widen it by building another lane. The promises did little to soothe the stress of the drivers stuck in the queues of vehicles, sometimes five or six miles long, on the M50 every day.

The precise terms of the 1987 agreement that bound the state's hands so tightly were still unknown when the West Link campaign was launched. We beat down the doors of National Toll Roads, the National Roads Authority, the Department of the Environment and Dublin City Council in search of the offending document. In early

January 2005 one of our best sources in the public service arrived unannounced to meet us, a brown envelope in his hand and a twinkle in his eye.

'I have something that might interest you,' he grinned. 'You may publish it on Sunday.'

The envelope contained a copy of the 1987 deal, a fifteen-page agreement between National Toll Roads, Dublin City Council and the Minister for the Environment. We started reading. Initially it seemed indigestible and soporific. Our source watched contentedly as we struggled to understand the legal terminology of the contract.

We were silently disappointed as we reached the end. The deal was heavily weighted in favour of the toll company on a first reading, but that wasn't news. Hidden costs to the state, buried in the small print, included 100 per cent capital allowances for the project's construction costs, where normally 50 per cent would apply; a waiver of VAT on tolls; and exemption for the bridge from local-authority rates. But there was no smoking gun that we could see, and it wasn't clear to us what our source was so excited about.

Then we discovered that we had overlooked two pages pinned to the back of the document. There lay the bombshell: the signatures. The agreement had been signed on behalf of Dublin City Council by George Redmond. It was signed on behalf of the government by the Minister for the Environment, Pádraig Flynn. We were stunned and delighted. We had our story.

The cocktail of Redmond and Flynn, two characters with deeply damaged reputations, was explosive. Flynn is remembered not just for his boast about how hard it was to meet the cost of maintaining three houses when he was European Commissioner; nor for his poisonous personal attack on Mary Robinson, accusing her of 'having a new-found interest in her family' when she sought the presidency in 1990. He is also remembered as the recipient of a £50,000 political contribution from builder Tom Gilmartin in 1989. Gilmartin told the Flood Tribunal that, although the cheque was for Fianna Fáil, Flynn had asked him to make it out to cash. Flynn denied it, testifying that it was always meant for his personal election expenses.

The name of George Redmond, meanwhile, prompts law-abiding

citizens to shudder. Redmond was the assistant city and county manager for Dublin who was savaged by the Flood Tribunal for taking money from builders and developers as well as for barefaced lying. Flood found that Redmond had accepted corrupt payments. (Later he was charged with corruption and sentenced to a year in jail, though he was acquitted on appeal.)

Now we had the signatures of Flynn and Redmond in front of us on a 1987 agreement that had blown up in the government's face eighteen years later.

Two days after our discovery the business section of the *Sunday Independent* led with a story headlined 'Redmond and Flynn Signed Off Toll Bridge Deal'. Fuelled by this revelation, the campaign to open the toll gates and reduce the misery of commuters moved up a gear. The campaign deliberately left the thorny issue of tolling itself for another day; the view was that commuters couldn't wait for electronic tolling or some other queue-cutting solution to be introduced. A few days after the Flynn–Redmond story appeared, the National Roads Authority posted the 1987 document on its website. All the details of the agreement, signed eighteen years earlier, were in the public arena.

Under the terms of the deal, the state gathered no revenue at all from the first 27,000 cars a day to pass through the West Link; it was to receive 30 per cent of the revenue from the next 8,000 vehicles, 40 per cent from the next 10,000 and 50 per cent from every car beyond the 45,000 mark. According to agreed projections, traffic was not expected to reach the 45,000 level until the bridge reverted to the state in 2020.

In reality, the projections (which evidently did not foresee the dramatic economic boom that commenced in the mid nineties) underestimated traffic flows dramatically; the 45,000 figure had been reached within ten years, in 1997. Both NTR and the state hit the jackpot.

But the jackpot proved a poisoned one for the state. Just as no one had anticipated so much toll-generating traffic on the M50, so no one had foreseen the problems associated with such traffic. The M50 was not wide enough to accommodate the upsurge, and the toll barrier made matters worse. Queues began to form.

Private companies love to see their customers queueing, but the
state recognized the queues as political irritants that needed sorting.
The only 'political' solution was a buyout: the toll bridge would be
run by the state, which could eliminate the physical toll gates, perhaps replacing them with electronic tolling. Under the terms of the
1987 deal the price of removing NTR from the pitch was a monthly
compensation payment equal to the monthly average of the tolls paid
during the previous twelve months. The compensation would be
index-linked all the way to 2020. In 2005 the ballpark figure for a
buyout was €500 million. The state could recover this by collecting
the tolls itself, but the question of how that was to be done remained:
leaving the toll barrier in place would only make its political problem
worse; and introducing electronic tolling would be both costly and a
major technical challenge for a state with a terrible record on anything related to IT. NTR had the state over a barrel.

Tom Roche, the boss of National Toll Roads, was a giant of Irish
industry. He started his business life when he and his brother Donal
bought a half-ton truck and ran a tiny coal and sand business. Next
they purchased a gravel company, Castle Sand and Gravel. It went
public in 1949 as Roadstone plc and – after several hiccups – was
merged with Irish Cement to become Cement Roadstone Holdings
(today CRH), later to develop into Ireland's largest publicly quoted
company.

Tom Roche took over as chairman of Cement Roadstone in 1971
after the death of the sitting chairman, former Taoiseach Seán Lemass.
He retired in 1974 at the age of fifty-eight, reputedly as rich as Croesus.

Instead of taking a rest, Tom took a punt. In the late seventies and
early eighties, onshore mining was all the rage in Ireland. Tom sank
nearly all his money into a little mining outfit called Bula, named,
appropriately, after a racehorse.

Delays in planning permissions and heavy borrowings eventually
left Bula bust. Both Tom Senior and his son-in-law – Bula's managing director Michael Wymes – took a bath in the collapse. The sheriff
arrived at Wymes's Meath ranch to seize his herd of pedigree Cha-
rolais cattle.

The family split badly, ending up at war in the Four Courts. While Wymes never recovered from the Bula disaster and the permanent rift in the family, Tom Roche Senior bounced back. Together with his son, Tom Junior, he began to build toll bridges.

In 1984 the father-and-son team had started to build the East Link toll bridge over the River Liffey, connecting Ringsend and the North Wall. It was the first ever toll bridge in Ireland. The Roche family company, Conor Holdings, struck an agreement with Dublin Corporation and Dublin Port and Docks Board to build the bridge at a total cost of £8 million.

Under the terms of the deal, the local communities were to be given £50,000 a year from the proceeds of the toll and no toll increases could be agreed without the go-ahead from the local councillors.

After it was opened by Taoiseach Garret FitzGerald in 1984, the East Link printed money for the Roche family, lifting them back off their uppers. Instead of resting on their laurels, the father-and-son team decided to double up. If one toll bridge worked, why not another? Construction was about to begin on the first phase of the M50, between Blanchardstown and Tallaght. NTR entered tripartite negotiations with Dublin County Council and the Department of the Environment to build a toll bridge at the M50's Liffey crossing as part of that stretch of road.

Tom Roche Senior needed a good deal, but he also needed a speedy one – not easy to achieve when dealing with Dublin County Council on planning matters in the brown-envelope era of the eighties. According to Liam Collins, writing in the *Sunday Independent* in 2006, he handed over an envelope containing £10,000 in cash to none other than George Redmond, the assistant city and county manager in charge of planning, to hurry things up.

We also learned from the Flood Tribunal that National Toll Roads had paid the late Fianna Fáil TD, local representative and jailbird Liam Lawlor £74,000 in 'consultancy fees'. Lawlor claimed that it was a political donation, declaring that his father and Tom Roche Senior had been friends for thirty years. Despite their friendship, Lawlor said that he had never been asked, as a local representative, to make any decisions in their favour.

Most disturbing of the lot was NTR's 1992 donation of £8,000 to Pádraig Flynn, the minister who had signed the toll deal five years earlier.

The West Link deal was agreed without competition or tender. NTR was the only candidate for the job. Apologists for NTR continually plead that the Roches took all the risk on the West Link deal, ponying up £27.6 million (€35 million) to build a bridge in exchange for an unknown return at a time when the state coffers were empty and investment capital scarce. They point out that if the project went belly-up the state had no money on the line.

Quite true. But the terms on which the state gave NTR control of a public asset, and access to a thirty-year income stream from it, were generous: the tolls on the West Link were index-linked, unlike the East Link, where the permission of local councillors was needed for any hikes; 100 per cent capital allowances were granted on construction costs; no local-authority rates were payable on the bridge; no VAT was payable on the tolls.

According to the projections agreed by both parties at the time, there was little likelihood of the vehicle numbers even approaching the magic 27,000 mark for ten years, and the 45,000 figure was not expected to be reached for thirty years – by which time, in any case, the deal expired and operation of the toll bridge reverted to the state. When the bridge opened in 1990, there were only 6,800 cars passing through daily.

While traffic numbers in the early years were actually lower than expected, they soon dramatically exceeded all the projections. Both the state and NTR were reaping unforeseen rewards.

By 2005 the state had received €83 million directly in tolls, while NTR had earned €412 million. Even the most generous interpretation of the return to the state (including revenue from corporation tax, VAT and rates) showed a return of only €173 million for the taxpayer with €239 million for NTR. It had been a great deal for NTR, and the opportunity costs to the state were massive. And it left the state with a massive political problem.

Interestingly, at the time of the original deal the Roches had given the state an option of either a portion of the toll income or a slice of the equity in NTR. The government, apparently fearful of taking any risks at a time of economic weakness, opted for zero risk and minimum responsibility. The failure to take equity left the government and its successors without a say in how the company was run and unable to share any possible bonanza should NTR or West Link ever be bought out. The state chose the role of bystander, giving National Toll Roads the green light to enjoy the fruits of the deal, to squat on the bridge and to sit tight until somebody bought them out.

As the 2007 general election approached and the campaign to open the gates gathered steam, Bertie Ahern's outgoing coalition came under populist pressure to clear the backlog in traffic. Catherine Murphy, the successful independent by-election candidate in Kildare North in 2005, had made the turmoil at the toll a main plank of her platform, and single-issue toll-bridge candidates were threatening to challenge Fianna Fáil in the impending contest. Ahern and transport minister Martin Cullen knew that it was political suicide to abandon a hundred thousand voters a day – bursting blood vessels on their journey to and from work – to the mercies of NTR. Schoolchildren were getting caught up in the jams. Flights were being missed. Daily lives were being disrupted.

National Toll Roads gloated as they surveyed the queues. Not only did they smile as the coins filled their baskets, but they enjoyed the government's political discomfort. As the pressure built up from the punters, an expensive buyout became more likely; and as the vehicle numbers at the booths continued to rise, the price of any buyout soared.

By 2004 the numbers passing through had reached 85,000 a day. By 2005 they had passed 89,000 – nearly double the 45,000 figure originally forecast for fifteen years later.

As public protests increased, the battle between National Toll Roads and the government was joined. Tom Roche Senior had died in 1999; Tom Roche Junior and Jim Barry, a 39-year-old Harvard MBA, were now running NTR. Their well-paid public-relations spinners constantly heaped the pressure on Fianna Fáil, hinting to the punters through the media that NTR was happy to do a deal if the state coughed up the right amount of money.

The streetwise Barry had commissioned Davy Kelleher McCarthy consultants (DKM) to write a report on the West Link. Its findings were predictably sympathetic to its paymasters in NTR: 'despite viewpoints to the contrary', the state had negotiated a good deal with its clients. It pooh-poohed the very idea that poor NTR was bleeding the taxpayer and vigorously defended charges against NTR of causing congestion or profiteering. The DKM report emphasized that the Roches were entrepreneurs, and that in the early years the toll profits had fallen far short of forecasts. It subtly pointed the finger at the politicians, asserting that the state was now quietly making a healthy return and that NTR was much misunderstood. It stopped just short of hailing the Roches as members of the Legion of Mary or St Vincent de Paul.

NTR's clever strategy of keeping the spotlight on the government paid off. The message was clear: the government was creaming it from the West Link, so it was in the government's power to buy out the toll company and clear the gridlock.

Bertie Ahern and Martin Cullen were caught in a pincer movement of discontented commuters on one side and NTR on the other. The defects of the original deal were coming home to roost.

There was only one way out but it was lethally expensive. Although Bertie Ahern had told Pat Rabbitte in the Dáil in early 2005 that the government would not buy out the toll bridge, he would soon eat his words. In early 2006, after secret talks between the two sides broke down, the government announced that it was going to exercise the nuclear option and remove the toll gates. Compensation would be paid to NTR.

On 18 February 2007 the government announced that the price of the buyout had been agreed at €600 million, with the handover taking place in the summer of 2008. In line with the original deal's formula, the price was based on the amount of toll revenue gathered in the previous twelve months, extrapolated until 2020.

The timing was uncanny. February 2007 was the pinnacle of Ireland's boom. The property market was at its peak. The Irish stock market hit an all-time high in the same month. The government was awash with money. At that precise moment of giddy values, with traffic levels on the M50 also at an all-time high, Tom Roche Junior decided to cash in his chips.

It could all have been so different. When the government finally conceded the €600 million payout to NTR in February 2007, it was not buying an asset. It was digging itself out of a political hole by reoccupying the 3.2 kilometres of road surrendered to NTR back in 1987. It was retaking the right to toll a public road from a private company.

If Redmond and Flynn had insisted on a 50 per cent equity stake in National Toll Roads in the 1987 negotiations, the state could, by 2007, have been selling a valuable stake in a thriving company. It could have been selling its half-share to NTR or even to an outside company. Alternatively, it could have been buying out a mere 50 per cent share from the tolling company.

If the state had ignored NTR back in the eighties, found the €35 million construction costs and itself done what the Roches did, it would have reaped enormous revenues and retained the ability to address the traffic problem on its own terms. The overall opportunity cost to the state probably exceeded a billion euro.

Questions surrounding the West Link deal on the M50 will remain unanswered forever. No one should conclude that it was dodgy just because Pádraig Flynn later received £8,000 from National Toll Roads, or because Tom Roche Senior gave £10,000 to George Redmond, or because NTR paid Liam Lawlor £74,000 in 'consultancy fees'. These payments are in no way prima facie evidence that the deal the state struck with NTR was corrupt. In any case, it's not clear which idea is more depressing: that the West Link deal was a product of corruption, or that it was honest.

If the deal to build and run the West Link was a one-off failure of vision whose ultimate cost to the state and its citizens can never be accurately calculated, the National Development Plan (NDP) was a muddle of epic proportions in which every cent — and there are zillions of them — has been counted.

Back in June 1999, when the National Development Plan 2000–2006 was being worked out on the back of a beer mat, it was estimated that the roll-out of new roads and road improvements covered by the plan would cost the state about €5.6 billion. Five major inter-city roads would be developed, linking Dublin to Cork, Galway, Waterford, Limerick and Belfast; other main primary and secondary roads would be upgraded. The completion of the M50 Dublin ring road and the Port Tunnel were the final elements of this ambitious undertaking.

Within four years the cost of the works had trebled to €16.4 billion, and it was clear that the completion of the programme was going to take far, far longer than originally planned. The phenom-enal rise in cost saw the government transfer spending from other sectors into road-building, and more and more of our state infra-structure into the hands of multinational corporations brought in under public–private partnerships (PPP).

Inflation, labour costs and the increased price of materials were cited as reasons for the swelling budgets. Land costs were also a huge factor. Large chunks of the road-building programme were delayed for six months in 2001, as 8,000 farmers blocked plans to buy their land for road-building by refusing to allow road surveyors and plan-ners on to their property. The impasse was ended when the National Roads Authority (NRA), environment minister Noel Dempsey and the Irish Farmers' Association inked an agreement to give farmers far better rates when it came to the compulsory purchase of their lands for road-building. The deal was flamed in an *Irish Times* editorial on 3 December as 'a smash and grab raid on the public purse'. It was estimated that the farmers who benefited from the much higher prices also received €5,000 per acre as a 'co-operation payment'. The NRA estimated that this deal added €200 million on to the costs of the road-building programme.

It later emerged that the NRA didn't even use so much as a calcu-lator when coming up with its original estimates. 'At the time of the adoption of the NDP cost estimation was not well developed in the NRA,' a subsequent government report would note. 'The Authority had no dedicated in-house expertise to determine or validate the cost of projects included in the programme.' At the tiller for much of this squanderfest was Fianna Fáil TD Noel Dempsey of Meath.

Road-building and the NRA were under his aegis when he was Minister for the Environment. In 2002 responsibility for road-building was transferred to Séamus Brennan and later Martin Cullen in the Department of Transport. Dempsey got another stab at building roads when he left the Department of Communication to become transport minister following the June 2007 cabinet reshuffle. There is no doubt that, before the onset of the National Development Plan, Ireland's road system was in need of a serious upgrade, and the development programme was a justifiably massive strategic priority for the state. But the state showed no ability to cost the original plan accurately or to keep spending in check.

This does not bode well for the other major state infrastructure projects. The proposed Dublin Metro has seen its price rise from less than €2 billion to more than €5 billion. That project may never see the light of day, but the government's much trumpeted Transport 21 programme – the next phase of the NDP – is likely to cause sleepless nights. Some €34.4 billion has been earmarked for the vast array of shiny projects and big holes in the ground. It is also under the control of Noel Dempsey. Be afraid, taxpayers. Be very afraid.

Two of the most high-profile NDP projects also turned out to be two of the biggest turkeys. When the Dublin Port Tunnel was first priced up, estimates indicated that the 5.6-kilometre underground route – linking Santry with Dublin Port as a way of allowing trucks direct access to the M50 and the motorways without having to battle through (and exacerbate) traffic in central Dublin – could be done for about €220 million. The final tab was more than three times that amount, coming in at €789 million. A breakdown of the costs of the project shows that €485 million was spent on digging and building the tunnel. The remaining €304 million was spent on lawyers, land costs, construction supervisors and environmental reports.

Dublin City Council fronted the work, which was supervised by the US outfit Kellogg, Brown & Root, part of Halliburton, of which former US vice-president Dick Cheney was chairman and CEO from 1995 to 2000. Kellogg, Brown & Root has built parts of the US detention centre at Guantánamo, the US embassy in Kabul and army housing to the value of $200 million in Iraq. Japanese–British–Irish consortium Nishimatsu Mowlem Irishenco (NMI) did all the spade work. When the first sod was turned in June 2001, the tunnel was targeting a January 2005 opening. But January 2005 came and went. So did January 2006. Those in charge mouthed hollow excuses for the delays and cost overruns. Drilling time was reduced, they said, because of neighbourhood noise concerns, which meant that certain sections of the boring couldn't be conducted twenty-four hours a day. In 2006, as the tunnel neared completion, dramatic undercover film footage showed water pouring through cracks in the roof. This would lead to further costs and delays, as a giant cement Elasto-plast needed to be slapped on to the ceiling. While the boring was under way, a debate erupted over the height of the tunnel, which, at 4.65 metres, was too low for the next generation of supertrucks being developed on the Continent. Rather than increase the height of the tunnel – at a cost of €85 million – the tunnel has been fitted out with a warning system that detects the approach of a supertruck; barriers, signs and flashing lights all spring into action.

When the tunnel finally opened in December 2006, twenty-three months late, there was a great celebration; but there should have been a ritual disembowelling and a small number of crucifixions. Even as the ribbons were cut, more problems erupted. No sooner were the barriers raised than they came slamming down again: the tunnel's expensive IT and management systems had malfunctioned. There were also suggestions of serious safety flaws, with RTÉ's *Prime Time* highlighting a series of worrying issues. The programme found that the Port Tunnel had remained open despite jet fans – used to aid firefighting – failing on several occasions; safety cameras had been broken; vehicle cross-over points had been blocked with water con-tainers; and computer systems were on the blink. The NRA insisted the tunnel was safe, and a September 2008 statement from the Depart-ment of Transport read, 'The Minister is satisfied that the NRA has not and will not allow the Port Tunnel to be operated in circum-stances that would compromise the safety of the public.'

At a cost of €789 million, the Port Tunnel is looking like a mon-strously expensive boondoggle. In November 2009 a leaked traffic report showed that the number of five-axle trucks travelling through had slumped 47 per cent from the peak in August 2007. We've obtained a November 2007 briefing note from tunnel operators Transroute, which forecast that up to 20,000 vehicles would use the tunnel every day, including up to 9,000 articulated lorries. It was miles off the mark: in July 2010 the NRA told us that an average of 14,125 vehicles used the tunnel on weekdays, including 7,700 trucks. At weekends the figures fell to 8,500 per day, including 2,400 trucks. These figures are nowhere near the Transroute projections from 2007.

Based on these figures, the Port Tunnel – which is free for big trucks and costs €10 for cars on weekdays – will generate about €18.6 million in tolls this year – well short of the near €30 million per year it would have generated based on the 2007 Transroute estimates. All this money gets paid to the Department of Transport, with French group Transroute bagging a five-year €15 million contract to maintain and operate the tunnel. In March 2008 the tunnel-construction consortium launched a lawsuit against the NRA and Dublin County Council, seeking to recoup some of the extra costs they say they incurred when building the tunnel. In August 2010 it emerged that a settlement of €37 million had been agreed. The hole in the ground just keeps getting bigger.

When it was first crayoned on a map in the late nineties, the forecasts were that the Luas would cost €288 million: one of the most expensive tram systems ever constructed in a major city, despite consisting of just two lines. The construction cost per kilometre of the Luas line was more than double the average cost of light rail schemes in the UK.

In December 2001, public enterprise minister Mary O'Rourke – she of the Eircom flotation debacle – set up a brand-new quango to lead the Luas project, which had been bubbling away undisturbed in a CIÉ basement for a number of years. By this stage the projected cost had soared to over €670 million, due largely to rising land values. The new agency was chaired by former IDA boss Pádraic White, whose wife Mary is a Fianna Fáil senator. KBC Bank's head of infrastructure lending, Frank Allen, was brought in to run the show as chief executive.

Allen essentially took over from CIÉ light-rail chief Donal Mangan, who had been running the Luas project for seven years. This prompted Mangan to launch a lawsuit against the Railway Procurement Agency. It took nearly two years to reach a settlement. Despite having no role in the company and nothing to do, Mangan went in to work every single day and sat in an office for the next two years. He was paid €150,000 per annum, with a secretary and company car during this period.

A report by economic consultants Fitzpatrick Associates for the Department of Finance has found that the costs of many Luas construction elements were not identified early enough, so budgets were dramatically underestimated. At the last minute it was decided not to join up the Sandyford line with the Tallaght line. Instead there was to be an underground train line – the Metro – running from St Stephen's Green to the airport, thus creating a fiddly connection between the two Luas lines. Despite government protestations to the contrary, the €5 billion Metro project is now about as likely as finding a polar bear flipping burgers at a barbecue. So passengers wishing to travel on the Luas from a location near the Sandyford line to one along the Tallaght line will continue to be forced to make the fifteen-minute walk from St Stephen's Green to Abbey Street. As high-speed transfers go, this is just plain embarrassing.

But, despite being over budget, years late and unintegrated, at least the Luas was built. The same cannot be said for another state deal that unravelled spectacularly. The Marine Tourism Grant Scheme was a government initiative initially designed to boost yachting tourism around the coast of Ireland. It was press-ganged by Fianna Fáil politicians for their party's gain and descended into farce. As usual, the taxpayer took a bullet for back-office political dealings; and, as usual, nobody took a beating when the scheme went horribly wrong.

In mid 1999 a fund of €25 million was allocated under the National Development Plan 2000–2006 to boost 'marine tourism'. But the funding process hadn't been activated. In late 2000 Frank Fahey, the Fianna Fáil Minister for the Marine and Galway TD, moved to set up a scheme to fund marine-tourism projects, which would be run by his department; the plan was for it to be separate from the NDP funding programme. About sixty projects applied for grants under this scheme, but only four were told that they would be getting money. One was at Rosses Point in County Sligo; a second, at Round-stone in Connemara, was in Fahey's own constituency; and the other two were in independent TD Jackie Healy-Rae's Kerry South con-stituency, at Kenmare and Cahirciveen. Healy-Rae was one of a number of independents in that Dáil whose support was essential for the survival of the Fianna Fáil–Progressive Democrat government. Each of the independent TDs had agreed deals with Ahern for their continuing support; marina developments in Kenmare and Cahir-civeen were just part of Healy-Rae's long list.

In late 2001 the promoters of the Kenmare marina received a €332,000 tranche of their funding. By mid 2002 the Department of the Marine was made aware that work appeared to have stopped at the site. It sought an update from the promoter on two occasions but did not receive an answer. A site visit was arranged in December 2002, with an inspector arriving to view the works. He found that the building was in breach of planning procedures and future funding was put on hold until these issues could be resolved. In February 2004 the department was informed by the marina promoter that the unauthorized building – an adventure-training centre – had been demolished on the orders of Kerry County Council. The big pile of smashed bricks and rubble on the quayside in Kenmare was all that remained of the €332,000 in taxpayers' money.

While the Kenmare project was ricocheting from disaster to disas-ter, the projects at Rosses Point and Roundstone entirely failed to get off the ground. That left Cahirciveen. The state funding for this €3.1 million project accounted for 75 per cent of the total sum, far above the 40 per cent limit for projects funded by the National Devel-opment Plan: the developers had failed to raise enough money for the capital spending required. Even before the marina had been con-structed, the Department of the Marine was expressing worries about its financial viability. Bord Fáilte was also concerned. The state tour-ism body had declined to fund the project when first approached in

1999. The plans for the marina were eventually scaled back after discussions with the department and local authorities. In the end, just thirty-eight of the ninety-three berths were used for tourism purposes; the rest were sold to private boat owners. In 2004 the Comptroller & Auditor General questioned the 'unorthodox' manner in which Fahey's department had divvied up the €5.72 million in grant money for the marinas without first properly appraising the various proposals. It also found that department officials had raised concerns over the projects' viability and soaring costs.

In one case, Fahey issued a letter on ministerial notepaper to the Kenmare marina's financial advisers stating that he would fund the project. Department of the Marine assistant secretary Michael Guilfoyle formally warned that this letter could create 'unwarranted expectations' and leave the department open to a lawsuit. Given that civil servants are specially bred never to stick their heads above the parapet, this was a highly unusual occurrence.

In March 2007 the Oireachtas PAC investigated the marina handouts. 'Effectively what we have here is a very large subsidy paid by the taxpayer to people who own yachts,' Fine Gael's Michael Noonan said. 'It raises serious questions that have to be answered.' The PAC heard the dismal news that more than half of the berths at the Kenmare marina were rented out to private yacht owners and that there was little or no information available on how the project had benefited tourism in the area. The criteria for selection of the four marina schemes chosen by Fahey 'were not communicated to the Department's officials' and 'virtually no relevant information on the viability or tourism value of the projects was made available to the Department at the time assistance was announced.' In other words, money was just shovelled out to these four pet projects without due diligence. It was Fianna Fáil local politics at its shabbiest.

The state's record when it comes to spending money on big ships is nothing short of disastrous. Thank God we're not an island. The state-owned training vessel *Asgard II* sank in September 2008, having kept the Coiste an Asgard quango afloat for three decades (see Chapter 9). But we're still lumbered with the *Jeanie Johnston*.

The idea of constructing a replica Famine ship was first proposed in 1993. It took five years to line up funding from heavy-hitting sponsors including Athlone drug company Elan, Shannon Development, Tralee Urban District Council, the government and FÁS. In May 1998 President Mary McAleese officiated at the keel-laying ceremony, with the ship finally launched two years later. The government lobbed in €2.5 million in grant aid. But the project sprang a leak: lengthy delays ensued, and costs rose. When key sponsor Shannon Development pulled out, the state came up with another €2.5 million handout, bringing public funding up to €9.8 million. The ship ended up costing over four times its original estimate, most of it state money, with bank-borrowing guarantees by Kerry County Council and Tralee Urban District Council as well as direct grants accounting for around €6 million.

Eventually, in January 2003, it made its maiden voyage, sailing to the US to commemorate the suffering of the millions who were forced to emigrate during the Famine. And then it ran out of useful stuff to do.

But that wasn't the end of the state's involvement. In September 2005 the Dublin Docklands Development Authority splashed out €2.7 million to buy the ship, which now lies docked on the Liffey. Minutes from the DDDA later revealed that after buying the ship, the financially crippled agency didn't have the faintest idea what to do with its new toy. Eventually it was offered to the Department of Defence as a replacement for the *Asgard II*, but the department wouldn't touch it with asbestos gloves. The DDDA also considered tarting it up for sale, overseas charter, corporate hospitality or as a Famine Museum. Fine Gael TD Phil Hogan described the DDDA's purchase of the *Jeanie Johnston* as 'very puzzling'. Utterly pointless might have been more accurate.

One of the more unnecessary pieces of infrastructural waste under the Fianna Fáil government took place less than fifty yards from the

Dáil chamber, a few steps from the people who are elected to ensure that the money we pay in taxes isn't squandered on frippery. The tiny glass-framed kiosk at the Kildare Street entrance of Leinster House – which has a canopy outside for politicians to stand under if it rains when they do interviews, and a nice bit of decking – cost more than a four-bed redbrick terraced house in Ranelagh. 'An Siopa', the imaginatively titled sweetie shop for politicians, has cost the taxpayer almost €1.3 million. The OPW had initially estimated that the shop would cost €800,000 plus VAT. At forty square metres, the building cost €32,500 per square metre. By comparison, a new house costs about €3,000 per square metre to build.

The Leinster House edifice, which was designed by award-winning architectural firm Bucholz McEvoy, was opened in January 2008 – appropriately by wasters-in-chief Bertie Ahern and Ceann Comhairle John O'Donoghue. A cost breakdown, retrieved under the Freedom of Information Act, shows that the main contractor was paid almost €496,000, with the glazier earning €413,000 and the electrical supplier €97,000. The interior was a separate expense altogether, with the final bill for that hitting more than €50,000. The state also lashed out €180,000 in 'fees' for this little monument to an out-of-control spending culture.

The contract to build the million-euro sweetie shop was won by Philip Earle's Dublin-based Glenbeigh Construction, which is better known for having won prison-construction projects worth €100 million that never went out to tender. These included a €21 million contract to build a 64-cell block at Castlerea Prison and various works at other prisons, including a snazzy all-weather football pitch.

But the state's irregular practices in prison construction were nothing compared to the catastrophic cock-up at Thornton Hall. It had all sounded so clever, when first aired. The ancient Mountjoy Prison, located near the centre of Dublin, was to be sold to developers, with the inmates transferred to a brand-new €400 million 'campus' on a site in north County Dublin. This new prison – sorry, campus – would house up to 2,200 villains of various degrees of nastiness, more than four times the capacity of Mountjoy. Apart from allowing the state to decommission an overcrowded Victorian prison, the real deal clincher was in the potential savings: it was estimated that a new prison would shave about €30,000 a year off the €92,000 annual cost of incarcerating someone. Instead, it turned into a political potato of unprecedented heat and one that has cost the taxpayer well over €42 million.

In January 2005, after a lengthy process of dithering, the government spent close to €30 million buying a 150-acre site in Kilsallaghan near Swords, County Dublin. The price at almost €200,000 per acre came under particular scrutiny when it emerged that another site – once shortlisted for acquisition for the prison – had sold in March 2007 for just €100,000 per acre, or half the amount paid for Thornton Hall. It also emerged that CB Richard Ellis executive Ronan Webster, the property adviser to the state on the Thornton Hall deal – who had bagged fees of up to €150,000 – was related by marriage to the family of the landowner.

Thornton Hall was to be built and operated using a public–private partnership. After a lengthy tendering process, the contract for Thornton Hall was awarded to the Léargas consortium, made up of former Fianna Fáil councillor Bernard McNamara's construction firm Michael McNamara, Barclays Bank, the late Frank O'Kane's Mercury Engineering and private-prison operator GSL. Under the proposed deal Léargas would have built the prison, maintained it, and provided operational and consultancy services for twenty-five years in return for an undisclosed annual payment.

But the timing couldn't have been worse. The credit markets slammed shut in August 2007, which meant that banks weren't lending to each other and they most certainly weren't funding Irish prison PPPs. Meanwhile, according to government sources, the price demanded by the Léargas consortium kept rising – by May 2009 it had gone up by 30 per cent. This was the point at which the deal finally collapsed and the government admitted that plans to develop the prison would have to be 'phased'. 'Phased' is government-speak for banjaxed.

A further €11 million has already been spent on the site, between consultants and linking services to the main systems some miles away. Close to €440,000 has been racked up on landscaping, with the taxpayer hit for €18,000 for buying and pruning 2,200 new woodland plants. Some 3,700 'linear metres' of trees and shrubs have been planted; according to justice minister Dermot Ahern, in an answer to a parliamentary question posed by Fine Gael's Denis Naughten, officials decided to increase the planted zone 'to mitigate the visual and aural impact of the development'. These plants must be terribly valuable: the cost for security at the site has now passed the €500,000 mark, even though construction has not even started. So we've spent close to €11 million on a big field with some flowers and shrubs in it. Excellent.

But the government and numskull civil servants have learned something from the Thornton Hall debacle. Apparently they accept that the state 'was seen coming' in the deal, and the Department of Finance now insists that government departments should use agents or intermediaries when buying property for the state. 'The acquisition of property should be pursued on a commercial basis including the use of intermediaries to ensure confidentiality in high value cases, since sellers to the state in such situations tend to consider they are in a strong negotiating position and look for higher prices,' states one departmental memo.

While most people in Ireland have, by now, heard of the PPARS disaster, where the taxpayer ended up paying close to €130 million for a useless IT project for the HSE, few will have come across another dog of a system known as the Public Services Broker (PSB) project.

PSB was set up in 2000 and designed to provide members of the public with a single website from which to access all state services. Not a bad idea. Some €18 million was paid to consultants in the opening five years of the project's existence but they got bogged down. The Revenue used it for online PAYE services and the Department of Social Welfare used it for death notices. However, by the time all the working parts of PSB were ready, other government departments and agencies had already bought far more advanced bits of kit.

The taxpayer took a €27.3 million hit when the Department of Finance wrote off the huge expenditure on computers and related hardware needed by the defunct project, which was finally unplugged in 2008. Costs for maintaining the system hit €15 million in 2007 and 2008. When it was scrapped the Department of Finance had to cough up €1.5 million to extricate itself from a maintenance contract with an external IT firm.

It also emerged that the taxpayer had spent €500,000 on a website – reachservices.ie – for the PSB system that duplicated another one – citizensinformation.ie – run by the same government department. At one stage the four-year-old reachservices.ie site had attracted just 18,000 visitors per year, compared with 2.5 million at the rival citizensinformation.ie.

The lack of joined-up government thinking was made painfully clear when in 2008 it emerged that the state had hired a total of ten different IT companies to essentially supply the same service at an annual cost of €3 million. Just three government departments had been using the state's shared services centre in Killarney, with the remainder hiring their own IT financial-management outfits, including Fujitsu, Oracle and IBM. The Department of Defence had been a big spender, as had the Department of Community, Rural and Gaeltacht Affairs, which had actually retained three separate firms to handle financial-management systems at a cost of €153,000.

When the Comptroller & Auditor General scoured the labyrinthine state computer and IT spending budgets and programmes, he found that 161 online projects were funded by the state between 2000 and 2005 at a cost of €420. Just seventy-four of these projects – or 46 per cent – were fully up and running by 2006, 44 per cent were partially working, and just over one in seven had been abandoned.

The government's tendency to become completely dazzled by new-technology projects was never more obvious than during the seemingly endless e-voting fiasco. Was anyone sacked? Nope.

In 2002 environment minister Martin Cullen spent €52 million to buy 7,491 electronic voting machines to replace what Bertie

Ahern referred to as those 'stupid little pencils'. The groundwork for the project had been done by his predecessor in the department, Noel Dempsey. Under the new system, election results would be known almost instantly; there'd be no need for a whole day of RTÉ pundits analysing exit polls, historical transfer patterns and swing-ometers.

A limited number of the machines were trialled during the 2002 election, most memorably in the Dublin North constituency. One of the enduring images of that election night was the moment when, at the flick of a switch, Fine Gael's Nora Owen was told that she had lost her seat. It was cruel, and yet it failed to satisfy the usual general election television bloodlust.

After the election doubts began to appear about the reliability of the machines. They could be hacked into, and there was no adequate paper trail as a back-up in the event of electronic failure. The government decided the machines were a mistake and sought to get some of its money back from the Dutch manufacturers.

In the meantime county returning officers were given the job of finding homes for the machines – with close to €3 million already having been spent on storage. When questioned by the PAC, Department of Environment secretary general Geraldine Tallon admitted that, in a minority of cases, there were 'relationships' between some returning officers and the owners of premises where the machines were stored. In Monaghan one returning officer signed a 25-year lease to store the machines in premises owned by her nephew. Returning officers in Cork and Dublin stored machines in buildings they owned. Cyberspace is also cluttered up by our e-voting machines. The website www.electronicvoting.ie cost the Department of the Environment €40,000 to create in 2004, with a further €12,000 in maintenance over the following six years. The website remains operational.

The cost of e-voting machines had become a major political issue when the new Fianna Fáil–Green coalition took shape in 2007. In one of his first moves on becoming environment minister, Green TD John Gormley ordered that machines be moved from twelve separate locations into one central warehouse in the Gormanstown army camp. However, machines remain at thirteen other separate locations around the country; this cost €204,000 in 2008 alone. While the machines themselves have a shelf-life of just twenty years, the leases for their storage are for twenty-five years in some cases. Piss-ups and breweries spring to mind, don't they?

9. The Wasters' A–Z

A is for Abbotstown

Long before we ever realized that Bertie Ahern's legacy would be long dole queues, a bombed-out economy and the most expensive bank bailout in history, it looked, for a time, as if he would be best remembered for a spectacularly ambitious sports complex in West Dublin. Campus Stadium Ireland – the so-called 'Bertie Bowl' scheme – would feature a fifty-metre pool, a velodrome for cyclists and an 80,000-seat stadium on a 500-acre site in the previously obscure suburb of Abbotstown. It was a time of grandiose projects – the Brits had just built the Millennium Dome. But in 2001, as the technology bubble popped and tax revenues fell, questions began to be asked about the cost of this vast scheme. The PDs, Bertie's partners in government, were opposed to the size of the project, especially when it emerged that the final bill could top €1 billion. The government had only a slim majority, and after considerable political wrangling plans for the Abbotstown campus were scaled down dramatically.

The €62 million National Aquatic Centre opened on the site in 2003, costing more than twice the original estimate of €30 million that had been calculated in 2000. Phased development of other facilities was planned, but Abbotstown was bumped down the government priority list and progress was extremely slow. In January 2007 the government reheated the remains of the project and set up the National Sports Campus Development Authority (NSCDA) to replace Campus Stadium Ireland. Its watered down remit was to redevelop the vast Abbotstown site surrounding the National Aquatic Centre, building headquarters for sports bodies and a few football pitches and facilities. Athletes would flock to Ireland and train here in our space-age facilities before heading off to compete in the London Olympics in 2012. The quango was allocated €4.4 million by the Department of Arts,

Sport and Tourism in 2009. The board includes Miriam O'Callaghan – not the RTÉ presenter but a somewhat less glamorous Fianna Fáil councillor from Brian Cowen's Offaly constituency; serial state board member Bernadette Cronin; and ex-SIPTU enforcer Billy Attley. The body is chaired by former Enterprise Ireland boss Dan Flinter.

Things ground to a halt in 2009, when the government's Sport Capital Programme was put on ice as the recession emptied the Exchequer. But quangos are not easy to eradicate, and this one is no exception. Although targeted for the chop by An Bord Snip Nua, the agency will receive €7.75 million in state funding in 2010, including €1.6 million to cover day-to-day spending and a further €1.03 million as an 'operational subsidy' to the National Aquatic Centre.

Buried in these figures was a legal settlement for one of the few bits of the campus that had actually been built. In March 2010 it emerged that the state had coughed up €1.5 million to Dublin International Arena Ltd (DIAL), which had been the under-bidder for the contract to build the National Aquatic Centre. In 2000 DIAL had tendered for the contract to build and run the €64 million swimming pool, but the gig had gone to Dublin Waterworld – which, it would later emerge, was a €4 shelf company with no assets. The identity of its owners was masked by a British Virgin Islands company – normally a major no-no when tendering for government contracts. DIAL unleashed its lawyers, claiming that Dublin Waterworld should not have been awarded the contract in the first place.

It got worse. After part of the roof of the centre blew off in a storm in early 2005, an engineering report revealed that it had not been constructed to the original specifications. Management of the aquatic centre was taken away from Dublin Waterworld following a lengthy court battle. Grass continues to grow out at the Abbotstown campus, but little else.

B is for Bord na gCon

Bord na gCon, the Irish Greyhound Board, has lapped up over €100 million in funding over the last decade, but this quango is a pup.

It's caused more trouble than most of the other agencies put together through shoddy governance and management errors.

In 2006 the quango buried a report that revealed two dogs had tested positive for the banned substance EPO. After Aidan Tynan, the board's boss, wrote to sports minister John O'Donoghue expressing his horror at this situation, he was promptly sacked by the board. Bord na gCon chairman Paschal Taggart denied that the sacking had anything to do with the letter, but a government report resoundingly criticized the board for its actions. It also raised other issues that were subsequently investigated by the Comptroller & Auditor General. Two years later the C&AG report revealed a staggering series of 'irregularities' in the governance of the semi-state body. It found that security guards were paid in cash, which led to the agency having to reach a settlement with the Revenue Commissioners. It also discovered some pretty ropy tendering practices, which resulted in Shelbourne Park, the dog track in Ringsend, Dublin, paying €124,000 for a new generator that turned out not to be new at all. Another €280,000 was spent jazzing up Shelbourne Park without any obvious tenders having been issued. The report also criticized an arrangement whereby the managers of the two Dublin dog tracks were each given a car by a local garage. They were required to cover running costs, but despite this arrangement the Shelbourne manager subsequently claimed mileage expenses and was paid for them.

Fianna Fáil has traditionally been as thick as thieves with Bord na gCon. Sean Collins, brother of former Fianna Fáil minister Gerry Collins, served as the body's chief executive for a number of years. One of Collins's deals ended up going rather badly for Bord na gCon. He rented out agency property to his daughter-in-law, in breach of board procedures. Sometime later the agency needed back the premises for a new laboratory and was forced to pay Collins's daughter-in-law €95,000 to end the lease.

C is for Car Park

Beaumont Hospital was one of the first state bodies to dip its toe into the world of public–private partnerships, making a deal with Brendan

Murtagh's Winston Properties to build a multi-storey car park on its grounds in June 1998. It created a new entity called the Beaumont Hospital Car Park to handle the project.

An investigation by the Comptroller & Auditor General and later the Public Accounts Committee found that by building the car park by this method, the net cost to the state was between €9 million and €13 million greater than it should have been, due to the unnecessary granting of tax breaks. The C&AG lashed the hospital management, saying that its failure to fully scrutinize the deal left the state with its trousers down. Management had got in over their heads in the deal, 'even with all their banks of advisers'.

We dug deeper into the story, and in August 2007 revealed that Beaumont's management had also made a cringe-worthy cock-up with regard to the transfer of the car park from the subsidiary quango back to the hospital itself. This transfer did not formally occur until November 2003, years after it had been completed. This left the cash-strapped hospital exposed to a tax bill of some €970,000 for income received from the car park – a bill that would not have existed had the car park been transferred to the hospital, a state charity, upon completion. The new multi-storey car park, which cost €8.6 million to construct, had 600 spaces. But, given that it had been built on the site of Beaumont's existing 370-berth car park, the hospital gained only 230 new spaces. Between construction costs and the loss to the Exchequer from the developer's tax breaks, each of the extra 230 spaces cost a whopping €93,900.

D is for Dormant Accounts

The Dormant Accounts Board was set up as a flying wing of Gaeltacht-poverty outfit Pobal to take all the money that people had forgotten about in various bank accounts around the country and dole it out to various schemes. Some €75 million was allocated in this way in 2008. The quango has been chocka with political appointees in recent years, including ex-Fianna Fáil general secretary Pat Farrell, Fianna Fáil's solicitor of choice Frank Ward and the Green Party's

Des Gunning. Other interesting board members have included former IAWS finance chief David Martin and the inevitable social-partnership appointment in ex-CPSU brass Rosaleen Glackin – now with the Labour Relations Commission. The old Fianna Fáil links are very profitable, as Q4, the public-relations outfit set up by former FF insider Jackie Gallagher, won the contract to spin for this quango.

It costs more than you might think to allocate the proceeds of dormant accounts. Over a three-year period board fees and expenses climbed to nearly €245,000 – more than was handed out by the commission to the Canal Communities Partnership cultural centre, the Open Door Network's efforts against domestic violence and a Killenarden drug-prevention programme. Among the commission bills we have uncovered was one for €997.80 for 'catering for a board meeting' in 2006. It must have been quite a board meeting.

Goodbody Economic Consultants produced a long and wordy report on the activities of the Dormant Accounts Board just in time for inclusion in the body's annual report. They must have wished it had been delayed in the post. It found that 'where measures funded a large number of projects for small amounts, there must be some doubt as to whether the most pressing needs were always prioritised.' It also warned that 'a majority of operational projects have sustainability issues' and that there was little evidence to show how the grant-aided schemes actually performed. 'A more rigorous approach needs to be undertaken in the measurement and reporting of performance, especially in the period following the disbursement of funds.'

This quango was also targeted by An Bord Snip Nua, which figured that the government could save €1.7 million a year by shuttering it.

E is for Europe

Now that we need Europe more than it needs us, it would be a shame to leave EU quangos out completely. Ireland bagged only one decent European pseudo-organization when they were being handed out:

we host the headquarters of the European Foundation for the Improvement of Living and Working Conditions (Eurofound). Honestly we do. The agency, which was set up in 1975, was specifically targeted by two British think tanks, the Economic Research Council and Global Vision in their eminently readable *Essential Guide to* EU *Quangos 2009*. The report estimated that European agencies and bodies cost €1.979 billion in 2009. Ireland's quango, Eurofound, had a budget of €21 million in 2008, with staff costs eating up an extraordinary 45 per cent of the pie. The report suggests that this body could be completely outsourced to the private sector, noting that it duplicates the functions of 'any number of consultancies, which specialize in offering ways to improve company working conditions'.

F is for Fish

There are many weird and wonderful creatures at the bottom of the deep blue sea – and the same is true of quangolia. The Department of Communications oversees a morass of overlapping authorities that look after river- and lake-fishing issues, ranging from the seven regional fisheries boards to the central fisheries board and the cross-border Loughs Agency. A monster created by the Good Friday Agreement, the Loughs Agency is funded to the tune of €7 million per year by the Irish and British governments. Members of the board pocket about €8,100 per year and include all manner of Fianna Fáil activists and supporters, including former Senator Enda Bonner and Louth councillor Jacqui McConville.

The Central Fisheries Board is also crammed like a tin of sardines with Fianna Fáil loyalists, including Leitrim councillor Mary Bohan and Donegal party secretary Naul McCole. Administration costs hit €4.1 million in 2008. But then there are all the little regional boards too, stuffed to the gills with local political appointees and with overlapping administration costs. Each of these burned through up to €3 million per year in grants and other spending. It was an utterly wasteful situation, and the government finally moved to restructure the orgy of intermingled bodies by amalgamating them into a single jumbo one. Given that large chunks of the duties of these bodies involve water-quality issues, it'd make an awful lot more sense to move the new organization into a wing of the Department of the Environment.

The Department of Agriculture, a paragon of joined-up government at its finest, oversees offshore fishing. The quangos include Bord Iascaigh Mhara (BIM), a kind of fish-promotion board, which paid its chief executive €122,000 in 2008. It does stuff like tell people that fish is good for you. It also runs loss-making refrigeration units in the country's key fishing ports. All this for just €65 million a year in state funding. An Bord Snip Nua recommended that BIM be smacked with a mallet, after which its promotion duties should be handed over to Enterprise Ireland and the other bits hived off to the Department of Agriculture. But God knows what they can do with their new €20 million office block in Clonakilty, to which the agency moved as part of the grand decentralization wheeze.

G is for Grangegorman

The Grangegorman Development Agency has spent €14 million of taxpayers' money concocting a master plan for an unlikely looking property-development scheme in Dublin's north-west inner city. The agency – stacked full of local politicians and activists, including Fianna Fáil's Mary Fitzpatrick and Green Party dog-poo campaigner David Geary – was established to roll out a fancy scheme that would see the Dublin Institute of Technology move into a new campus and the Health Service Executive open up a new treatment centre on the site of the former mental hospital in Grangegorman. Bertie Ahern's close pal and Fianna Fáil fundraiser Chris Wall was even on the board for a bit when it was being launched. Earlier this year one of the former hospital buildings was refurbished and renovated. It's now a laundry. Progress or what?

Although planning has been secured for chunks of the proposed development, the government has been dragging its heels about signing a big fat cheque. Delays in reappointing board members haven't exactly been indicative of strong support for the scheme. With the economy down the U-bend, the chances of the shiny new 73-acre Grangegorman campus being on the top of any party's programme for government are slim. But at least we've a cracking master plan and loads of glossy brochures.

H is for Horses

Revelations of outrageous overspending at the Irish National Stud, the semi-state horse-breeding agency, hit the newsstands in May 2010. It emerged that the taxpayer spent more than €130,000 to cover household bills, including electricity and heating, for the former chief executive of the Irish National Stud over ten years.

John Clarke and his wife Monica lived in the five-bedroom Tully House in the grounds of the National Stud in Kildare. The Stud coughed up over €97,000 to redecorate the house and buy new furniture and carpets for the residence. This included an April 2005 bill of more than €4,000 for 'dishwasher lights' and €8,000 for shelves. Another bill in 2007 saw the state pay €2,819 for a new sofa chair, with a rosewood table and footstool costing €3,400 a year later, according to a list of detailed expenditure released under the Freedom of Information Act to the *Irish Times* in May 2010. The agency also spent €22,000 to build a new patio at the Clarkes' residence in 2008. Some €37,000 in taxpayers' money was used to pay electricity and heating bills at the house over the ten-year period, with Clarke contributing a modest €133 per month towards the running costs.

The National Stud also spent more than €800,000 to cover the travelling costs of Clarke and his wife over an eight-year period, which saw them travel abroad forty times between January 2002 and January 2010, when Clarke left the semi-state company after twenty-seven years. His wife's flight and chauffeur costs totalled €95,000. The trips were undertaken so that Clarke could visit race meetings and horse sales abroad, travelling to the US, Japan, UK, Italy and France. In May 2004 Clarke visited London, Florence, Nice, Paris and Tokyo, with his credit-card bill hitting €18,000 for the month.

His flights to Tokyo – via Paris – cost the state a cool €9,000. Five trips to the US for Clarke and his wife between 2002 and 2007 cost a staggering €46,000. Although he had a company car, Clarke took a chauffeur-driven limo from Kildare down to Cashel in February 2006. This cost €440. Another limo bill, for a two-day rental in Illinois in 2002, cost a hefty €1,800. It has also emerged that the semi-state company – which lost €2.3 million in 2008 – has paid out €700,000 in legal costs and settlements related to internal-staff complaints over a five-year period to 2009.

I is for 'inexplicably dismal'

Media Lab Europe, like the Bertie Bowl, was a grandiose and wasteful project pushed by the Taoiseach in his home city. Unlike the Bertie Bowl, it actually went ahead.

Media Lab was a joint venture between the world-famous Massachusetts Institute of Technology (MIT) and the Irish government. It had offices in a former Guinness warehouse in the Liberties. Bono joined the board in 2000, stepping down in 2003 to be replaced by his U2 colleague The Edge. The state invested €35 million. But it soon became clear that Media Lab Europe's reliance on corporate funding to meet its running costs was a really dumb idea, given that the venture was launched just as the tech bubble burst. The quango was forced to go cap-in-hand to the state for a €10 million bailout – in those days bailouts were in the millions rather than billions. The government flipped it the bird and, in January 2005, the operation collapsed, with the loss of fifty jobs. The PAC steamed in to have a look. Its excoriating report said the fault lay with the 'Government collectively, and the Taoiseach's Department, and the Taoiseach personally'. It revealed that in 1999 an internal Department of Finance report advising on potential state involvement in the scheme had described the plans for the proposed project as 'inexplicably dismal', 'mediocre' and 'flaky'. Bertie went ahead with it anyway, and €35.5 million in taxpayers' dosh was flushed away.

The PAC probe into the affair revealed that the liquidator of Media

Lab had sold the organization's portfolio of patents to a consultant who had been brought in to advise on what to do with the ideas generated by the project during its short life. The consultant paid €40,000 for the entire block. Department of Communications chief Brendan Tuohy told the PAC it was unusual 'to sell to the guy who came in to advise you. It would not be something that a Government department would do. Normal practice would be to put the patents out to tender.' We don't know if any of these patents has turned into a new Google or Facebook, but the fact that all the patents developed by the venture fetched no more than €40,000 tells its own story.

Media Lab Europe was subsequently replaced with Media Lab Lite: the National Digital Research Centre (NDRC). It took a long time to get up and running – in fact, in 2007 the Department of Communications requested it to surrender €1.75 million in state funding, in light of the 'slower than anticipated rollout'. It was a rare instance of a quango actually being pressed to give some of its funding back rather than being forced to spend it all.

Media Lab's landlord, the Digital Hub Development Agency, remains in existence, chaired by Dr Joyce O'Connor, an academic and the sister of former Anglo Irish Bank boss Seán FitzPatrick. The Exchequer pumps about €2 million per year into the agency, which also generates close to €3 million in rents, sponsorship and other commercial income; most of this is eaten up by a seriously heavy payroll and administration costs, which left the quango nursing a €286,000 deficit at the end of 2008, according to its latest annual report. An Bord Snip Nua didn't pull its punches on this agency, recommending that it be merged into either Enterprise Ireland or the IDA, saving the state about €1.8 million per year.

J is for Junkets

If there's one thing we've learned about all these state bodies and agencies, it's that the top people really like to go abroad. Preferably far, far away.

In July 2010 we revealed the mind-boggling levels of expenditure on foreign travel at Dublin City Council. Despite libraries closing, swimming pools being shuttered and sewage flooding some of the poorer estates in Dublin, the city council had racked up travel, accommodation and conference bills of €625,000 between January 2008 and February 2010. The recession was well and truly savaging the country at this stage. Documents received under the Freedom of Information Act showed that Dublin City Council staff members and councillors had been on the pig's back, with trips to Istanbul for the UEFA Cup Final weekend in 2008, weeklong visits to Boston and New York, and even a trip to Reykjavik to visit a Viking festival. Dublin City Council had just announced that it would have to close three municipal swimming pools, at Crumlin, Sean McDermott Street and Coolock, because it couldn't afford to keep them open. The council would save €800,000 per year by closing these three pools – only slightly more than it cost to send staff and councillors off on visits abroad over a two-year period.

The C&AG's report into FÁS contained a mysterious buried reference to a state agency – unnamed – that had paid for fifty-two spouses to travel abroad at the taxpayer's expense. PAC chairman Bernard Allen called for the mystery agency to come clean. On the Wednesday after our story, the Central Bank issued a statement. It confirmed that it was the agency in question, but it also claimed that the C&AG had botched the information it had been given about the travelling partners. The fifty-two spouses hadn't gone off on one 'super junket', the Dame Street institution explained. It had been a series of mini-junkets. So that's all right, then.

This wasn't the only long-haul jolly for groups charged with keeping an eye on the knitting. In 2008 the Competition Authority splashed out €11,100 to send off three people to an International Competition Network beano in Kyoto, Japan, an annual get-together for global-competition regulators. Two of the top suits travelled business class all the way, with a poor old researcher being stuck in steerage. Flights alone cost a total of €8,377. We would also reveal details of a May 2010 Competition Authority junket to Istanbul – complete with a poolside drinks reception in a five-star hotel, a visit to the historic Topkapi Palace and a cruise on the Bosphorus for delegates. This was an agency that slashed staff and costs in 2009 but still managed to have a €90,000 budget for travel and conferences in 2010 including nearly €39,000 in overseas travel.

When he's not busy with lengthy – and we mean really lengthy – probes into banks, the director of corporate enforcement, Paul Appleby, has been known to go abroad. His office spent a whopping €31,000 on travel in 2008. In 2009 Paul and Colette Appleby, along with two other people from the office, made the trip to St Petersburg for the arduous four-day conference of the International Association of Insolvency Regulators. It must have been dreadfully dull, but the conference also offered visits to the Hermitage Museum, boat trips and a jaunt to St Isaac's Basilica as part of the 'social programme'. At the time of writing, pictures from the trip were still available on www.insolvencyreg.org. Appleby is smiling in the middle of the third row if you want to look at the main photo.

Brendan Logue – the man who put the 'logue' into 'travelogue' – represented the Registrar of Credit Unions at the five-day annual World Council of Credit Unions shindig in Hong Kong in the summer of 2008. The Registrar of Credit Unions office is part of the Financial Regulator's operation, which spent €775,000 on travel and expenses in 2007 alone. The Credit Unions headed off to Las Vegas for their annual knees-up in July 2010.

The Law Reform Commission does what it says on the tin. It considers and evaluates potential changes to laws in Ireland. This, it seems, necessitates an awful lot of long-haul travel, as we discovered from our trawl through the organization's annual reports over the last decade. In 2000 the Law Reform Commission dispatched delegations to Ottawa in Canada, Washington, DC and Basle. It was Ottawa again the following year, with The Hague thrown in for good measure. Sydney made for a cracking 2003, although the mood may have dimmed after a visit to Belfast. Victoria in Canada was the jolly in 2004, followed by a splendid outing to Cape Town. The Law Reform Commission jetted again to Sydney and to London, not once but four times in 2006. However, the world began to go down the plughole the following year, with no long-haul travel at all. There were, as compensation, little visits to beautiful Padua in Italy, Durham with its fine cathedral, Kent, London and Armagh. In 2008 travel was restricted to London and Edinburgh. It's quite an extraordinary amount of jet-setting for such a weenchy quango and one that has some particularly opaque financial statements, restricted to the amount of grant allocation it receives each year. A parliamentary question reveals that between 2003 and 2007 the Law Reform Commission cost the state almost €12 million. Did we mention that it had produced thirty reports between 2000 and 2008? That's more than three a year.

But the real prince of the junketeering regulators was former financial ombudsman Joe Meade, who retired from his office at the start of 2010. The *Sunday Independent* charted Meade's trips, from his days journeying out to Australia when he was the data protection commissioner to his jet-setting career as financial ombudsman. We revealed that the Office of the Financial Services Ombudsman spent an extraordinary €103,000 on 'conferences and travel' over a two-year period. Meade certainly liked Australia, having splashed out the taxpayers' money to head back to its beautiful gold coast for yet another jolly with the International Association of Financial Ombudsmen in 2007.

K is for Kingdom-Building

One of the fastest-growing quango kingdoms is the Review Body on Higher Remuneration in the Public Sector. These are the guys who dole out pay rises and bonuses to our highly deserving top civil servants. This originally cost €31,774 back in 1996 and again in 1997 – about the same as a secondhand Beemer. But in 2006 the bill for this lot exploded, hitting €480,000, or a nearly Zimbabwesque jump of 1,280 per cent over a decade. Over ten years, the Local Government Management Service board saw its spending rise 861 per cent, while the Health Research Board budget inflated by 451 per cent. The Competition Authority had a 441 per cent hike in its budget – and it still doesn't do anything useful. Most of these rising costs are to pay for burgeoning staff numbers at these ever-expanding agencies.

L is for Language

An Foras Teanga is one of those Irish-language organizations that few people have heard of and fewer really understand. It promotes the Irish language on a cross-border basis, as part of the Good Friday Agreement, and through it we fund about 75 per cent of Foras na Gaeilge and 25 per cent of the Ulster-Scots Agency. Just over €20 million was allocated to these organizations in 2005.

While Foras might be absolutely smashing at promoting the Irish language, quite frankly it stinks at transparency and accountability. Its 2005 annual report was published in February 2010. The ridiculously outdated accounts show that the then chief executive, Seosamh Mac Donncha, saw his salary rise from €97,000 in 2004 to €130,000 in 2005. (This was double the fee paid to his counterpart across the border for running the Ulster-Scots Agency.) The agency's rather limp approach to financial management seems to have the blessing of its departmental masters: one Foras document notes that the Department of An Gaeltacht 'didn't consider it appropriate to set key financial targets for Foras na Gaeilge for the year ending December 2005'.

Corporate-governance practices are also extremely worrying. The latest review notes that no register of members' interests was maintained. This means that we didn't know if any organizations connected to the body's executives and board members received any grants. Well, at least we didn't know until we looked into it. One of the biggest recipients of grant aid in 2005 was Forbairt Naíonraí Teoranta, the Irish schooling organization, which received €1.08 million – the second biggest award in 2005. The Foras deputy chief executive sits on the board of Forbairt Naíonraí Teoranta. There's no suggestion of any mischief, but we should be told where state money is going and whether there are any connections between the funders and the funded.

A 2005 Government Value for Money report discovered that many of Foras na Gaeilge's funding activities overlapped with those of Ciste na Gaeilge, an organization that bagged €15.3 million in funding from 2000 to 2005. They were both financing extraordinarily similar projects, and sometimes they were funding each other: the biggest recipient of Ciste funding was the Foras unit Bord na Leabhar Gaeilge, which picked up €5.9 million over the period.

Our favourite remains An Coimisinéir Teanga, which recently appointed its boss Seán Ó Cuirreáin for a second six-year term. The 'Coimis' is an Irish-language hit squad, set up to bollock out any state bodies that aren't doing their bit for the language. It is far more organized that its peers, with a shiny new 2009 annual report, available for insomniacs. This shows that the body had dealt with 3,000 complaints about not being able to access state services in Irish since it was founded in 2004. The Coimis cost €865,000 in 2009.

M is for Media Advisers

In order to justify their existence, quangos need to have their work publicized. The taxpayer, as usual, gets suckered for the bill for this promotion. The National Consumer Agency – the quango to which Bertie Ahern's former mot Celia Larkin was appointed – paid close to €562,000 to Q4 Public Relations from May 2007 to February 2010. That's nearly €18,000 per month. Despite being the state body charged with ensuring that consumers got the best value, the NCA didn't shop around, having employed Q4 PR since 2005. The PR agency – headed up by former Fianna Fáil general secretary Martin Mackin and Bertie Ahern's former adviser Jackie Gallagher – was proposed by Celia Larkin at an NCA board meeting. It also emerged that while Q4 was advising the National Consumer Agency it was also working for grocery behemoth Tesco. 'There's definitely a potential conflict of interest where you have Q4 representing the NCA, which is doing price surveys on Tesco products, and at the same time putting out ads telling you how cheap Tesco is,' Fine Gael's Leo Varadkar pointed out. The NCA has said that it is satisfied that its PR company had 'Chinese walls' to separate the two accounts.

N is for the National Statistics Board

Every country needs up-to-date data relating to its economy, population and trade. Fiscal policy is planned using these figures. But few will have heard of the rather low-key National Statistics Board (NSB) – a body established to oversee the Central Statistics Office and help in 'developing its statistical strategy'. There are eight people on its board, which is made up of social-partnership worthies, civil servants and stray economists, including former Irish Farmers Association bean-counter Con Lucey. There's a nice picture of the board standing in front of the Taoiseach's office on its website. The statutory body, set up in 1994, is chaired by Pat O'Hara of the Western Development Commission – an outfit itself targeted by An Bord Snip Nua for extinction. The NSB publishes an average of two documents per year. Its last press statement – 'NSB Supports Use of PPS Number' – was issued in July 2003. This enormously productive board cost the taxpayer over €190,000 between 2003 and 2007.

O is for Overlap

Overlapping and duplication are some of the key attributes of any self-respecting quango. In several sectors it's damn difficult to tell one statutory body from another. There's a phonebook of agencies dealing with workplace and labour-relations issues. The Labour Court, Labour Relations Commission and the Employment Appeals Tribunal are stuffed full of ministerial appointments and former trade-union officials. Former LRC boss Maurice Cashell, in the 2007 annual report, admitted that 'the very multiplicity of bodies can be confusing, not least to the employee with a grievance'. An Bord Snip Nua recommended that a rationalization of these overlapping bodies could save €3 million a year.

Then there's the Health and Safety Authority and the National Employment Rights Authority, both doing rather similar tasks. Merging these two bodies would save €5 million a year. Training and

jobs-support projects and schemes are funded by a stack of over-
lapping and conflicting agencies ranging from FÁS, Skillnets and
Enterprise Ireland to the thirty-five county enterprise boards. An
Bord Snip Nua suggested that the 'County and City Enterprise
Boards, the Business Innovation Centres, the Western Development
Commission and the enterprise functions of Údarás na Gaeltachta,
Shannon Development, Bord Iascaigh Mhara, LEADER and Tea-
gasc, as well as sector-specific agencies such as the Irish Film Board,
should be merged within a reconstituted Enterprise Ireland.'

It makes it rather easier to hide if your organization has almost
the same name as the one next door. When Bertie Ahern created the
National Economic and Social Development Office (NESDO), he
managed not only to duplicate but to triplicate a quango. Under the
umbrella of the NESDO huddles the National Economic and Social
Council (NESC), the National Economic and Social Forum (NESF)
and the National Centre for Partnership and Performance (NCPP).
Each of these three inexplicable bodies has its own board of directors.
Rory O'Donnell heads up the NESC as well as the mothership
NESDO, on €150,712. Seán Ó hÉigeartaigh, the NESF leader, earns
€118,872, while Lucy Fallon Byrne at NCPP is paid €114,366. See if
you can figure out what they do: 'The primary role of NESDO is to
add value to the work of its constituent bodies through collabora-
tive policy development initiatives,' the website notes. It is also
involved in 'facilitating and promoting complementary programmes
of research, analysis and discussion by the NESC, NESF and NCPP'.
NESDO got a €5.4 million grant from the government in 2008 and
€5.8 million a year earlier. It lashed out €1.1 million on consultants,
€1.5 million on PR and advertising, and almost €120,000 on taxis,
couriers and post over a two-year period. Money well spent for 'col-
laborative policy development initiatives'. Or something.

P is for Pointless

One of Bertie Ahern's final thoughts as Taoiseach was that Irish
people weren't happy enough. So he set up the Active Citizenship

Taskforce to see what could be done. Some real heavy hitters were drafted in to join the taskforce – and its interim steering group. These included former NIB boss John Trethowan, ex-Bank of Ireland director Mary Redmond, GAA president Sean Kelly, ICTU beardie David Begg, Mary Davis of the Special Olympics, former PD TD Bobby Molloy, secretary general of the Department of the Taoiseach Dermot McCarthy, National College of Ireland boss (and Seán Fitz-Patrick's sister) Joyce O'Connor, plus a stack of charity types. The body cost €383,000 between 2006 and 2007. Around €15,000 was spent on official entertainment. The question of whether we are happier since this taskforce was created has yet to be answered, but higher taxes, Seánie FitzPatrick and the horrors of NAMA may weigh heavily on the answer. Following the report by An Bord Snip Nua, the taskforce was earmarked for closure in 2010.

Q is for Queueing Up for Grants

The Family Support Agency (FSA) is a big fat ATM machine for family centres and counselling services. In 2007 – the year of the latest annual report – it approved 553 of the 569 applications it received for grants. That's a 97 per cent success rate. The 3 per cent that failed to bag a grant must have been quite outstanding in their ineptitude.

The FSA, which vies with a clatter of other similar-sounding bodies, is one of the top quangos earmarked for closure by An Bord Snip Nua. Its demise would deliver the biggest single saving of any quango cull. Colm McCarthy and his Bord Snip team calculated that the state could save €30 million per year simply by chopping the agency. That's an awful lot of money. It'd cover the child-allowance payments for about 170,000 kids for a week.

The agency was set up in 2003 by the Department of Social and Family Affairs and is presided over by former Fianna Fáil minister Michael O'Kennedy, who also sits on the Refugee Appeals Board. Past board members include Fianna Fáil's Maria Corrigan, who was nominated by Bertie Ahern to the Senate in 2007 (she also had a relationship with Bertie's close pal Joe Burke for a number of years while he was chairman of Dublin Port, but that's another story), and Long-ford Fianna Fáil councillor Paddie Connellan. The board cost nearly €210,000 in a two-year period, with admin and payroll costs for the fifty-odd staff at its St Stephen's Green headquarters costing a stonking €4.84 million in 2007.

R is for Refugee Appeals Tribunal

They clearly weren't thinking about acronyms on the day they set up the Refugee Appeals Tribunal in 2000. The organization, which was created to provide a service for those whose application for refugee status had been turned down, is to be phased out and replaced by a brand-new quango called the Protection Review Tribunal. The high level of pay received by members of RAT – all of whom are barristers or solicitors appointed by the Minister for Justice – came under increased scrutiny after it emerged that one member, James Nicholson, had pocketed €780,000 in fees over a five-year period. This came to light in 2008 when a case was brought to the High Court by three asylum seekers who 'perceived bias' on his part. The case was settled but Nicholson resigned.

Nicholson wasn't the only one making a decent wedge out of the quango. Most recent figures showed that almost €1.24 million was paid out in fees to its members in 2008, with Michelle O'Gorman bagging €180,097. RAT has also taken flak over its lack of transparency, particularly about the absence of information on decisions by various members, the number of judicial reviews taken against certain members and the wildly different sums of money snagged by the members.

S is for Shannon Foynes

If the Shannon Foynes Port Company (SFPC) was a schoolboy, chances are it would be sitting down the back of a class, flicking spitballs at the teacher. It is constantly in trouble.

Shannon Foynes is the second largest port company in the country, responsible for the whole of the Shannon estuary. In 2004 the chief executive Brian Byrne went looking for a pay rise. The government wouldn't budge, but Shannon Foynes figured that Byrne would leave if he didn't get more money, so it looked for an alternative method of 'bridging the gap'. It hired Byrne's Targa 33 cruiser as a backup and service boat. Deloitte & Touche subsequently were unable to find any evidence of a tendering process, or indeed of any need for the boat, for which over €50,000 was paid in 2005 alone.

Byrne was suspended on full pay in October 2006, after allegations were made by two port users about the circumstances of the sale of a 44-acre site in Limerick's docklands. The port company launched an investigation into the conduct of both Byrne and non-executive director Morgan Leahy. That move prompted Byrne and Leahy to launch a High Court action against Shannon Foynes, calling for the investigation to be abandoned because it was 'manifestly unfair' and had gone 'off the rails'. After more than a year of legal wrangling, the company settled. Byrne was paid two years' salary – about €400,000 – and all his legal costs. His legal bill from Arthur Cox came to €930,000, with SFPC's own legal bill hitting €600,000. Deloitte's investigation bill was €125,000, meaning that the whole affair had cost the taxpayer more than €2 million.

In summer 2010 news broke that a former deputy chief executive at Shannon Foynes had been paid up to €400,000 between 2001 and 2006 even though she was no longer working at the semi-state company. Margaret McNamara had taken injunctive proceedings to prevent Shannon Foynes from removing her from her position. Shannon Foynes had made her an offer to stay at home and not go in to work pending the full hearing of the court case – which did not hit the High Court for five years.

T is for Toothless

The National Property Services Regulatory Authority is quite a mouthful. But it's a mouth without any teeth. The agency was set up in 2005 by justice minister Michael McDowell to deal with estate agent and auctioneering mischief. However, the legislation to support the agency and to give it powers has yet to be passed by the Oireachtas. Despite this, a director designate was appointed in June 2006 and the agency has nine staff at its Navan headquarters. The office was allocated a budget of €700,000 for 2007, €930,000 for 2008, €657,000 for 2009 and €738,000 for 2010. That's a total spend of just over €3 million on an utterly powerless organization.

U is for *Údarás*

The hundreds of state agencies and bodies that give out grants and awards could be taught a thing or two by Údarás na Gaeltachta. Údarás is like a mini FÁS, IDA and Enterprise Ireland just for the rapidly shrinking Irish-speaking bits of the country. It provides money to companies to support jobs in the Gaeltacht. But Údarás jobs cost a lot more than normal jobs created by the IDA or Enterprise Ireland: latest figures suggest that it costs €10,800 in grants to support a job through Údarás, as against €6,100 at Enterprise Ireland. So €10 million would support 925 jobs in the Gaeltacht or 1,639 anywhere else in the country. Apples and oranges, says Údarás – or should that be *úlla agus oráistí*?

Údarás has a remarkably bulky board, made up mostly of local politicians and government appointees. In 2007 and 2008 fees and expenses for the agency's board members hit a staggering €1.01 million. It also spent €1.3 million on travel expenses and a further €890,000 on PR and advertising in the period.

Fianna Fáil is – obviously enough – the dominant player on the board. But the Gaeltacht is clearly a very small place. Our research into Údarás has shown that companies or enterprises associated with various board members have received close to €8.2 million of taxpayers' money through Údarás grants over the last ten years.

In April 2010 it emerged that the outgoing chief executive Pádraig Ó hAoláin snagged a €3,900 bonus in 2009, despite the freeze on bonuses in the public sector. Ó hAoláin was being paid an annual salary of €158,000 and had a company car worth almost €40,000.

The Comptroller & Auditor General roasted the agency after it emerged that there had been irregularities over the sale of thirteen holiday homes in Connemara in 2004. The agency made a right mess of the tendering process and tried to sell the homes to a local Gaeltacht group, even though it had not made the best bid. On legal advice, Údarás cancelled the sale. Eventually it put the homes back on the market, finally shifting them for just €1.645 million. By making a dog's dinner of the sales process, the C&AG found, Údarás had lost out on €300,000.

In 1998 the organization gave a grant of €70,000 to Moycullen-based quarry firm M & M Caireal Teoranta for business development and discovered only later that the company wasn't even in the Gaeltacht. Doh! Údarás told the PAC in 2005 that it had been an 'innocuous mistake'. It had decided not to try to retrieve the grant, despite spending staff time worth €10,000 on the issue. Chief executive Ó hAoláin told the committee that it would be a waste of taxpayers' money to pursue the matter further. An Bord Snip Nua figured that if Údarás's job-support function was sucked into Enterprise Ireland, the state would be €6.9 million better off per year.

V is for Vacant

In November 2009 we received a tip-off at the *Sunday Independent*: look at the empty office space at science and enterprise quango Forfás. After doing so, we revealed that the outfit was wasting up to €1.2 million per year in rent on unused offices. The agency, which has included former FÁS boss Rody Molloy and ex-Anglo Irish Bank director Ann Heraty on its board, was paying property developer Bernard McNamara and his partners rent for vacant office space in Carrisbrook House in Ballsbridge. The agency also paid rent for space in the grotty Knockmaun House on Lower Mount Street, having taken over the leases in 1990. It sublet these offices, but when tenants left the offices sat vacant. In 2009 it paid up to €990,000 in rent on the largely empty Carrisbrook House and €243,000 for Knockmaun House.

The Office of Public Works, which manages the state's property assets, has been ruthlessly inefficient over the last decade. A 2005 probe by the Oireachtas PAC revealed that the OPW had squandered €19 million on accommodation for asylum seekers without a single person being housed in any of the properties. The government body also splashed out €1.5 million tarting up new offices – ten times the original estimate – only for legal complications to keep them vacant for three years.

W is for Wages

The pay of the top civil servants who run the vast assortment of state agencies, taskforces, semi-states, regulatory bodies and ombudsmen is quite frankly obscene.

The former senator Maurice Manning is paid €237,000 as president of the Human Rights Commission. By comparison, Ban Ki-moon, secretary general of the UN, is paid just €171,000. David Gunning, chief executive of Coillte, which essentially watches trees growing in forests and cuts down a few of them, was paid €407,000 in 2008. That's more than President Obama gets. How about HIQA – the Health Information and Quality Authority? Its boss Tracey Cooper bagged €199,502, or about €50,000 more than US Federal Reserve chairman Ben Bernanke. Andrew Kelly of the Blood Transfusion Board trousered almost €168,000. Across the Irish sea, the chief executive of the British Blood Service earned €146,000, according to its most recent annual report. The British service got 2.1 million people to donate blood, compared to just 95,000 people here.

The Irish Aviation Authority paid Eamonn Brennan €350,000 in 2008, some €125,000 more than the British prime minister earns. Airport regulator Cathal Guiomard got €203,279 in 2007, or more than his boss, transport minister Noel Dempsey, earned last year. Horse Racing Ireland paid Brian Kavanagh €163,000, or about four times as much as a staff nurse. Digital Hub boss Philip Flynn was paid €187,000, close to what cabinet ministers earn.

Dublin Airport Authority, which has lumbered us with the

€200 million great white elephant of Terminal 2, paid Declan Collier an extraordinary €638,000 in 2008, and €698,000 in 2007. Despite DAA losing a stonking €13 million in 2009 and having its €1.25 billion gross debt-pile downgraded by ratings agency Moody's over fears that tumbling passenger numbers might hamper its attempts to pay back loans, Collier bagged a €51,000 performance bonus as part of his €568,000 pay packet. This was in a year when all staff earning over €30,000 were hit with a pay cut and the semi-state introduced a voluntary redundancy scheme to skim off excess staff.

The former oil executive has been at the front of a €2 billion splurge to make Dublin Airport capable of handling 30 million passengers a year. But in the real world, passenger numbers have fallen from 23.5 million down to the 17 million forecast for 2010. Collier's salary is far more than Angela Merkel's and Nicolas Sarkozy's wages combined.

X is for X-rated

Despite a messy legal action when it tried to ban the porno movie *Anabolic Initiations 5*, the Irish Film Classification Board remains a cracking ministerial award to be divvied up to loyal political servants or party activists, who get paid to sit around watching films. The film watchers include a stack of former Fianna Fáil politicians, such as P. J. Sheridan, a former councillor, as well as three former Fianna Fáil senators, Olga Bennett, Tom Fitzgerald and Marian McGennis. Green Party candidate Elizabeth Davidson is also a film classifier. The lucky ten officials got close to €40,000 each for sitting around viewing films and deciding on age ratings for them in 2008. The ten assistant classifiers were paid fees of €306,683 and expenses of €52,569 in 2007; fees of €339,608 and expenses of €49,898 in 2008.

Apart from the ten specially appointed film classifiers, the agency had eleven other staff members. An Bord Snip Nua recommended that €500,000 per year could be saved by merging the IFSC with the Broadcasting Authority of Ireland and throwing ComReg in for good measure.

Y is for Yacht

On 11 September 2008 the *Asgard II*, a state-owned sail-training vessel, sank in the Bay of Biscay. The official cause was a hole in the hull,
but the ship might have sunk under the burden of keeping an entire
quango afloat.

Coiste an Asgard was set up to run sail-training programmes on
the ship. It was under the command, so to speak, of the Department
of Defence. So when the *Asgard II* sank in the Atlantic on that September morning in 2008, there really wasn't much point in keeping
the organization open. But Coiste an Asgard was able to hang on.
And on. In February 2009 it was proposed that the €3.8 million insurance payout could be used to buy a brand-new training vessel. Plans
to refloat the vessel were also considered but were ultimately torpedoed when the country's top naval officer, Commodore Frank Lynch,
expressed concerns about the safety of a refloated ship. A frantic lobbying process to buy a new training vessel began, with Minister for
Defence Willie O'Dea writing to Minister for Finance Brian Lenihan
asking for the green light to make a purchase. But the quango was
finally zapped in the December 2009 budget, a full fifteen months
after the ship sank, saving the state €800,000 per year.

Z is for Zapped

In late June 2010 the Institute of Public Administration (IPA) – a
quango funded to the tune of €3.8 million a year by the taxpayer –
produced a report on various state agencies, bodies and organizations.
Organizations rather like itself.

The IPA's definition of 'national non-commercial state agencies'
left a lot of state agencies out of the mix, but the exercise was useful
in that it allowed a comparison with 2007, when it last conducted its
census. In the intervening three years, eighteen quangos had been
shuttered. As well as Coiste an Asgard, the other victims are the
National Salmon Commission, the Advisory Council for English

Language Schools, the Centre for Early Childhood Development and Education, Integrate Ireland Language and Training Centre, the International Education Board Ireland, the National Adult Learning Council, the Advisory Board for Irish Aid, the Board for the Employment of the Blind, the ever-busy Poisons Council, the Garda Síochána Complaints Appeal Board, the National Consultative Committee on Racism and Interculturalism, the National Crime Council, the sadly missed NDP Gender Equality Unit, the Registration of Title Rules Committee, the National Forum on Europe, the Active Citizenship Office and the Irish Newfoundland Partnership. But, while these agencies have bitten the dust since 2007, the government in its infinite wisdom has created eight brand-new shiny quangos, including the Science Gallery in Trinity College, the Grangegorman Development Agency, the Management Development Council, the National Paediatric Hospital Development Board, the utterly pointless and powerless Property Services Regulation Authority and the Office of Confidential Recipient, a quango set up to handle whistleblower information from within the ranks of the Gardaí and headed up by President Mary McAleese's former secretary general Brian McCarthy. Newborn agencies also include An Foras Orgánach, an organic food advisory group with nineteen members including former Green Party secretary Stiofán Nutty, and the National Transport Authority. The members of the board of this last new quango will earn €12,600 per year apiece and include Damian Usher, a bank manager from Meath, who canvassed for his friend Fianna Fáil minister Noel Dempsey . . . who appointed him to the board.

10. The Property Players: DDDA and NAMA

In its heyday, the Dublin Docklands Development Authority was a bit like FÁS . . . but for a posher type of person. The executives and board members of the DDDA squandered hundreds of millions of euros of taxpayers' money on fine wines, lavish foreign travel, pretentious art installations and quite possibly the dumbest land deal in the history of the state, if not the world.

The DDDA replaced the Customs House Development Authority in 1997, the year that Bertie Ahern became Taoiseach. Its brief was to lead a major project of social and economic regeneration in Dublin's docklands, which at that stage had become bandit territory. 'They eat their young down there,' wealthy developer Harry Crosbie told viewers of RTÉ's *Late Late Show* in 2005, as he outlined his flashy plans to benefit the area by building lots of two-bedroom flats and shops. Under the aegis of the DDDA, the docklands would become a Klondike for developers: those in the loop would make fortunes. The scheme would attract €3.35 billion in private and public investment, making it by some distance the single largest urban project in the history of the state.

Crucially, this new quango was granted statutory autonomy for development planning: it could make its own master plans and grant certificates to developers, allowing them to skip the step of seeking planning permission from Dublin City Council. This planning 'super ray' needed to be exercised with care, to ensure that it was used in the public interest rather than to benefit a few property tycoons. But the authority got far too close to Seán FitzPatrick's Anglo Irish Bank and its developer pals, becoming known as 'the downtown branch of Anglo'. Misguided government appointments and lax oversight saw the state agency all but annexed by key bank executives. FitzPatrick sat on the DDDA board, and the DDDA's chairman Lar Bradshaw became a director of Anglo. Bradshaw's replacement at the DDDA,

Donal O'Connor, became chairman of Anglo. The government – through the Department of the Environment, which is responsible for the DDDA – could have done something about this dangerously incestuous situation. But it did nothing.

The authority was a useful bit of political grease: as well as the nine-member board there was a 25-strong council – all political appointees. It was located in Ahern's own constituency. And the Drumcondra man got extraordinary mileage from the political goodwill the various docklands schemes and projects created in the good times.

'There's no doubt about it, it had an awful lot of clout,' a political source told the *Sunday Tribune* in 2006. 'Anyone on the council could get trips abroad and get invited to canapés and champagne in the docklands. There were pots of money to be thrown at communities to keep them happy. Every summer and every Christmas, those people in the docklands were guests at Bertie's cheese 'n' wine parties in St Luke's. It was run as a separate city down by the water.'

But, while the authority was good for political schmoozing, it was also the mother of all gravy trains for the insiders, who partied and travelled abroad at taxpayers' expense. Internal DDDA documents obtained by the *Irish Independent* under the Freedom of Information Act revealed a shameful binge with our money. Expenses clocked up by the authority included vast quantities of wine bought for board meetings, booze bills at Lillie's Bordello nightclub, a trip to Paris for the 2007 Rugby World Cup, golf outings, jewellery from Weir's and an eye-popping €2,200 blown at Claridge's in London on a two-day splurge. Some €1,077 was spent to buy tickets to the West End show *Billy Elliot* in September 2006. Exactly how that benefited urban regeneration is not clear.

Between August 2004 and October 2009 DDDA staff and executives racked up bills of €518,000 on company credit cards, which had limits of up to €40,000. Company cards were held by former chief executives Peter Coyne and Paul Maloney, as well as finance director David Higgins and his predecessor Martin O'Sullivan, and the cards were often used to pay bills for others in the organization. The sheer scale of this expenditure is even more extreme, given that the DDDA had a staff of just fifty-five people. The task of rejuvenating the docklands cost the taxpayer €210,000 in flights for the insiders, €116,000 in hotel bills and a further €82,700 in restaurant bills.

In April 2007, as jobless numbers began to rise with the slowdown in the construction sector, the DDDA was oblivious to the darkening clouds. It thought it appropriate to spend €2,847 on a meal at the rather splendid Michelin-starred Restaurant Patrick Guilbaud, where the pan-roast duck foie gras with stewed apple, *pain d'épice* and muscat grapes cost €44. And that's just a starter. Snouts were also buried in the trough at the Ely CHQ restaurant, including one outing for €6,447 in March 2007 and another costing €5,247 the following month.

The DDDA spent close to €600,000 on foreign travel for its key members, including the Anglo Irish Bank duo Seán FitzPatrick and Lar Bradshaw. One flight to Vancouver, for board member Joan O'Connor, cost a staggering €5,505. That's more than a primary-school teacher earns in a month.

In 2004 FitzPatrick and his wingman Bradshaw were part of a thirteen-strong fact-finding team sent by the DDDA to visit Helsinki and St Petersburg. The travellers blew €6,000 on restaurants in just three days, with an obscene bacchanal at St Petersburg's Noble Nest restaurant, featuring lashings of caviar and Bollinger champagne, coming to €2,578. The jaunt to the Baltic saw the travellers stay in the opulent €450-per-night Corinthia Nevskij Palace in St Petersburg and the Hotel Kamp in Helsinki. The flight for Fitz-Patrick cost €2,635, with Bradshaw's coming in slightly cheaper.

In October 2003 Bradshaw and FitzPatrick were among a party of fifteen that flew business class to the US to view harbour developments in New York and Baltimore. The flights cost €3,800 each. The travellers stayed in a plush hotel on New York's Madison Avenue, with the final bill for restaurants, drink and accommodation hitting €27,000. The piers-and-beers junket must have exhausted the jet-lagged revellers.

FitzPatrick and Bradshaw were among the junketeers who stayed in the €580-per-night Amstel InterContinental Hotel in Amsterdam during a boozy October 2005 jolly, when bottles of Chablis, at €63 each, were downed with gay abandon. They jetted to San Sebastián and Bilbao in October 2006, and produced hotel bills for €450 per night. FitzPatrick went on a junket to Glasgow in May 2005 that featured a slap-up meal in the exclusive Etain restaurant, where the travellers glugged back bottles of wine at €60 apiece. There was a €2,065 champagne-and-dinner blowout in Cannes, although the Anglo duo didn't make that one.

The extravagant meals and luxury hotels weren't all abroad. The DDDA did its bit for the Irish tourism industry by holding a series of 'annual strategy' board meetings in Wexford. The DDDA racked up a bill of €7,785 for just one day at Dunbrody House in 2006, and €10,733 for just one day at Marlfield House in 2007 as the recession was hitting these shores. While people were losing their jobs, the DDDA dined in Marlfield's wonderful restaurant and necked bottles of wine costing €85 each. Rarely has the taxpayer treated a state agency to such fine wine. Rarely has the taxpayer been treated with such utter contempt.

The company credit cards were used to make payments to Manchester City and Middlesbrough football clubs, as well as Smyths Toys and Newbridge Silverware. The DDDA indicated that the football club payments were part of a schools project, with the expenditure at Smyths Toys in December 2005 related to 'props for a teambuilding exercise'. The Newbridge Silverware spending was on pens and picture frames for presentations and gifts, according to the DDDA.

While the DDDA was squandering money on its executives and board members, it was doing things on the cheap for the little people. In 2006 the DDDA took community representatives and school principals to a Viking festival in northern France, but only coughed up for Ryanair and three-star hotels.

Wasting taxpayers' money on champagne and caviar is inexcusable, but the problems in the DDDA were much more deep-rooted than that. The authority was at the centre of billions of euros' worth of big business deals that involved alarming conflicts of interest.

In early July 2009 Nick Webb had an afternoon pint in Davy Byrnes pub with a rather well-known property player, who had been lunching for most of the day. In the course of the discussion about how screwed everything was, they talked about the docklands. As a throwaway line, the property guy mentioned talk about Lar Bradshaw being involved in owning a few buildings down in the docks. The following morning, none the worse for wear, Nick went straight up to the King's Inns and the Registry of Deeds office. After sifting though land records for a while, there was a hit. The documents showed Bradshaw was a member of the Liffey Partnership, which owned a major €70 million car park and office development in the heart of the IFSC. The DDDA had approved major changes in the scheme to allow an office block to be built on top of the car park. Bradshaw's fellow investors in the Liffey Partnership included Derek Quinlan and hotelier Francis Brennan. We obtained documents that showed that the deeds to the land had been transferred from the DDDA's forerunner, the Customs House Development Authority, to Bradshaw and the Liffey Partnership on the day before Bradshaw was appointed chairman of the DDDA. We also discovered that Bradshaw owned a stake in the key retail unit at the entrance to the IFSC, where his fellow shareholders included RTÉ's Pat Kenny and builder Seán Dunne.

It was an extraordinary situation: the chairman of a state agency had major financial interests in an area that he was tasked with overseeing as part of a €10 billion development plan. The DDDA had the power to take decisions affecting businesses that could have competed with Bradshaw's premises. Bradshaw's car park in Manor Street is the only multi-storey car park in the whole of the IFSC.

Other potential conflicts of interest were rife within the authority, which adopted the government-wide ethics policy of asking key members to declare what they owned, and then doing nothing about it. We reported that Seán FitzPatrick's family had bought property in the new developments in the docklands, including a luxury flat in Customs House Square, while he served on the board of the authority. It emerged that the authority had paid out almost €1 million to companies linked to its board of directors over the period 2006–8. Board member Niamh O'Sullivan is a director of Arup Consulting, which pocketed €682,000 in consultancy fees from the body. Donal O'Connor saw his main employer, accountancy group PricewaterhouseCoopers, earn €149,000 in internal audit and consultancy fees in 2007. Sheila O'Donnell's family-owned architectural firm bagged more than €132,000 from the DDDA during the three-year period. Among other docklands board members, Dónall Curtin, Catherine Mullarkey and Angela Cavendish all had strong Anglo connections.

PR woman Mary Finan – a former head of the RTÉ Authority – was a member of the DDDA council in 2005 and 2006. From 2003 she was also chairwoman of Wilson Hartnell PR, which had a major contract with the authority, earning €630,000 between 2006 and 2009. Wilson Hartnell certainly has a history of charging quangos big fees. As recounted in Chapter 4, this was the PR company that had bagged €318,000 from the HSE for the design of a leaflet on pregnancy and sexually transmitted infections.

Despite the obvious overlaps between the authority and its board members' private interests and investments, the DDDA believed that it had the situation under control. It was as clean as the proverbial whistle, according to former DDDA chief executive Peter Coyne, who left in 2005. 'There was never even a hint of any kind of corruption, nothing at all,' he told Justine McCarthy of the *Sunday Tribune*. 'It was something the board was quite conscious of. No disrespect, but we used to ask ourselves what would a journalist who wants to have a pop at the board say about what we're doing now. We used to actively ask ourselves that question.' Coyne claimed that conflicts of interest were addressed and avoided. 'Regularly at board meetings, someone would step out and stand in the corridor.'

In February 2009 Lar Bradshaw rejected claims that there was a conflict of interest between his position on the state board and his directorship at Anglo Irish Bank. He told the *Sunday Times* that an inquiry by a Dáil committee into the relationship between the bank and the state agency would find that 'absolutely nothing' improper had taken place. 'Everything that we did in the Docklands was by the book, by the rules,' he said. 'Any potential or perceived conflicts [of interest], everything was out on the table before there was any discussion.'

Bradshaw said: 'Down through the years there would be situations where, because of things that people were involved in either on a professional or a personal basis, there could have been potential conflicts.

We had set processes which were best practice around how perceived conflicts would be dealt with, and those policies would be always followed to a tee.'

But the increasingly intense Anglo connection would cause many of the authority's subsequent problems and lead to its near collapse. The agency had adopted a 'pro-developer' stance for planning practice, partially because of the influence of FitzPatrick and Bradshaw, according to Niamh Brennan, who was levered into the organization as chairman in April 2009 to find out what had gone so horribly wrong. She said that there had been 'a significant influence by the bank on the culture of the authority'. Two independent reports into the running of the organization had identified significant shortcomings in the DDDA's operations, particularly in relation to planning. 'The planning function of the authority was used to facilitate development and may not have been operated as independently of development as it might have been,' Brennan said. 'Planning standards, as result, were compromised.' The reports also showed that there had been 'very loose internal financial controls' in the quango.

Anglo's fingerprints are everywhere. A search of the mortgages and loans borrowed by the major development companies working in the area turns up the same name over and over again: Anglo was bankrolling an extraordinarily large share of the developments.

Anglo Irish Bank was the chief lender in the syndicate that provided Richard Barrett and Johnny Ronan's Treasury Holdings with more than €390 million for the development of Spencer Dock. At the time this was the largest secured property loan in the history of the state. Anglo was also involved in the financing for another Treasury tower project in Grand Canal Quay.

The bank funded much of Paddy Kelly's development in the area, including the Clarion Hotel and apartments, which were once valued at €125 million by Kelly's Redquartz Group. Anglo also lent more than €13 million for a recent redevelopment of the hotel. Kelly's Haytonvale Developments, which constructed the €75 million Ivory Building and Quality Inn (now Maldon Hotel) block, was also backed by Anglo, as were the Kelly-fronted €150 million Gallery Quay apartment and office block and the €175 million SJQ complex on Sir John Rogerson's Quay.

Paddy Kelly won the contract to build the National College of Ireland in the IFSC with the McCormack family's Alanis company and Ged Pierse's building group Pierse Contracting. The complex was built on a two-acre site provided for free by the DDDA, with Kelly and his partners building a block of apartments at the side. The €25 million cost of construction was funded through tax breaks and a big wodge of money from – guess who? – Anglo Irish Bank.

Liam Carroll was also an Anglo customer. Before his empire came tumbling down, Carroll was working on a deal to build a new €200 million headquarters for Anglo as part of a €1.5 billion complex on the north docks.

It wasn't just office blocks and apartments that Anglo bankrolled. In 2002 the DDDA secured one of its key residents when the National College of Ireland (formerly the National College of Industrial Relations) moved from Ranelagh to the IFSC. The college was headed up by Joyce O'Connor, who also sat on the board of another state quango, the Digital Hub Development Agency. She is also Seán FitzPatrick's sister.

The connection between O'Connor and FitzPatrick was out in the open. 'Everybody knew that Joyce and Seán were brother and sister,' DDDA chief Peter Coyne said in 2009. 'Joyce was president of the only college that fitted the bill for what we wanted to do in the docklands in that it would be very proactive in bringing in the local community. The college was going to relocate anyway because it was on a short lease in Ranelagh. Joyce managed to get the money in. High-net-worth individuals had their arms twisted for donations.' Paddy Kelly, who won the contract to develop the college, was one of those donors: he handed over a cheque for €250,000 after a fundraising dinner in Patrick Guilbaud's restaurant.

Some of the agency's dealings with developers were alarmingly secretive and opaque. Developer Liam Carroll and the DDDA agreed a confidential deal in 2007 that effectively allowed him to ignore the 2002 North Lotts Planning Scheme, which specified a maximum building height of eight storeys, and build the new Anglo headquarters to sixteen.

Carroll's rivals in the area, Seán Dunne and Treasury Holdings' Johnny Ronan, went ape when they discovered the secret deal and unleashed a barrage of lawsuits. In his legal action, Dunne claimed the permission given to Carroll to build to a greater density than permitted by the 2002 development plan would lead to a situation where his own planned residential apartment block would look out on to office blocks rather than a garden area, while access to his site would be restricted. Treasury Holdings was equally miffed. An affidavit sworn by Treasury director John Bruder claimed the secret agreement gave Carroll a competitive advantage over Treasury, Dunne and other developers in terms of negotiating with prospective tenants in the area.

The High Court ruled that the DDDA's fast-track permission for the site – known as a Section 25 certificate – should be quashed because the authority's executive had reached the secret agreement regarding building height before the Section 25 application had even been considered by the DDDA board. Despite this decision, Dublin City Council cleared the way for the building to continue. An Bord Pleanála appealed the planning approval, but, just as the lawyers were clocking up big fees, external events rendered the whole question irrelevant: the financial crisis and collapse in the property market brought Carroll's empire tumbling down. The hulking frame of the Anglo building sits unfinished, weeds carpeting the site, one of the most poignant symbols of a country that lost the run of itself.

But why did the DDDA agree this secret deal? This has never been explained satisfactorily. Carroll called a halt to his plans to build a major development that would have competed directly with the DDDA's proposed headline-grabbing U2 Tower, but the DDDA denied that there was any link between this and Carroll's preferential deal at North Lotts.

The U2 Tower was another mad idea – not as mad as Harry Crosbie's wheeze to have a cable car running along the Liffey all the way up to Heuston Station, but pretty silly all the same. When U2's studio building on Britain Quay in the south docks was bought out for development, the DDDA decided to run another one of its international competitions to find a suitably grand building for the site. It made an absolute pig's ear of the whole thing, including losing the entries. It was excruciatingly embarrassing, but, given the ineptitude of the DDDA, not all that surprising. This snafu led the DDDA into a multimillion-euro arbitration dispute over the original plan and design for the vast project. The chosen design was later scrapped and architecture firm BCDH issued a claim against loss of fees.

A consortium called Geranger – which included members of U2, Sean Mulryan's Ballymore and Paddy McKillen – won the gig to build the €200 million tower on the site. McKillen, who would later become one of the so-called 'Anglo 10' to whom the bank lent money in order to buy up part of Seán Quinn's unstable holding in the bank, was also involved with members of U2 in the Clarence Hotel. The U2 Tower would be mirrored on the north side of the river by another giant edifice being planned by Harry Crosbie as part of his Point Village, and this led to many, many funny jokes about whose erection would be bigger. Ultimately, neither Crosbie nor U2 were able to get theirs up, as the financial contagion killed the scheme, and just over a year later it was shelved indefinitely.

In its quest for a signature building for its bailiwick, the DDDA developed a rather inflated sense of its own importance. It believed that it was doing something splendid for a run-down area of Dublin, rather than just building flats and offices. Its pompous attitude was nowhere more evident than in its constant search for landmark schemes and ideas. The DDDA blew almost €343,000 developing the giant *Wire Man*, a 46-metre-high steel sculpture by British artist Antony Gormley that was to stand bang in the middle of the Liffey. The project, with its €1.6 million budget, has now been kiboshed by the cash-strapped authority. Gormley, who produced the *Angel of the North* sculpture in Gateshead, had already been paid over €54,000 to develop the project, following an international competition costing more than €80,000. The DDDA then spent more than €205,000 shuffling the steel-mesh sculpture scheme through the planning process. This included a €36,000 spend on 'public consultation'.

The aborted but still costly *Wire Man* wasn't the DDDA's only ludicrous spend on art. In June 2008 the cash-strapped quango splurged €170,000 on arranging a vast nudie photograph by renowned artist Spencer Tunick: some 25,000 people took off their clothes in South Wall harbour in the docks and were photographed as a group. He was paid €31,768 for his contribution, and a further €63,000 was spent on 'project management' and other production costs. The DDDA was taking the mickey.

If it made a mess of pretentious art, the DDDA's attempt to lure yuppie shoppers to the IFSC was even more hapless. Plans to turn a warehouse building known as Stack A into a commercial development had been under way since the early noughties. At one stage top-end British department store Harvey Nichols was pencilled in as a potential tenant, but it wisely opted for the Dundrum Shopping Centre instead. The eventual development, named CHQ, lured the likes of Meadows & Byrne, Carphone Warehouse, Louis Copeland, Mitchell's Wine, Starbucks, Fitzpatricks Shoes and the rather excellent Toss'd noodle bar, but since opening in November 2007 it has struggled, with occupancy rates falling below 50 per cent in January 2010. Internal DDDA estimates have shown that the value of CHQ had fallen from €60 million to just €17 million by the end of 2009. DDDA advisers expect the complex to miss its €775,000 rent forecasts by €465,000 in 2010 once 'potential tenant default and ongoing negotiations' are factored in.

The DDDA and its board of Anglo bankers will be remembered forever, not only for the failed shopping centre and the never-built towers, but also for the utterly insane move to borrow money to invest in development land at the apex of an overheated property market. The deal to buy into the Irish Glass Bottle site will go down as one of the worst business decisions in Irish corporate history.

In November 2006, after weeks of negotiations, it was announced that a Bernard McNamara-fronted consortium, Becbay, would pay almost €412 million for a 24-acre brownfield site in Ringsend, formerly occupied by the Irish Glass Bottle Company's plant. McNamara owned 41 per cent of Becbay (via a deal with private investors rounded up by Davy), with Derek Quinlan and his backers holding a 33 per cent stake. The DDDA had 26 per cent. The deal was structured as a company takeover rather than as a land purchase, which meant that Becbay paid only 1 per cent in stamp duty instead of the standard

9 per cent for a land transaction. In the penultimate line of the *Irish Times* report on the deal, Anglo reared its head: 'The transaction is being funded through a combination of new debt issued by Anglo Irish Bank and the sale of more equity and loan stock to Becbay's current shareholders.' The deal was tidied up and put to bed in the early months of 2007.

On 22 April 2007 we published the revelation that ethics campaigner Michael Smith – the man credited with sparking the Flood Tribunal – had made a formal complaint to the Standards in Public Office Commission (SIPO) about Lar Bradshaw and Seán Fitz-Patrick's conflict of interest at the DDDA. 'It is clear that the future of the Docklands seems to be largely in the hands of under 15 development companies,' Smith's complaint stated. 'It is clear that Anglo Irish lends money to a considerable number, perhaps a majority of them.' He wanted to know if Bradshaw and FitzPatrick had absented themselves from key meetings and whether they had made full declarations of their interests to the DDDA.

It wasn't the first time that Anglo's links with the DDDA had been queried. In 2004 the late Tony Gregory TD asked a question in the Dáil about the potential conflict facing FitzPatrick and Bradshaw. Dick Roche, the environment minister at the time, said he had no knowledge of a breach of the DDDA code of conduct.

SIPO picked up the ball, and then promptly dropped it. 'While it may be that both [Seán FitzPatrick and Lar Bradshaw] held substantial shareholdings in the bank,' SIPO found, 'there was no evidence that either held "control" of the bank.' It was clear that SIPO was a watchdog without much of a bark.

But the appetite for developing grandiose property schemes was ebbing fast, as Ireland's property bubble quickly began to deflate. By the end of 2008 it was clear that the DDDA and Becbay had paid far too much for the site. It was also evident that Bernard McNamara and Derek Quinlan were gasping under the weight of their debts.

In December 2008, after the revelation that Seán FitzPatrick had hidden €87 million in personal loans from the bank – by transferring them on to the balance sheet of Irish Nationwide, so that they would not come to the attention of the bank's shareholders – former

PricewaterhouseCoopers managing partner Donal O'Connor stepped down from the DDDA in order to replace FitzPatrick as chairman of the fatally wounded Anglo. All FitzPatrick's off-piste dealings were suddenly under enormous scrutiny. 'The Government should now revisit the issue of whether the public interest is served by the DDDA continuing high-level – including board-level – membership cross-overs with Anglo when the board makes decisions that have such a big effect on the bank balances of many of Anglo's developer clients who have property in Docklands,' Michael Smith said after the FitzPatrick revelations.

Private clients of Davy stockbrokers had lent €52 million to Bernard McNamara to buy his chunk of the Glass Bottle site, and early in 2009 the broker informed them that the value of the site and their investment had fallen 60 per cent. The DDDA had figured that its stake was worth €117 million in 2007; based on Davy's estimates, this share was worth only €47 million in 2009. This was beginning to look like a catastrophic investment.

Fine Gael TD Phil Hogan and the Oireachtas Committee on the Environment summoned the DDDA boss Paul Maloney to give an explanation. Maloney stunned the normally sedate committee when he revealed that the DDDA had not paid any interest on its loans for the Irish Glass Bottle site for eight months. It took the decision because its fellow shareholders in the deal had stopped paying interest too. Here was a state agency that was technically in default on its borrowings. And it had kept this bombshell quiet.

Hogan cornered Maloney about possible conflicts of interest on the part of FitzPatrick and Bradshaw. The DDDA boss revealed that both men had taken part in an October 2006 conference call among board members regarding the decision to take a share in the Ringsend site. He added that they had absented themselves from a meeting the following month that agreed to deal with Anglo as the lender, rather than Bank of Scotland and Bank of Ireland.

Further revelations about links between the key players in the deal emerged. Lar Bradshaw was part of a consortium that had bought the Atrium Building in Sandyford in 2006 – along with Paul Coulson, the Glass Bottle site leaseholder who made €273.5 million from the sale, and Derek Quinlan and Bernard McNamara. Bradshaw had also invested in Derek Quinlan's purchase of the Four Seasons Hotel in Ballsbridge.

As Hogan and the Oireachtas committee trawled through the DDDA's sorry finances, it emerged that environment minister John Gormley was seeking to parachute Gerry McCaughey in to the DDDA as its new chairman with a brief to crack some heads and find out what had happened. McCaughey turned out to be one of the most embarrassing state appointments of all time. A mere twenty-one days after his appointment in March 2009, he stepped down when it emerged that his tax affairs were complicated, to say the least. Leaked documents revealed details of a legal but convoluted scheme to reduce his tax bill from the €100 million sale of his timber-frame house-building company to Kingspan in 2005. McCaughey insisted that there were 'sinister forces' who wanted to make sure he would not take on the DDDA role. It was a cringeworthy episode that left free-range egg splattered all over Gormley's face.

He was replaced by the formidable Niamh Brennan, the Kevlar-plated UCD expert on corporate governance. Paul Maloney stood down as chief executive, despite having eleven months left on his five-year contract.

By this time, relations between the DDDA, McNamara and Quinlan had deteriorated drastically, as developers felt the full force of the property-market collapse. In September 2009 McNamara started legal action against the DDDA over guarantees about which members of the consortium should pay the interest on the €288 million borrowings from Anglo Irish Bank. McNamara alleged that the DDDA had not honoured its commitment to fast-track planning permission for the development – an undertaking that, McNamara claimed, was what had made the Glass Bottle site so incredibly valuable.

At the same time as he was suing the DDDA, McNamara was fighting a lawsuit against the Davy private clients that had lent him the money for the deal. In Christmas week 2009 the Commercial Court ordered him to pay €63 million to the Davy investors, who included Glen Dimplex boss Martin Naughton, ESB chairman Lochlann Quinn and Riverdeep chief Barry O'Callaghan, according to McNamara's court filings. In January 2010 McNamara revealed what the dogs on the street knew: he was broke and couldn't pay the investors back.

It was squeaky-bum time in the plush new offices of the DDDA on Sir John Rogerson's Quay. The authority released its annual report, which outlined the true extent of the critical financial situation it faced. The quango had losses of €27 million and had taken an €186 million writedown on the value of its assets. It also wrote off a €43 million loan to Becbay to fund works on the site. It was well under water.

The figures continued to disintegrate for the DDDA when a team of surveyors valued the Glass Bottle site at just €60 million – some €352 million less than it had paid for it three years earlier. Tens of millions of euros invested by the DDDA had gone up in smoke. The authority told the courts that it would need to be bailed out by the state if it was to continue in existence. The Comptroller & Auditor General began an investigation in the summer of 2010, following two independent reports into corporate-governance failings at the quango. Environment minister John Gormley said these reports described 'serious weaknesses' in the authority. The reports also raised questions over the legality of the planning process that had led to some of the shimmering docklands developments. The DDDA now has a skeleton staff and is hanging on by its fingernails. The taxpayer has been left with a debt of over €213 million and some rather large holes in the ground.

NAMA is no DDDA. The National Asset Management Agency has none of the corrupt practices discovered at CIÉ, the extravagances of FÁS or the endemic waste of the HSE.

NAMA is desperate to be painted as a model of propriety, thrift and efficiency. This picture had better be accurate, because NAMA is almost the last throw of the dice in the nation's deadly game of solvency.

It takes years of practice and flying below the radar to perfect the worst habits of the state sector. NAMA, however, has been under the microscope since birth. The Minister for Finance, Brian Lenihan, and NAMA's chief executive, Brendan McDonagh, have been hauled before the media and Oireachtas committees at every turn since the state's 'bad bank' was conceived in early 2009.

Not a penny of expenditure has gone unchallenged.

Not a board member has escaped scrutiny.

Yet NAMA has the potential to be the biggest semi-state corpse ever invented.

The initial charge against NAMA was that the state had invented a fairytale quango: that an 'asset-management' body had been invented simply as a roundabout way of bailing out the banks by paying fairytale prices for the bank's toxic assets, and that it would have a fairytale ending, with everyone – the banks and the taxpayer – emerging a winner by 2020.

No one really believed the fairytale story, but nor did anyone understand the fairytale calculations that assumed a recovery in property prices. No credible alternative was offered to the fantasy world, bar nationalization of the five guaranteed Irish banks that had not already been nationalized; and this option was swiftly dismissed by Taoiseach Brian Cowen.

Independent economists who understood the detail of NAMA, such as TCD Professor Brian Lucey and UCD Professor Karl Whelan, took to the airwaves to oppose it. Indeed, they gathered a group of forty-six academics to sign a piece in the *Irish Times* arguing against what they saw as a fantasy solution to the banking crisis.

But not everyone joined the two academics in opposing NAMA. Economists from banks, stockbrokers, insurance giants, auctioneers or government agencies were notably missing from the ranks of those lining up against it. A clear division had emerged. The familiar old property interests were firmly pro-NAMA; academics with less to lose were against it. Economic views, as usual, seemed to depend on the employer of the economist.

Not long after the decision was taken by the government to go down the NAMA road, one solid number did emerge. Lenihan's draft NAMA business plan of October 2009 revealed that the total cost of fees to be paid to 'professionals' hired by NAMA would come in at €2.4 billion over ten years.

With that one sentence, any scepticism from bankers, brokers, accountants, estate agents and lawyers was forgotten – or at least went underground. The scene was set for a monstrous NAMA industry on a scale to leave all the other semi-states in the shade.

Bankers were euphoric at the sight of the lifeboat. Auctioneers starved of commissions, solicitors deprived of conveyancing fees, auditors without audits, valuers without valuing opportunities, tax advisers, even public-relations spinners – all spotted the openings. They wanted a slice of the €2.4 billion waiting to flow their way from the NAMA fountain of riches. FÁS, even in its glory days, could not match such mighty expenditure.

All the old chancers suddenly smelled that they might be back in the game. The state agency set up to put manners on the guilty would end up enriching them.

Perfectly correctly, NAMA put contracts for valuers, solicitors, auditors and other advisers out to tender. All appointments were sensitive, given the nature of the contracts and the record that Ireland had for political trickery when it came to state gigs. But the most sensitive role of all would be played by the valuers: as the valuation of the assets being transferred to the taxpayer from the banks was the flashpoint of the entire NAMA debate, it was imperative that the abilities and integrity of NAMA's valuers be beyond question.

A media leak suggesting that no Irish auctioneer would be allowed to take part in the process of valuing the loans caused consternation among members of the cabal. The lifeboat was cutting their lifeline. Whether or not the leak was accurate, some fairly sturdy arm-twisting followed. The disproportionate number of Oireachtas members and county councillors with auctioneering licences flexed their muscles. Ireland's discredited auctioneering firms were allowed to apply for both the national and local NAMA valuation panels.

The tenders were accepted during a quiet three weeks in August 2009. Most of the selections were announced during that eerie lacuna between Christmas and the New Year.

It was a comeback to make Lazarus blush. The valuers' panel turned out to be a lap of honour for many of the culprits of the boom. The five selected were CB Richard Ellis (CBRE), Jones Lang

LaSalle, Lisney, Savills and DTZ Sherry FitzGerald. All five estate agencies had made a mint during the Tiger years. Many had done it while giving starry-eyed valuations. Part of their brief during the years of plenty had been to predict future prospects and prices for the property market.

NAMA was now paying them to estimate not only today's prices – by way of determining the amount that it should pay for the banks' assets – but also to give an estimate of the 'long-term economic value' of the properties held as securities.

Presumably those interviewing the estate agents tendering for the NAMA gigs had a look at the past records of these so-called experts.

Top of the list of NAMA valuers is CB Richard Ellis. This group of property consultants was outspoken in its criticism of non-believers who suggested during the boom years that the property market was heading for a fall. In April 2007 CBRE dismissed Richard Curran's prognostication of a possible property crash in his *Future Shock* TV programme on the subject. It was CBRE's contention that the slowdown in the property frenzy being experienced in 2007 was simply a levelling out in the extraordinary pace of growth previously experienced.

The company's 'head of research', Marie Hunt, was positively vitriolic when it came to Curran's programme. 'The sensationalist approach of last night's programme is in our view irresponsible as property is a very important issue and ultimately the general public will take the sentiments expressed last night on board when deciding whether or not to make what will essentially be the biggest financial decision of their lifetime. Would-be first-time buyers who have heeded equally dramatic and incorrect predictions in the past have lost out significantly as they sat on the fence and watched prices escalate because of the underlying fundamentals in Ireland. All we ask is that the media consider these fundamentals and adopt a balanced, informed and considered approach when dealing with such an important issue.'

She went on: 'It is also irresponsible to suggest that the negative equity scenario that occurred in the late eighties in the UK could occur in Ireland considering that Irish lending institutions are work-ing under the remit of the Central Bank and continue to stress-test potential borrowers to 2 per cent above ECB rates.'

Quite a put-down for Curran. Quite a vote of confidence for the Central Bank. Quite a hostage to fortune on negative equity, which, by 2010, was rampant.

NAMA should have asked Richard Curran to become an adviser. Instead, they put Marie Hunt's CBRE on to the NAMA gravy train. They wanted the guys, who had called it so wrong two years earlier, as experts to value the NAMA properties. You would never have spotted Marie Hunt's name at the bottom of the article in the *Irish Times* opposing NAMA.

NAMA opted for other local auctioneers with similarly flawed pedigrees. It is difficult to explain why the NAMA interviewing board wanted DTZ Sherry FitzGerald to value its properties. But it did. Sherry FitzGerald had been among the most enthusiastic sup-porters of the housing boom. It was a champion of the dubious practice of publishing guide prices for properties that were invariably too low but that seduced buyers into viewing and entering the auc-tion room. It ran its own mortgage agency, selling houses for vendors while lending purchasers the money to buy. Above all, it was a bull of the market to the last. No economist from DTZ Sherry FitzGerald would have put his or her signature on an article in the *Irish Times* opposing NAMA.

Its photogenic chief economist Marian Finnegan had been on message for years, seeing no evil in the Irish property market. In an interview with the *Irish Independent* in 2006 she rated the Irish prop-erty market '10 out of 10' and went on to say that 'Property still looks like providing fantastic opportunities in the years ahead.'

Finnegan thought that the initial fall-off in market prices in 2007 didn't mean much. In a statement on 1 October 2007, when the mar-ket was seven months into its long tumble, she acknowledged the 'more challenging market place' but asserted that any slowdown was minor: 'We remain absolutely confident,' she insisted, 'that the fun-damentals underpinning the market remain sound, a factor that will underwrite performance in the medium term.'

In 2008 Finnegan was a little more circumspect. After property prices had been falling for over a year she used more tortuous language to temper her bullishness. In a July press release she told clients: 'The results of the price barometer illustrate that the reprieve in the pace of price inflation in the first quarter has abated.'

Perhaps the NAMA interviewers never asked Finnegan and the other geniuses at DTZ Sherry FitzGerald how they had reached such bullish conclusions in the face of so much contrary evidence.

The others selected for the NAMA valuations – Lisney, Savills and Jones Lang LaSalle – were all bulls of the property market for far too long as well.

Perhaps it will suit NAMA to welcome such people on board. Perhaps it will mean that they will always be conveniently upbeat about short-term or long-term economic value. According to Lenihan, NAMA's success depends on property prices rising over a ten-year period – which could mean that the state agency's agenda will best be served by a valuer whose mood music is appropriately upbeat. NAMA can expect a sympathetic outlook from CBRE and DTZ Sherry FitzGerald.

The awards of other professional contracts followed a similar pattern. The legal-advice contract went to Arthur Cox, a long-established favourite for government gigs. Arthur Cox was already advising Bank of Ireland on NAMA. Now it was advising NAMA on Bank of Ireland. The legal firm claimed that its team working for NAMA would be 'ring fenced'. Somehow they seemed to have hogged the inside track.

The same firm had been advisers to the Department of Finance on the bank-guarantee scheme and on the banks' recapitalization. Now it had landed the big one. Critics were vocal in denouncing the choice, pointing out that Arthur Cox had already been paid €3.87 million for advice about reforming the banks.

KPMG won the job as auditors to NAMA. KPMG was also auditor to AIB. Other awards went to PricewaterhouseCoopers, long-time auditors to Bank of Ireland.

It should be remembered that NAMA had the power of life or death over the bankers and their clients. Each loan bought by NAMA would be considered on its merits. The information produced by KPMG and PricewaterhouseCoopers would undoubtedly influence these two companies' own fates. PricewaterhouseCoopers had received €100 million in fees from Bank of Ireland in the previous ten years.

Even Ernst & Young got a slice of the action. The auditors – who were under investigation for not spotting the transfer of as much as €122 million in loans from Anglo boss Seán FitzPatrick's personal account to the Irish Nationwide at the year-end – were appointed to one of the panels on Loan and Associated Valuation Services.

It was not as though we had not been warned. John McManus of the *Irish Times*, possibly the most prescient financial journalist in Ireland, foresaw the problems early on. Two months before the NAMA gigs were dished out he warned: 'NAMA both directly and indirectly is going to be the single biggest employer of lawyers, accountants, auctioneers, and other professionals over the next ten years. The potential conflicts of interest for a country whose business culture is already riddled with them really does not bear thinking about.'

McManus is right. It would do your head in to contemplate the possibilities.

And then he continued: 'It is obvious that the Government should act at this stage to make sure that NAMA does not become some sort of bonanza for the same firms that participated so unthinkingly in that which led to its creation. NAMA's market power will allow it to be a price setter, and any firm quoting fee rates from any time this side of 2000 should be sent packing.'

Conflicts of interest were going to pop up all over the NAMA industry in the next decade. And NAMA bosses simply told us to accept them. Chief executive Brendan McDonagh reassured the world that there were 'procedures' for managing conflicts.

They will need them.

In early April 2010 Nick Webb started to investigate whether any of the NAMA top brass had needed to make declarations of interest or even remove themselves from the pitch. He started pretty near the top. John Mulcahy, the man appointed head of portfolio management at NAMA, had a bit of a problem: he held shares worth more than €2.31 million in Jones Lang LaSalle and had formerly chaired the company's Irish operations.

A NAMA spokesman stated that Mulcahy had 'absented himself from any discussions concerning Jones Lang LaSalle during the tender process to establish this panel and he is not involved in the allocation of work to firms chosen for the panel'.

Nick also discovered that Donal Kellegher, one of NAMA's portfolio asset managers, had held 22,264 shares in Savills. As of mid April 2010 that number of shares was worth €88,000. NAMA refused to say whether Kellegher had sold the shares since they were last registered in his name at the end of December 2008.

So much for conflicts among NAMA's top executives. It was no great leap to surmise that its board was likely to be stuffed with holders of bank shares.

Michael Connolly had been appointed to the board of NAMA with all the initial directors in December 2009. As an ex-Bank of Ireland chief, his appointment as a director of NAMA raised immediate questions. Did he have a bond of affection with his old bank? Or did he have a prejudice against them? Could he be neutral on one of the two biggest banks in NAMA's universe?

Connolly turned out to hold 20,000 shares in his former employer, worth €37,000. (At one stage they were worth €360,000.) The spotlight on Connolly's shareholding in Bank of Ireland also brought the rest of the board into focus. The politically appointed directors were certainly not the usual party-political hacks, nor were they drawn from the ranks of the slothful social partners. All had credentials for the job. NAMA was, after all, a life-or-death quango, not just an outfit to pamper cronies and trade unionists. NAMA was protecting the national interest.

Yet there was a slightly unnerving pattern to the selection process. Politicians appeared to have influenced it in an unusual way. While the original applications had been vetted by two civil servants and whittled down to thirty-six candidates, the final selection had been left to Minister for Finance Brian Lenihan.

Lenihan made no bones about Connolly. His credentials were clear. He had banking experience at the top of Bank of Ireland, and he ran a banking-consultancy service that had advised ACCBank, Bank of Ireland and Anglo Irish Bank since its nationalization.

The government had chosen Connolly for the board. But who had proposed the others?

It appeared that their colleagues in coalition, the Greens, had been allotted one member, Fine Gael another and Labour a third. In a desperate effort to secure all-party assent, the government had accepted a large measure of party-political input into the make-up of the board.

NAMA was already a political football, with the parties controlling seats on the board.

That left the chairman.

There had been widespread speculation that the chair of NAMA would be held by a foreigner. The dangers of conflicts of interest with an Irish chairman were obvious. The whole organization was, as we have seen already, riddled with them. The reluctance of the selection committees to pick independent outsiders ensured that NAMA would be cursed with these conflicts from cradle to grave.

But Lenihan took the local road by selecting the local man, Frank Daly. Despite Daly's reputation for integrity, it was probably a bad choice.

Frank Daly is a favourite of Lenihan and of Cowen. The Taoiseach appointed him to the chair of the Commission on Taxation in 2008. Lenihan has not allowed him a day's rest since he retired from the Revenue Commissioners, giving him a key post as a director of Anglo Irish just before the mass exodus of disgraced chairman Seán Fitz-Patrick's board. Hardly a wet day at Anglo, Daly was plucked out of the Anglo frying pan and thrust into the NAMA fire.

Daly's reputation was impeccable, but he knew many of the bankers personally. He had locked horns with them over several offshore issues. His short term on the board of Anglo might raise minor questions. He had been given a send-off dinner by the Irish Bankers Federation when he left the Revenue at which David Drumm – then Anglo's chief executive – was present. Small beer, but an outsider would have been better shielded from any past links with Ireland's rogue bankers.

The remaining board members included chief executive Brendan McDonagh, John Corrigan of the NTMA and William Soffe, chairman of the Dublin Transportation Office and former county manager of Fingal County Council. Only one overseas board member sits at the directors' table: Steven Seelig was appointed to the board in May 2010 after he retired from the International Monetary Fund. His nomination had a whiff of tokenism.

The directors are paid handsomely. Their fees shot up within three months of their appointment. It was announced that Daly's part-time chairman's fees would rocket from an original estimate of €100,000 a year to a phenomenal €170,000. The rest of the board were hiked from €38,000 to €50,000 at a time when other public servants were being cut back.

An inspired leak revealed that Michael Connolly was to be given a fee of €150,000 to chair the NAMA credit committee on the understanding that he worked 'no less than 3 to 4 days a week'. The NAMA board is already on the gravy train.

The parochial feel of the NAMA board, the political flavour of several of the nominations, the obvious conflicts of interest surfacing among the top staff and the lack of information forthcoming from NAMA itself – all of these things bode very badly for its future.

NAMA now enjoys the same priceless protection as CIÉ, the Financial Regulator and the Central Bank: it is not covered by the Freedom of Information Act. Just like the old Central Bank fortress down in Dame Street, it can parry all questions about its operations by refusing to answer on the grounds that the information is commercially sensitive.

In her 2009 annual report ombudsman Emily O'Reilly was withering in her criticism of NAMA's exemption from the Freedom of Information Act. Her words fell on deaf ears.

Such featherbedding is not in NAMA's interests. Its immunity from challenge could be its eventual undoing. Its insistence on appointing Ireland's insiders could send it down the same road as the old regulator. It is already looking too cosy.

NAMA spokesmen are starting to sound like the voices of an organization under siege. Its reluctance to select more than a handful of external companies for the professional advisers' jobs has left it compromised. Its top staff are cursed with conflicts of interest. Insiders are backing the NAMA project to the hilt in the hope of gaining crumbs from its €2.4 billion treasury of patronage. It has been exempted from the Freedom of Information Act. With its insider executives and contractors, its giant budget, its licence for secrecy and its political protection, NAMA could turn out to be the ultimate wasters' quango.

Epilogue

The Office of the Comptroller & Auditor General is supposed to be the state's spending Rottweiler. It is the body tasked with growling at government departments and agencies and making damn sure that they aren't wasting money.

Given that the Office of the Comptroller & Auditor General is responsible for scrutinizing state expenditure, we thought it might be a plan to check its chief's own expenses. We lobbed in a Freedom of Information request for the travel expenses of the C&AG from January 2007 to February 2010. A huge green folder of photocopied receipts arrived in the post some weeks later.

John Purcell, who retired as chief C&AG auditor in May 2008, was quite the traveller. In April 2007 Purcell spent five days abroad, visiting San Francisco for a meeting of the Global Working Group – according to its website, 'a forum which provides a select group of Eighteen Auditors General to meet for organised yet informal discussions on current and emerging issues of concern to their governments and offices, and to explore opportunities to share information and work closely together' – with his flights costing a cool €2,822. He also filed a subsistence claim for €821 largely related to his stay at the Serrano, a luxury boutique hotel in San Francisco.

Purcell was back a month before hopping on a plane to Ljubljana, the capital of Slovenia, for a visit to the Slovenian Court of Audit. He stayed in the Hotel Lev – Ljubljana's only five-star hotel, filing a €481.32 subsistence claim for his three-night stay. Three weeks later he was back in the air, flying off to Sofia in Bulgaria, where he paid a visit to the country's national audit office. He rested his weary head on the downy pillows of the upmarket Sofia Sheraton during his three-day stay.

In November, Purcell and his wife (whose expenses Purcell covered himself) travelled to Mexico City, with flights costing €788. The seven-day trip for the annual knees-up of the International Organization of Supreme Audit Institutions saw Purcell file a claim for €1,456.92, largely for his room at the swanky Hotel Nikko.

The year closed out with a five-day trip to Helsinki and London, with flights worth €559. Purcell stayed in the elegant Scandic Hotel in Helsinki before running up a bill of about €550 for three nights in the Crowne Plaza in London. The junket to Helsinki was for a meeting of the Contact Committee, an assembly of the heads of European audit offices of EU member states. The London trip was to hook up with the British National Audit Office, which was in turmoil following the revelation in *Private Eye* magazine of the travel expenses – including a flight on Concorde and sojourns in luxury hotels in the Bahamas – of the NAO's chief Sir John Bourn.

In 2008 Purcell travelled to Marrakech, with flights costing €978.50. There was also a €969 subsistence claim, largely for the Marrakech Plaza Hotel. The documents we received also showed a €50.18 excess-baggage bill on his return flight. (His wife's fares were not included in the expense claim.)

Over the last year and a half of Purcell's tenure as chief auditor, the taxpayer coughed up close to €10,000 so that he could go on long-haul trips and stay in fancy hotels. The money would have been better spent on new batteries for the office calculator to prevent stuff such as the CIÉ integrated-ticketing fiasco or the National Stud behaving like the National Lottery.

When Purcell stowed his bean-counting kit for the last time, he was replaced by John Buckley. Despite the new blood and the new climate of austerity in public spending, the C&AG's office showed no sign of diminished wanderlust. The state's new chief auditor and his wife Noreen jetted up to scenic Bergen on the fjords of western Norway in May of 2009. The six-day trip saw flights worth €1,056 billed to the C&AG's office. John and Noreen stayed in the Rica Hotel for one night before checking in to the Ullensvang. A handwritten note attached to the claim indicates that Buckley didn't seek his subsistence for the final three days of the journey. The hotels cost over €700, with Buckley refunding €528 for his wife's airfare and a further €200 in respect of the 'accompanying person's fee'. Thanks. In November,

Buckley jetted off to Budapest, spending two nights in the Inter-Continental Hotel at a cost of €339 to the taxpayer. Buckley's travels also included visits to Edinburgh, London, Luxembourg (twice) and Cardiff, where his hotel bill of €332 included two bottles of water.

The Office of the C&AG also spent the taxpayers' money treating visiting dignitaries to meals in some of Dublin's most exclusive restaurants. We took Poland's top government auditor out for dinner, Campari, pints and a cheeky Cabernet Sauvignon in Roly's in Ballsbridge, at a cost of €232.07. The was also a meal for the New Zealand spending watchdog in Jay Bourke's excellent Eden restaurant in the heart of Temple Bar, where the bill came to €116.

Purcell claimed for meals in the classy Mermaid Café and in Peploe's, where his dining companion was none other than the secretary general of the Department of Finance, David Doyle. One of the diners feasted on the suckling pig; the cost of that dish alone would have covered the weekly drop in child allowance for a one-kid family.

While it is accustomed to hauling others across the coals, traditionally there is no set procedure for holding the C&AG's office to account for its activities. It has never been asked to answer about itself to others. There is an aura of infallibility about the office that should be challenged. The C&AG has a chequered history of cock-ups, pulling its punches and simply being ignored. The scandal at FÁS highlighted these failings. Former FÁS head of internal audit Terry Corcoran felt so incensed by the C&AG's report that he wrote to the PAC to point out that the watchdog had wimped out of giving the FÁS management a deserved spanking. FÁS board member Niall Saul later said that if FÁS had been a private company and the C&AG had been its auditor, it wouldn't have had its contract renewed. The C&AG had audited the books of FÁS from the year dot. It was on site in FÁS offices for six weeks of every year. Never once did it pick up even the slightest sniff that something was wrong. The sound of snoring must have been deafening.

The C&AG also mucked up the infamous 'fifty-two spouses' junket, when it indicated that one state agency had taken a ridiculous number of wives and husbands abroad on a super-jolly at the taxpayer's expense. It refused to name the jet-setting agency, waffling and hiding behind flawed procedures for the best part of a week before the Central Bank confessed. The C&AG was showered with egg as it emerged that it had got the wrong end of the stick completely. There was never a single junket of fifty-two wives, as the C&AG's original report stated, but rather a total of fifty-two trips involving Central Bank spouses over a two-year period.

With Ireland's public finances shot for the foreseeable future, politicians' junkets, boozy lunches and boondoggles are even less acceptable now than they were in the good times. Spending ought to be supervised by a body that has no questions to answer in this area.

Acknowledgements

Most of the people who talked to us while we were working on *Wasters* did so under the strict condition that all conversations would be anonymous. We'd like to thank all of them, especially those who took a real risk in helping us lift the lid on the excesses at FÁS and the corruption at CIÉ. Without them this book would not have been possible.

Our publishers Penguin were right behind us all the way, geeing us up whenever we stumbled and offering valuable advice. Penguin Ireland managing director Michael McLoughlin played a stormer, and a special thanks to our editor Brendan Barrington, who kicked the book into shape with real finesse; he even found a way of raising his voice through the medium of email. Brendan's contribution to this book has been immense, so thank you.

We'd like to thank *Sunday Independent* photo editor David Conachy, Gerry Mooney and Willie Brennan for their amazing work with the photos and some late, late dig-outs. Thanks also to *Sunday Independent* editor Aengus Fanning for helping to light the fire in our bellies and to all at Independent News and Media who have been hugely supportive of our work. We'd also like to thank the readers of the *Sunday Independent*, who over the years have supported us and given us some jaw-dropping bits of information about waste in the public sector.

Nick

I'd also like to thank my family, particularly Rebecca, who put up with me vanishing off to write whenever nappies needed to be changed or homework needed to be supervised, and the kids, Tom, Sarah, Millie and Edward, who got to watch a lot more television than they could have dreamed possible for the best part of nine months. Thanks also to my mother Monica and sister Emma, who read chapters, gave me ideas and were hugely supportive.

Shane

Sincere thanks to my personal assistant Nuala Walsh, who for the second year running gave of her own time to unravel many messes of my creation. Her ability to rescue me was priceless.

To Joey Facer, who worked full time for six months researching the chapters on cronyism and the semi-states, I am deeply grateful. She left the country immediately after her task was completed, hopefully not in despair.

To the staff of the Oireachtas Library, who sourced and suggested obscure books that were essential for the history of the semi-states.

To my wife Ruth for constantly pricking my ballooning ego as I bored my family – one by one – with the detailed wonders of each chapter as it was being written. They sorted out the problem by organizing a rota and sharing the burden in half-hourly shifts.

Photo Credits

Tom Burke, *Irish Independent*: p. 2, bottom; p. 4, bottom; p. 7, top left.

David Conachy, *Sunday Independent*: p. 1, bottom left; p. 2, top; p. 3, bottom; p. 5, top.

Tony Gavin, *Sunday Independent*: p. 4, top; p. 5, bottom.

Frank McGrath, *Irish Independent*: p. 3, top; p. 6, bottom; p. 8, bottom.

Maxwell Photography: p. 8, top.

Ken O'Halloran, *Irish Independent*: p. 7, top right; p. 7, bottom left.

Jim O'Kelly, *Irish Independent*: p. 1, bottom right.

Senan Doran O'Reilly, *Evening Herald*: p. 7, bottom right.

Mark Stedman, Photocall Ireland: p. 6, top.

Thanks to the above-named newspapers and agencies for permission to reproduce images, and to Sean O'Connor for permission to reproduce the photograph of Seán Lemass on p. 1 of the inset.

Index

Federated Workers Union of
    Ireland 137
Finan, Mary 233
Finance Bill (2008) 53
Financial Regulator 144, 172, 213, 251
Financial Services Ombudsman 214
Fingleton, Michael 40, 99
Finland 125
Finn, Billy 55
Finnegan, Marian 246–7
Finucane, Marian 100
fishing 207–8
FitzGerald, Garret 49, 115, 136–7
FitzGerald, Mark 49
Fitzgerald, Tom 225
Fitzpatrick, Mary 208
Fitzpatrick, P. J. 82
FitzPatrick, Seán 211, 219, 230–31, 232,
    234, 235, 239–40, 248, 250
Fitzpatrick Associates (consultants) 192
Flanagan, Charles 95
Flavin, Jim 143
Flinter, Dan 203
Flood Tribunal 180, 181, 183, 239
Florida:
    FÁS Science Challenge branch 2,
        51–2, 54
    junkets to 2, 5, 6, 51–2, 54, 56, 57
Flynn, Pádraig 180–81, 184, 187
Flynn, Phil (labour relations adviser
    and financier) 86, 143–4
Flynn, Philip (Digital Hub
    CEO) 224
Foir Teoranta 9
Foley, Michael 33
Food Safety Authority 101
Foras Forbartha (National Institute for
    Physical Planning and
    Construction Research) 20
Foras na Gaeilge 215–16
Foras Orgánach 227

Foras Teanga 215
Forbairt Naíonraí Teoranta 215
Foreign Affairs, Department of 101,
    114, 117
Forfás 71, 72, 141, 223
Fox, Noel 7, 11, 17
Foxe, Ken 112, 118
Freedom of Information Act (FOI) 4
    exemptions 146, 251
Freeman, John 152
FSA *see* Family Support Agency
Future Shock (TV programme) 245–6

GAA (Gaelic Athletic Association) 22,
    68–9
Gaffney, Maureen 82
Gallagher, Denis 129
Gallagher, Jackie 40, 206, 216
Gallagher, Paul 127
Gallagher, Terry 129–30
Garda Síochána Complaints Appeal
    Board 227
Geary, David 208
Gender Equality Unit 227
Geoghegan, Brian 44–5, 57, 118–19,
    121, 142
Geraghty, Des 50, 132–4, 135
Germany 135
Gilmartin, Tom 180
Gilmore, Eamon 113
Gilroy, Brian 77, 78, 79, 80, 97
Glackin, Rosaleen 148, 206
Glenbeigh Construction 196
golf 5, 51, 54, 78, 106
Good Friday Agreement 105, 140,
    207, 215
Goodbody Economic Consultants 206
Gorman, Sean 55
Gormley, Antony 237
Gormley, John 124, 127, 129, 200–201,
    241, 242